Football's
New York Giants

Football's New York Giants

A History

Lawrence A. Pervin

McFarland & Company, Inc., Publishers
Jefferson, North Carolina, and London

LIBRARY OF CONGRESS CATALOGUING-IN-PUBLICATION DATA

Pervin, Lawrence A.
　　Football's New York Giants : a history / Lawrence A. Pervin.
　　　p.　　cm.
　　Includes bibliographical references and index.

　　ISBN 978-0-7864-4268-3
　　softcover : 50# alkaline paper ∞

　　1. New York Giants (Football team)—History.　I. Title.
GV956.N4P47　　2009
796.332'64097471—dc22　　　　　　　　　　　　　　　2009011917

British Library cataloguing data are available

©2009 Lawrence A. Pervin. All rights reserved

No part of this book may be reproduced or transmitted in any form or by any means, electronic or mechanical, including photocopying or recording, or by any information storage and retrieval system, without permission in writing from the publisher.

On the cover: Giants fullback Bull Karcis scores as New York defeats Washington at the Polo Grounds on December 4, 1938 (Associated Press)

Manufactured in the United States of America

McFarland & Company, Inc., Publishers
　Box 611, Jefferson, North Carolina 28640
　　www.mcfarlandpub.com

Table of Contents

Preface	1
1. In the Beginning (1925–1953)	3
2. The Glory Years (1954–1963)	20
3. "Fifteen Years of Lousy Football— We've Had Enough" (1964–1978)	48
4. George Young, Bill Parcells, and the March to Two Super Bowls (1979–1990)	73
5. The Times They are A-Changin' (1991–2003)	118
6. The Coughlin-Accorsi-Manning Era and Super Bowl XLII (2004–2008)	145
Chapter Notes	193
Bibliography	199
Index	201

To my partners in rooting for the team,
Bobbie, David, and Levi,
and to all those who stick with
the Giants throughout

Preface

I was born and grew up in Brooklyn, so of course I was a Dodgers fan (still am) and a Giants football fan (again, still am). My two sons came along and joined me in the excitement of watching Giants football, though to tell the truth, my older son, born in Boston, also has a strong attachment to the Patriots. Super Bowl XLII was something of a challenge for him but not for the rest of the family. When my sons went off on their own, Sunday afternoons and occasional Monday nights were "holy times," with me watching the games by myself, praying, twisting and turning with each play, exhausted by the end of the game since I had played both offense and defense. My wife was not a football fan. The times I was "playing" she was out shopping—for clothes, not food. My enthusiasm for Giants football turned out to be very expensive! However, over the last few years she too has become a Giants fan. It was Tiki Barber who did it. She found someone "cute" who she could root for and thereby begin to become both enthusiastic and knowledgeable about the game. Together we would go to the Giants training camp in Albany and during the season watch the Giants and yell "Go, Tiki, Go."

So how does this end up as a book on the history of the Giants? I'm a retired professor and have authored many scholarly books on personality psychology. When I retired, I wanted to combine two things that I love, writing and Giants football. I read some of the books on the Giants and realized that there was no book on the history of the Giants, the team and the family, that focused on specific eras, particular games, and specific players, as opposed to a description of each game of the season over the course of many years. Could I capture the ups and downs of a team over the years and the excitement of critical games? I read everything I could get hold of, in particular every book I could find authored by a Giants coach or player, or written about them. I talked with a former consultant and scout, and gained insights from them about the Mara family and the frustrations of trying to draft players who will contribute to winning. I also learned about some of the internal battles that go on inside the organization, part of the dynamics of any organization. And I heard that "NFL football is an entertainment business," something I should have been aware of but never thought about as I twisted and turned with each play.

My writing the history of the Giants started in about 2004 and was completed in 2008. It was totally luck that the Giants won the Super Bowl in 2008. Nice to be able to end on a championship, but totally chance.

I hope that readers, young and old, male and female, will enjoy reading the history of the team as much as I have enjoyed writing it, and that they will relive, as I have, the many ups and downs of the team. Finally, if the readers gain some new insights into the team, its owners, management, coaches, and players, and occasionally twist and turn as they read about a critical point in a critical game, then my goals for the book will have been achieved.

1

In the Beginning (1925–1953)

In a Philadelphia performance, the British comedian Eddie Izzard expressed puzzlement at the American game of football. He asked, "How come it is called football when the ball almost never touches anyone's leg and in fact never touches any part of the body of most players?" Of course, he was contrasting American football with what the British, and most of the rest of the world, call football, known to us as soccer, where kicking the ball by all players is fundamental to the game. Since in our football at least some of the players use their hands, in contrast with soccer, why isn't it called handball?

The answer to the British comedian's question has to do with the roots of American football, a combination of English/European soccer (known by the British as a game of gentlemen, played by hooligans) and English rugby (known by the British as a hooligans' game played by gentlemen). Thus, the game of football that we know today is vastly different from that played between Rutgers University and Princeton University in 1869, the first college football game.[1] In that game a round ball could be batted or dribbled but not thrown or carried. Points were scored for kicks over a goal line rather than by carrying the ball over the line or kicking it through uprights. Sounds remarkably like what today we know as soccer. A few years later a Canadian influence entered as players were allowed to run with the ball and be tackled, as in the game of rugby. By 1890 football playing was increasing among college teams with rules that began to take the form of what we know as football today—downs, yards to gain, blocking, tackling below the waist, touchdowns. In 1906 there was an effort to standardize the rules. These rules included allowing the forward pass, establishing the length of the football as the neutral zone between offense and defense, and establishing ten yards as the necessary distance for a first down.

Key to many of the changes that came around that time was Alonzo Stagg, former All-American end and then coach at the University of Chicago. He is credited with such fundamental innovations as the forward pass, varied backfield formations including men in motion, and the use of uniform numbers, tackling dummies, and blocking sleds. One story has it that when he was on the same train as President Herbert Hoover, a train that was greeted by hundreds upon its arrival at the train station, he was amazed to learn that these were football fans greeting him rather than citizens greeting the president. Stagg field at the University of Chicago was the site in 1942 where members of the famed Manhattan Project created the first controlled nuclear reaction, leading the way to the development of the atomic bomb. Today a sign at the University of Chicago reads "Alonzo Stagg Field"—it is used for playing softball. Also significant in the development of the game were Glenn (Pop) Warner, after whom the boys' football league is named, and John Heisman, after whom is named the Heisman Trophy. Warner invented many of the early formations such as the single wing and double wing. Heisman built Georgia Tech into a football powerhouse during the early 1900s and helped to popularize the game throughout the country prior to the formation of the NFL.

By 1915 football had started to be played on a professional level. A game in Canton, Ohio, between the Canton Bulldogs and the Massillon Tigers featured Jim Thorpe on the Bulldogs and Knute Rockne on the Tigers. Thorpe, a Native American, was a bruising running back as well as a great all-around athlete who won gold medals in the 1912 Olympics. Rockne, a Norwegian immigrant who grew up in Chicago and went to Notre Dame, was a determined tackler and sure-handed receiver. At the time, of course, players played both offense and defense and by now forward passes were allowed. In the game between the two teams, Thorpe kicked two field goals for a 6–0 Bulldogs victory. Rockne went on to become a legendary coach at Notre Dame, coaching the team to five unbeaten seasons and two national championships (1924, 1930). One of his teams included the legendary Four Horsemen. Also noteworthy was the 1928 victory in which the team would "Win One for the Gipper." George Gipp was the nation's outstanding college player in 1920 who developed pneumonia. Before dying, he told Rockne that some day there would be a critical game in which Rockne might ask the players to "win one for the Gipper." In such a game against Army at the Yankee Stadium, Rockne asked his team to do just that. Sure enough, the team won one for the Gipper. The story later was made into a film in which Ronald Reagan, future president, played George Gipp.

In 1920 the NFL was founded as a professional league. Prior to then there had been some successful professional teams but the enterprise remained a financial risk—players could jump at will from one team to another, driving up salaries. This was at a time when most players were paid fifty to seventy-five dollars a game, approximately six hundred dollars a game in current terms. In addition there was a public relations problem— college players played in professional games under assumed names. In all, the makeup of teams could change from week to week, and even from game to game when multiple games were played in the course of a week.

In 1920 there was an attempt to stabilize the situation. Men from twelve Midwestern cities met in an auto showroom. A few sat on chairs, the rest on running boards that then were part of the auto exterior. The result was the formation of the American Professional Football Association. The association had the stated purposes of coordinating schedules, eliminating bidding for football players, and preventing the signing of college players still in school.

In 1921 there were teams playing on dirt fields in Chicago, Green Bay, Cleveland, Cincinnati, Detroit, Buffalo, Canton, Akron, Dayton, Columbus, Rock Island, and Rochester. Noticeably lacking were teams in major east and west coast cities. As few as a couple of hundred fans or as many as a couple of thousand fans would attend a game. Following that first season the name of the league was changed to the National Football League—the NFL. With attendance ranging between a few hundred and a few thousand fans, financial difficulties remained for many teams. By 1925, however, there was a sellout game at Wrigley Field in Chicago in which over thirty thousand fans came out to see the Galloping Ghost, Red Grange, play for the Bears, then owned by the legendary George Halas. The following year, 1926, Grange was part of an effort to form a rival league, the AFL. The league folded after one year. Although there was interest in professional football, the sport clearly remained overshadowed by interest in college football and professional baseball.

1925: Tim Mara Brings Professional Football to New York

With the newly formed league having mixed success and many teams in financial distress, the NFL owners felt that a team in a major city on the east coast was necessary for the future success of the league. The owners dispatched the league president, Joe Carr, to find someone who could establish such a team. Carr contacted Billy Gibson, the manager of boxer Gene Tunney, soon to become the heavyweight champion of the world. Gibson was reluctant to take on the risk associated with establishing a team in New York and suggested that Tim Mara, who Gibson knew from Mara's efforts to invest in Tunney, might be interested. The rest is history.

In 1925 Tim Mara purchased the Giants, thus bringing professional football to New York. Mara was a successful businessman and bookmaker at a time when bookmaking was legal. The cost of the franchise was a reported five hundred dollars, with an estimated additional $25,000 necessary to actually get the team going. In 2007 dollars that initial purchase amount would have been approximately three hundred thousand dollars—not a bad investment, given that in 1991 half the team was sold for a reported seventy-five million dollars, and in 2007 its estimated value was in the area of one billion dollars! Mara had figured that the rights to any New York franchise was worth the price he paid. According to his son Wellington, he also figured that an empty store in New York City was worth that.[2] At the time, however, most people considered this a risky investment and, in fact, there would be difficult financial times before the team and the league achieved their current success.

Mara, who reportedly had never seen a professional football game until his purchase of the team, named the team after baseball's New York Giants. The team immediately became a family affair with Tim Mara's two young sons, Jack, then 17, and Wellington, then 9, taking an active interest in the team. Wellington told the story of his attendance at the first home game, played in the Polo Grounds against the Frankford Yellow Jackets: "I sat in the stands behind the Giants bench with my mother, and in the second half I joined my brother Jack on the sidelines.... I remember it was a little chilly that day, and my mother, after the game, complained to my father that we had sat in the shade. Why couldn't we go over to the other side of the field and sit in the sun, where we would be nice and warm? she asked. The next game, and from that point on, the Giants sideline in the Polo Grounds was on the sunny side of the field."[3]

Mara, an experienced promoter, recognized that the fledgling team would require a player of name recognition to bring in the fans and signed the great Jim Thorpe to play for the Giants. Thorpe, by now thirty-seven and hardly able to play a full game, was paid $200 per half. As it was, he was only able to play in three games. The early years were difficult for the Giants, both professionally and financially. In that opening season they lost their first three games, including a 14–0 loss to the Yellow Jackets in their first home game. However, they went on to win their next seven games and by the end of the season had outscored their opponents by a considerable margin.

From a financial standpoint, the team was operating at a loss and Mara was being urged by many to give up the enterprise. Then they hit "pay dirt" in a December game against the Chicago Bears. The Bears were led by Red Grange, the legendary "Galloping Ghost." More than seventy thousand fans packed the Polo Grounds to see the three-time All-American—a crowd beyond capacity and the largest to ever attend a professional football game. The game was close until near the end when Grange intercepted a pass and raced thirty-five yards for a touchdown. The final score was Bears 19, Giants 7. Although a disappointing loss, the game allowed Mara to wipe out his losses. It similarly was a financial success for Grange, whom Mara earlier had tried to sign for the Giants. He reportedly made thirty thousand dollars in the game—more than Tim Mara's costs to purchase and finance the start of the Giants team. Dissatisfied with the contract offered to him by the Bears for the 1926 season, Grange joined the American Football League's Yankees, playing in Yankee Stadium, for the one season that the league existed before its collapse.

During the rest of the decade the team had mixed professional and financial success. On the positive professional side, the team won its first title in 1927, with the league now down to twelve teams from an earlier twenty-two. The following year, 1928, the team, now with its third head coach, was badly outscored by its opponents and ended the season with a losing record. In addition, it lost money for the third year in a row. Desperate to improve things on both the professional and financial fronts, the team hired a new coach, got rid of many players, and bought an entire team, the Detroit Wolverines, so that they could acquire a star quarterback, Benny Friedman.

Small, at five foot eight inches and one hundred and seventy pounds, Friedman was considered the best passer in the game, described by Red Grange as the best quarterback he ever played against. During the 1928 season Friedman led his team, the Wolverines, to a victory and a tie in their two games against the Giants. In the first game Friedman led the team with his running and passing to a 28–0 victory. In the second game, he brought them from behind with two touchdown drives, both ending with his throwing touchdown passes. Thus, the Giants knew first-hand what they were getting when they landed Friedman. And Friedman did not disappoint them, leading the league with nineteen touchdown passes, eight of them to Ray Flaherty, the star end the Giants also obtained for the 1929 season.

In addition to his league-leading passing, Friedman led the league in kicking extra points. Friedman was well worth the league-leading salary of ten thousand dollars he was paid for the season. In addition to the improvement in team play there also were financial dividends from the addition of Friedman, with the team showing a profit for the first time since the 1925 season. Thus, by the end of the decade, the Giants were a rejuvenated team and had weathered the 1926 intrusion of a rival league and a team in their home territory.

The Steve Owen Era: 1931–1953

In 1931 Steve Owen became head coach of the Giants. The deal was made with a handshake and Owen continued as head coach without an actual contract for the next twenty-two years. Owen had joined the team as a lineman in 1926. Known as "Stout Steve," he stood at 5'10" with a reported playing weight of 225 pounds—not small for the time. He anchored the defensive line during the championship 1927 season when the team had an 11-1-1 record and held the opposition to twenty points.

The Giants were not very successful during the first two years of Owen's tenure as head coach. Benny Friedman played only part of the 1931 season and not at all during the 1932 season. Prior to the latter he had asked to become part owner of the Giants and signed with the rival Brooklyn Dodgers when Mara committed the team to remaining a family operation: "Benny, I'm sorry, but this is a family business and the Giants are for my sons."[4] A few years later the young Wellington was about to make his first contribution to the team. His mother had given him a movie camera for Christmas. He began taking movies of the team which then were used for team analysis. Wellington became the official cameraman of the team and then, with the advent of Polaroid instant pictures, he would take pictures of alignments from the press box and sixty seconds later send them down to the sidelines on a weighted sock.

Things turned for the better in the 1933 season with the team winning the division championship with an 11–3 record. The team was led by ends Ray Badgro and Ray Flaherty, center Mel Hein, halfback Ken Strong, and quarterback Harry Newman. Flaherty played offense and defense for the Giants for seven seasons (1928–1934). Badgro played during many of the same seasons as Flaherty and was an All-Pro during the 1931, 1933, and 1934 seasons. Both Flaherty and Badgro became members of the Pro Football Hall of Fame.

Hein joined the Giants in 1931, the same year that Owen became head coach. In addition to playing linebacker, he was recognized as a great center, being named All-Pro for eight consecutive years (1933–1940). Hein had originally signed with another professional team when he hadn't heard anything from the Giants. While playing in a basketball game he was informed by Ray Flaherty that the Giants were making him a better offer, one hundred and fifty dollars a game. He was able to intercept his signed contract with the other team and sign with the Giants: "I think at that time $150 was probably the highest pay of any lineman in the league. It was pretty good money, even though it would not sound that way now, but you could buy a loaf of bread for a nickel and get a full meal for thirty-five cents in the Automat back then. And you had no income tax."[5]

Strong, another Hall of Famer, was described by Wellington Mara as one of the greatest halfbacks of all time—a great runner, passer, and kicker. Whereas the Giants only almost missed out on signing Hein, they initially missed out entirely on signing Strong. When Strong was signed after playing three years with another team, he was asked by Tim Mara why he had signed originally with another team for less money. Strong was puzzled by the question, thinking he had been offered five thousand dollars when actually he had been offered twice that amount. Apparently the employee was either going to pocket the difference or was attempting to save the club some money. Finally, Newman was an All-American from Michigan who led the Giants in rushing and passing in both 1933 and 1934.

Although 1933 was a very successful one for the Giants, it ended on a disappointing note with a loss to the Chicago Bears, 23–21, in the first NFL championship game. Three plays were of particular note in a game that saw the lead change hands six times. In the first, the center Hein hiked the ball to Newman, who had come under him to take the snap. Newman immediately returned it to Hein between his legs. Hein then hid the ball under his shirt and ran downfield. Most of the Bears defense focused on Newman, who was faking a pass. Unfortunately for the Giants, one of the Bears defenders spotted Hein and tackled him downfield before a touchdown could be scored.

In the second play of note, a Bear player, playing without a helmet, caught a pass and then pitched it back to another Bear who took it in for a touchdown, putting the Bears ahead in the game. In the third play, with but a few seconds remaining in the game, Red Grange, playing defense, stopped Badgro before he could pass the goal line on a completed pass from Newman. For the game, the individual player shares were $210.34 for the Bears and $142.22 for the Giants.

In 1934 the Giants again won their division championship, entitling them to a repeat contest against the Bears, again winner of their division championship. The Giants already had lost twice that season to the Bears, the second before a crowd of fifty-five thousand at the Polo Grounds. The game also was noteworthy for an injury to Newman—broken bones in his back. With Newman out of the game and lost for the rest of the season, the Giants had to turn to Ed Danowski, new to the team this year. Nevertheless, in the NFL championship game the Giants were able to prevail against the Bears in what came to be known as the "Sneakers Game."

1934 NFL Championship: "The Sneakers Game"

The Giants were playing the Bears in the NFL championship game for the second year in a row, having lost to the Bears the previous year in the closing minutes of the game. This year the Giants were playing at home before over thirty thousand fans who had braved the nine-degree temperature. The freezing rain the night before and the freezing temperatures of game day had turned the field into a sheet of ice. Playing without Harry Newman, their injured starting quarterback, by the end of the first half the Giants had fallen behind by a score of 10–3. The larger Bears, led by their fullback Bronko Nagurski, had been able to push the Giants defense back on the slippery field.

The Bears added a third-quarter field goal while holding the Giants scoreless, so that by the end of that period the Bears were ahead by a score of 13–3. Things did not look good for the Giants. Lo and behold, the Giants were able to score twenty-seven points in the fourth quarter, assisted by sneakers, of all things. Prior to the game, end Ray Flaherty had observed the slippery conditions of the field and remembered a college game in which his team, playing under similar field conditions, had been able to defeat a stronger team by wearing sneakers borrowed from the basketball team. Flaherty mentioned the idea to Steve Owen, the head coach, who thought it had merit. Without a basketball team to turn to, Owen dispatched Abe Cohen, a tailor then on the Giants' payroll in the role of making pants for the players, to find the sneakers for the team. As luck would have it, Cohen had access to the equipment room at Manhattan College, where he was able to "borrow" nine or ten pairs of sneakers from the basketball team. Rushing by taxi back to the Polo Grounds, Cohen presented his prized contraband to the Giants players.

As described by Wellington Mara, some of the players were reluctant to use the sneakers. However, observing the success of those who did wear them, most of the players turned to using them as well. Among those players was the halfback and kicker, Ken Strong, who lost the toenail on his big toe while kicking with the sneakers. In any case, the Giants now had better traction than the sliding Bears and were able to move the ball in a way that previously had been impossible. A desperate George Halas, coach of the Bears, told his players to step on the toes of the sneaker-clad Giants players. But to no avail. The Giants were able to score twenty-seven unanswered points and thereby to win their first NFL championship by the score of 30–13. Whereas the Bears had outrushed the Giants in the first half, sixty-seven to twenty-nine yards, the sneaker-wearing Giants were able to completely turn the tables in the second half, outrushing the Bears one hundred and twenty-eight yards to twenty-seven yards! A disheartened Halas immediately bought sneakers for his team, vowing that he would never get caught like that again.

Apparently the Giants were not only aided by sneakers but by whiskey as well. During the fourth quarter the Giants' trainer, Gus Mauch, decided that the players could use some whiskey to warm them up. Obtaining a bottle from Jack Mara, Mauch took the opportunity of a fourth-quarter timeout to pour some whiskey into paper cups. On the next play, Ken Strong ran for a touchdown. Seeking to duplicate his success, Mauch did the same thing on the following timeout, with another score the result. Feeling confident in their lead and fearing what could become a team of drunks, the Giants stopped imbibing while they were ahead.[6]

In the remaining five years of the decade, the Giants played in three NFL championship games, winning one and losing two. In 1935 Harry Newman left the Giants in a contract dispute. Newman's contract involved a percentage of the gate. With the Polo Grounds filled for big games, the Giants were reluctant to continue that arrangement with Newman. In addition they felt comfortable with Danowski at quarterback, although he had only thrown twelve passes in the championship game. Newman's holdout was unsuccessful and he rejoined the team later in the season, but by then Danowski had established himself at quarterback, completing fifty percent of his passes and rushing for over three hundred yards. Together with a strong defense that held the opposition to under one hundred points for the season, the Giants were able to win their third straight division championship. In the NFL championship game, played before a small crowd in Detroit against the Lions, the Giants lost by the score of 26–7. Under terrible weather conditions, the Giants were only able to muster one score — a touchdown pass from Danowski to Strong.

The 1936 season was noteworthy for the Giants for two reasons. First, they had a losing record for only the third time in twelve seasons. In part this was due to the loss of players such as Strong, Newman, and Badgro to the fledgling American Football League, and the retirement of Flaherty. Second, in what was the first year of the NFL draft, acting on the recommendation of a young Wellington Mara, the Giants selected the running back Alphonse "Tuffy" Leemans in the second round. Their first-round selection turned out to be a disappointment, playing in New York for only one season. However, in Leemans they found a back who would star for them in rushing and passing for much of the next eight years. In an otherwise disappointing season, Leemans led the NFL in rushing in his rookie season.

Given the disappointing previous season, the Giants made major changes for the 1937 season, having seventeen rookies on their twenty-five man roster. Led by Danowski and Leemans, and bolstered by rookie backs Hank Soar and Ward Cuff, the Giants were able to return to a winning record. Playing in the blue jerseys and silver pants that would become their hallmark for years to come, the Giants lost to the Washington Redskins, led by the legendary Slinging Sammy Baugh, at the end of the season and ended up as the runner-up in their division. This was the second of four straight seasons, 1936–1939, in which the Giants and Redskins would battle to the end for the division championship. The Redskins went on to defeat the Bears in the NFL championship game.

The Giants returned to their winning ways the next two seasons, winning their division and playing for the NFL championship in each of these years. In 1938 they again were led on offense by Danowski, Leemans, Soar, and Cuff. In addition, a strong defense held the opposition to an incredible low of seventy-nine points during the eleven-game season. Reversing their previous season's loss to the Redskins, the Giants shut out the Redskins to win the division championship. The NFL championship game, pitting the Giants against the Green Bay Packers, was played at the Polo Grounds before a record championship-game crowd of almost fifty thousand fans. Statistically the Packers far outplayed the Giants, outgaining them by over one hundred and fifty yards. However, in what was described as a barroom fight outdoors, the Giants won the game by a 23–17 score. The winning score came on a leaping goal-line reception by Soar in which he dragged the Packer defender over the line for a touchdown. Playing for the Giants for almost a decade, Soar went on to become a major-league baseball umpire. An additional note of glory was the naming of Mel Hein as the year's MVP of the NFL.

In the final season of the decade, the Giants again won their division but lost badly to the same Packers in the NFL championship game—27–0. The Giants again were led by their star backfield and a strong defense that held the opposition to under one hundred points in eleven games. In the championship game, however, the Giants seemed particularly bothered by the weather in the Packer stadium. Playing in gusting winds in a stadium with open ends, the Giants threw six interceptions and missed three field goals—a disappointing end to a decade for which they had much to be proud.

Four Giants of the '30s: Badgro, Leemans, Strong, and Hein

Three players from the Giants of the '30s are considered among the greatest NFL players of all time: Morris (Red) Badgro, Alphonse (Tuffy) Leemans, Ken Strong, and Mel Hein. Badgro, a 6' and 190-pound end, joined the Giants in 1930 after a year with the New York Yankees football team and two years in professional baseball. After finding that he could not hit in baseball as well as he thought, he signed on with the Giants for one hundred and fifty dollars a game—as he noted, "I didn't exactly get rich on that salary."[7] During his six seasons with the Giants, Badgro played both defensive and offensive end. He scored the first touchdown in the first NFL championship game (1933) and was named to the All–NFL team in 1931, 1933, and 1934. In 1934 he tied for the NFL's pass-catching title. He was elected to the NFL Hall of Fame in 1981, the oldest player to be so honored.

Tuffy Leemans was a halfback/fullback who played for the Giants from 1936 to 1943. He was scouted by a young Wellington Mara, who recognized the talent in this triple-threat running back while observing him in a game between George Washington, his college, and Alabama. Partly on Wellington Mara's recommendation, Leemans was selected by the Giants in the second round of the first NFL draft (1936). Although previously relatively unknown, Leemans was the MVP in the 1936 College Football All-Star Game. He immediately made an impact with the Giants, leading the NFL in rushing in his rookie season. He was named All–NFL in 1936 and 1939, and during his career the Giants won three division titles and one NFL championship (1938). During his career he rushed for over three thousand yards, passed for over two thousand yards and sixteen touchdowns, had over four hundred yards in receptions, and averaged almost fourteen yards per punt return. He was elected to the Hall of Fame in 1978 and his number has been retired by the Giants.

Ken Strong played for the Giants from 1933 to 1935, in 1939, and from 1944 to 1947. Not only was he a triple threat, he could do everything on the football field — run, pass, receive, punt and kick field goals, and play strong defense. As noted, the Giants missed out on signing him after college and for four years he played with the relatively unknown Staten Island Stapletons, being a virtual one-man team as he carried the ball most of the time, did the passing, did the punting and place kicking, and did much of the tackling. He played with the Giants for three seasons before jumping to the rival AFL and then returned to them in 1939. He retired at that time but came back as a kicking specialist during the years 1944–1947. At the time of his retirement he was the all-time leading scorer for the Giants, the points coming on touchdowns, field goals, and extra points. He was inducted into the Hall of Fame in 1967 and his number has been retired by the Giants.

Over the course of his fifteen seasons with the Giants (1931–1945), Mel Hein never missed a game, playing sixty minutes a game as center on offense and linebacker on defense. Hein was named an All–NFL center for eight straight seasons (1933–1940) and MVP in 1938, the year the Giants won the championship. Among the sidelights to his play with the Giants were his experiences with pay. Although Hein was a college All-American he was not heavily recruited by the NFL. He first signed and mailed a contract to play for the Providence Steam Rollers for $135 per game. Just after mailing the contract he learned that the Giants would pay him $150 per game, so he wired the Providence postmaster to have the Steam Roller contract returned.

Later, after being named MVP in 1938, Hein felt that a salary increase was in order. In addition to the MVP honor, he had been named All-Pro for six consecutive years. He also was one of the few Giants players to play the entire game, both offense and defense, every game of the season. Hein asked Jack Mara for a contract for three hundred dollars a game, which, adjusted for inflation, is less than a hundred thousand dollars for a sixteen-game season. Mara turned him down.

Although he liked Mara and the Giants, Hein was angry and he looked elsewhere. He was offered a job with the Los Angeles Bulldogs, a pro team not part of the NFL, that included a year-round position with the owner's business. Mara got wind of this and sent a number of telegrams to Hein with increased offers, all of which were rejected by Hein since they did not come to what he had requested. Finally, Hein sent a telegram to Mara saying: "Don't send any more telegrams or call me. My mind is definitely made up. I'm going to stay out on the Pacific Coast."[8] Immediately he received a telegram from Mara that gave him the contract he wanted. The rest is history.

Hein was enshrined in the NFL Hall of Fame in 1963 and his number was retired by the Giants.

The decade of the '30s was important for the league as the game increasingly took on the character of professional football as it would come to be known—the shape of the football increasingly one that enabled long spiral passes, the T-formation, the use of numbers on jerseys, the use of helmets by the players, the draft to select players, the Pro Bowl (1939), and at least one version of a platoon system.[9] For the Giants, clearly it was a time of success as they became one of the powerhouses of the league. At the same time that there was increased fan interest, however, the teams struggled financially. At one point there was a decline in the number of NFL teams due to financial difficulties. Tim Mara suffered substantial losses during the stock market crash and depression, leading him to hand over the franchise to his sons Jack and Wellington, then twenty-two and fourteen: "We managed to make it through the early years of the NFL and the Depression. Money, needless to say, was very tight in those days. But my father felt sports businesses might prosper somewhat in those economically depressed times because they offered the best entertainment around for the money. And he was right."[10]

The first half of the '40s was dominated by events surrounding World War II. The 1941 NFL championship game, in which the Bears beat the

Giants by a score of 37–9, was played two weeks after Pearl Harbor. It was the first of what would be a number of occasions in which national and world events would influence decisions concerning play in the NFL. For the 1943 season the league was reduced from ten to eight teams, with the Philadelphia and Pittsburgh teams combining to form the Steagles. During this period some players were lost to military service while others were dissuaded from retirement or brought out of retirement. For the Giants, among those drafted into the military in 1942 was their quarterback Danowski who, after retiring before the 1940 season, had come out of retirement for the 1941 season. Ken Strong, at the age of thirty-eight, was brought out of retirement to serve as a placekicking specialist. And Mel Hein, who had been with the Giants since 1933 and retired after the 1942 season, was convinced by coach Steve Owen to come out of retirement and play on weekends. Hein, thirty-five at the time, would teach physical education and play touch football during the week at Union College in Schenectady, New York, work out with the team on Saturdays, play on Sunday, and then head back to Schenectady on Sunday.

The Giants of the '40s were not the powerhouse they had been in the '30s. The powerhouse team of the period was the Chicago Bears, led by their exceptional quarterback Sid Luckman. Born in Brooklyn and graduating from Columbia, Luckman was a triple-threat back who flourished when head coach George Halas introduced him to the T-formation in 1939. After some initial difficulties, Luckman went on to become the first great NFL T-formation quarterback. Within their own division, the Giants were challenged by the Washington Redskins, led by their own great quarterback, Slingin' Sammy Baugh. A college All-American from Texas Christian University, he arrived as a rookie with the Redskins and was told by the coach to "hit the receiver in the eye." Baugh asked: "Coach, which eye?"[11]

Unfortunately, the Giants did not have a comparable quarterback of their own, at least until 1948 when Charlie Conerly, billed as "the new Sammy Baugh," joined the team. During the decade their record ranged from a high of 8-1-1 in 1944 to a low of 2-8-2 in 1947. Even when the Giants won their division they were beaten in the championship game. In 1941 the Bears beat the Giants 37–9, the lone Giants touchdown coming on a touchdown pass by Tuffy Leemans. In 1944, the Giants lost in the championship game to Green Bay, 14–7. And in 1946 once again they lost in the championship game to the Bears, 24–14. This game was of particular note because suspected of bribes to Giants players to throw the game. The day before the game the Giants learned that their quarterback, Frank Filchock, and their fullback, Merle Hapes, were under investigation in relation to the attempt to fix the championship game. Filchock that year had earned All-Pro honors as he passed for over one thousand yards and led the team in rushing. Hapes had been the Giants' leading ground gainer in 1942 and had just returned from military service for the 1946 season. As the story unfolded, Hapes had been offered a bribe, had not taken it, but had not informed the team or officials of the offer. In addition, he had allowed himself to be associated with the attempted fixer, a known gambler. He was suspended indefinitely by the new NFL commissioner, Bert Bell. Filchock claimed that he had not been offered a bribe and was allowed to play in the game. Playing his heart out and for much of the game with a broken nose, Filchock passed for two touchdowns but also was intercepted six times. In the end, Filchock as well as Hapes was banned from the NFL by Bell.

Two other events were of particular note for the NFL during this period. First, in 1946 a new league, the All-America Football Conference (AAFC) was formed. The league included the Cleveland Browns, headed by coach Paul Brown, and the Brooklyn Dodgers, whose owner Dan Topping left the NFL over a disagreement with Tim Mara over home dates for the two teams. He renamed his AAFC team the New York Yankees, after the baseball team of which he was a part owner. The AAFC only lasted through 1949, with three teams merging into the NFL in 1950—the Cleveland Browns, the San Francisco 49ers, and the Baltimore Colts. For the NFL, the three teams added would have storied histories. The Browns in particular became an immediate powerhouse, winning the NFL championship in their first year in the league. For the Giants, the merger meant the addition of four outstanding defensive players—defensive backs Tom Landry, Otto Schnellbacher, and Harmon Rowe, and tackle Arnie Weinmeister.

The second event worthy of note was the integration of the NFL. Blacks had played with some teams in the early years of the league but since the 1933 season not a single black player had played in the NFL, duplicating the segregation found in major league baseball. This was despite the fact that talented black players were performing with college teams and there was a manpower shortage during the war years. The spotlight of racism in the NFL fell on Kenny Washington, a black player who at UCLA led the nation in total offense in 1939. Washington had size, speed, and strength as a passer and runner. He was viewed by many, including Jackie Robinson, his former UCLA teammate, as the best football player of all time. Despite his accomplishments, Washington was not selected to any All-American team and was not drafted into the NFL. Some NFL owners, including Tim Mara, had been encouraged to draft Washington but none chose to break the racial barrier. From 1940 through 1946 Washington played with minor professional teams, hurting his knee so badly that he was disqualified from military service. Finally, in 1946 he was signed to a contract with the Los Angeles Rams.

The major breakthrough in terms of integration occurred with the merging of the AAFC into the NFL. Three players are particularly noteworthy. Marion Motley, of the Cleveland Browns, was the leading rusher of the AAFC for the four years of its existence and the leading rusher in the NFL in 1950. Not only was he an exceptional fullback but he also was an exceptional blocker for the Browns quarterback, Otto Graham, and an exceptional linebacker. In 1968 he became the first African-American to be elected to the NFL Hall of Fame. The second player, Buddy Young, played for the AAFC New York Yankees before the merger with the NFL. At 5'4" and 175 pounds, Young was small even for those times. However, he was fast and elusive, and could receive and return punts as well as serve as an occasional runner. Finally, in 1949, George Taliaferro, a running back and passer from Indiana, became the first African-American player selected in the NFL draft. Selected by the Chicago Bears, Taliaferro signed with the Los Angeles team in the AAFC. He then played with the New York Yankees with the folding of the AAFC.

For the Giants, integration occurred with the entrance of Emlen Tunnell into the Giants' office before the start of the 1948 season. The Giants, seeing his versatility as a punt and kick returner as well as a defensive back, signed him to a contract. He immediately began to make a contribution to the team, making seven interceptions in 1948 and ten in 1949. During the latter season he led the team in interceptions and averaged over twenty-five yards per interception. Over the course of his eleven years with the Giants (1948–1958) he had seventy-four interceptions and 257 punt returns, both Giants team records. He played his final three years in the NFL with Green Bay. Over the course of his career he became an All-Pro four times and set a number of records for a defensive back. He was elected into the Hall of Fame in 1967. At that point he was the first African-American and the first purely defensive player to be enshrined.

Entering the decade of the '50s, things did not look bright for the Giants— they had been outgained by their opponents the last three seasons and their quarterback, Charlie Conerly, had ended the '49 season completing less than fifty percent of his passes and throwing more interceptions than touchdowns. In addition, the powerhouse Cleveland Browns, led by their star quarterback Otto Graham, were now a part of the NFL's American Conference, the same conference the Giants were part of. At the same time, there was hope that an improved defense, led by the players who had been added from the AAFC, might carry the team forward. There was also hope that the switch in 1949 to a T-formation offense, and the addition that year of Allie Sherman to work with Conerly, might begin to pay dividends.

As it turned out, the hopes for the team were realized during the years 1950–1952. During these years the team had winning records, outgained their opponents, and, at least during 1950 and 1951, showed improvement on defense. The defense was particularly helped by Owen's introduction in 1950 of the umbrella defense in which two defensive backs played shallow and wide and the two other defensive backs played deep and tight. Of course, the success of this new defensive backfield arrangement was facilitated in no small part by the addition of Schnellenbacher, Rowe, and Landry from the AAFC, as well as the continued stellar play of Emlen Tunnell.

On offense, Conerly was not showing great improvement but there was improvement in the running game, led first by the addition of Eddie Price in 1950 and then by the addition of Kyle Rote in 1951. Frank Gifford, who later would play such an important role in the running and receiving game, arrived in 1952, but was used mainly as a defensive back in his first year.

While many of the hopes for these years were realized, the Giants still could not play to the level of the Cleveland Browns. Led at various points during this time by Otto Graham at quarterback, Marion Motley at running back, Dante Lavelli and Mac Speedie at receiver, and Lou Groza at kicker, the Browns won the conference championship every year between 1950 and 1955! In addition, during this time they won three NFL championships. Along with these and other stellar players, the Browns were led by their namesake coach, Paul Brown. Brown exercised complete control over the organization and team, introducing such innovations as classrooms and playbooks, film scouting, grading of players, face bars on helmets, and rotating guards as messengers to bring in each new play.[12]

By the end of the 1952 season there were signs that the Giants were weakening as a team, particularly on defense. Their record had gone from 10–2 in 1950 to 7–5 in 1952, and then there was he collapse in 1953 to a 3–9 record. The 1953 team was strengthened by the addition of three offensive linemen who would play a major role in future Giants successes—Rosie Brown at tackle, Jack Stroud at guard, and Ray Wietecha at center. However, once more the defense gave up more points than the offense scored and the offense had more interceptions than those produced by the defensive backfield, something that had last occurred in 1949. Following the collapse of the Giants, the Maras did something they had never done before and would be reluctant to do in the future—they fired their coach of twenty-three years, Steve Owen. Despite the poor season, the move came as a shock to Owen, the coach who was so close to the senior Mara that, rather than sign a contract before each season, the two just shook hands.

"Stout Steve"—Coach of the Giants 1931–1953

Born in 1898, "Stout Steve" Owen came from a small Oklahoma college, Phillips University, and began his pro football career with a traveling team, the Kansas City Blues. After a brief stay with another team he was sold to the New York Giants in 1926 for five hundred dollars, and thus began a career with the team that would last for twenty-eight years.

Owen began his career with the Giants as a star defensive tackle, captaining the 1927 NFL title team which held the opponents to a record low of twenty points. He was a player from 1926 to 1931, during which time he was a four-time All–NFL tackle. He was co-coach in 1930 with Benny Friedman, and then head coach for the next twenty-three years. Over the years Owen had a coaching record of 153-100-17, a record that included eight divisional titles and two NFL titles. Also included in his record was the 1934 victory over the Chicago Bears in the "Sneakers Game." He was an innovative coach, his innovations including the A-formation offense and the umbrella defense. The umbrella defense was particularly important in stopping the passing game of the Cleveland Browns, led by the great Otto Graham.

After ending his career as head coach of the Giants in 1953, Owen became a scout for the Giants for one year, then an assistant first at Baylor University, then with the Philadelphia Eagles for two years, then head coach of the Canadian Football League's Toronto Argonauts, and finally head coach of the CFL Saskatchewan Roughriders, all fulfilling his love of coaching. He died in 1964, and in 1966 was inducted into the NFL Hall of Fame.

In sum, during the period 1925–1953 the league generally, and the Giants in particular, had their ups and downs. However, overall professional football was on an upward trajectory. For the Giants, and the NFL, the best was yet to come.

2

The Glory Years (1954–1963)

The decade of 1954 to 1963 represents years of glory for the Giants: NFL champs in 1956; division champs in 1958, 1959, 1961–1963; an overall record of 86–35–5; Hall of Fame players such as Roosevelt Brown, Frank Gifford, Sam Huff, Andy Robustelli, and Emlen Tunnell; participation in what many consider to be the greatest game ever played, the 1958 championship game against the Baltimore Colts; and beginning of the chant of "Dee-Fense!" There were great teams and great players to be battled but the Giants held their own and then some. This was a period during which football became increasingly specialized and complex, during which attendance increased, and television became increasingly important.

The Players

Some of the players to be remembered from this era are, on *offense*: Charlie Conerly (Quarterback), Frank Gifford and Alex Webster (Halfbacks), Mel Triplett (Fullback), Kyle Rote (End), Rosey Brown (Tackle), Bill Austin and Jack Stroud (Guards), Ray Wietecha (Center). Those to be remembered from the *defense* are: Jim Katcavage and Andy Robustelli (Ends), Rosey Grier and Dick Modzelewski (Tackles), Sam Huff, Harland Svare, and Bill Svoboda (Linebackers), Emlen Tunnell, Jimmy Patton, Tom Landry, Dick Nolan, and Erich Barnes (Defensive Backs). Kickers were Don Chandler (Punts) and Pat Summerall (Field Goals).

Frank Gifford (1952–1960, 1962–1964)

Frank Gifford was a multitalented player—he could run, pass, and receive; he could play offense and defense. In fact, he was so multitalented that for a time it was unclear where he should play. His story is almost out of Hollywood, which is ironic since he almost became a Hollywood movie star and did become a famed television announcer on Monday Night Football.

As described in his autobiography, Gifford grew up poor, his father an oil field worker who moved from job to job without any financial security.[1] He drifted in high school until his football coach took him under his wing. He starred as a single wing quarterback and tailback who also could punt and return punts. He was heavily recruited by colleges but had not taken the necessary courses to meet the entrance requirements. Upon the advice of his high school coach, he enrolled at Bakersfield (CA) Junior College, where he became a junior college All-American. He was again heavily recruited by a number of major colleges, including an offer of a car and $500 a month by an alum of the University of Arizona. However, he decided to attend the University of Southern California (USC), his high school coach's alma mater.

At USC, Gifford's scholarship covered tuition only, so he worked mornings and evenings cleaning the gym to earn extra money. He started out as a defensive back, punter, and extra point kicker. In his senior year, a new coach switched him to a wing T and single wing tailback while also playing him as a defensive back. He gained considerable publicity as he led USC to an upset over the number-one ranked UCLA. In his senior year he rushed for over 800 yards, completed more than half his passes, had 11 receptions for 178 yards, had 3 interceptions, and kicked 26 extra points and 2 field goals. At the same time, he worked as a stunt man and bit player in several Hollywood films.

Wellington Mara was impressed with Gifford's play in the USC–Army game at Yankee Stadium, as was Vince Lombardi, who at the time was an assistant coach at Army. Mara also scouted the East-West Game and Senior Bowl after the old Giant Mel Hein recommended that he take a look at Gifford: "That's really how they scouted in those days. There weren't any combines or things like that, or even scouting departments for the individual teams. People like Wellington Mara relied on the coaches they knew, former players, and they listened to their recommendations."[2] So the Giants drafted Gifford with their first selection in the 1952 draft. The first question was how to get him. He was offered $7,500 by the Giants but almost twice as much by the Edmonton Eskimos of the Canadian Football League. So the Giants increased their offer to $8,000. with an immediate signing bonus of $250 and help in payment of doctor bills associated with his wife's pregnancy. This was the beginning of a long-term relationship of affection and trust between him and the Mara family generally and Wellington Mara in particular. The second question was where to play him. The Giants had drafted Kyle Rote as their halfback the year before, so Gifford was selected as a defensive back.

Gifford's introduction to the Giants was not an easy one. He had problems with the coach, Steve Owen, whom Gifford felt did not care about offense, and who believed in the intimidation of players. At the same time, he was resented by teammates who viewed him as a glamour boy. They treated him rough in practice, cursed him, and isolated him socially. In his first year he made the Pro Bowl as a defensive back but things got worse in 1953. That year the Giants won only three games. According to Gifford there was low team morale, the head coach Steve Owen had lost touch with his players, the equipment was poor (torn jerseys were patched and players had to replace their own worn shoes), and the owners were having financial problems. Attendance at the Polo Grounds averaged fewer than twenty thousand fans a game and "we weren't all that certain of our paychecks." Gifford considered quitting football, as he was playing for a losing team, taking a physical beating, and making $8,000!

Fortunately, things began to change in 1954 with the arrival of Jim Lee Howell as head coach and Vince Lombardi as assistant coach in charge of the offense. Lombardi made Gifford into a halfback and emphasized power sweeps, with two pulling guards around end, and option plays where the halfback had the option of running or passing. Gifford increased his rushing yardage, averaged 5.6 yards per carry, passed for three touchdowns in eight passing attempts, and had fourteen receptions for 154 yards in nine games. He and Kyle Rote were injured in the ninth game of the season, Rote with a concussion and Gifford with a torn ligament in his knee: "The second I felt my knee go, I thought, God, my career's over.... For the next nine years of my career, I never played one game without being aware of my knee."[3] It is interesting here that in his '93 book Gifford expressed the view that in later times surgery was done too readily and players rushed back into play too quickly. He seemed to favor Doc Sweeney's earlier treatment approach of time, nature, and good Scotch whiskey.[4]

Things really picked up for Gifford and the Giants in 1956, the year they won the championship and Gifford was named the Most Valuable Player. In that year Gifford rushed for over eight hundred yards, again averaging over five yards a carry, and caught 51 passes. Under Lombardi's guidance, the offense became more diverse, with more players involved. At the same time, the defense became the favorite of the fans who responded with the chant of "Dee-Fense." In the NFL championship game, the Giants beat the Chicago Bears 47–7, with Gifford scoring a touchdown on a pass from Conerly. For Gifford it was a magical year: "It was like waking up one morning to find your most impossible fantasy come to life.... Heady stuff and I loved it."[5]

Throughout the '57–'59 seasons he continued his pattern of success in rushing and receiving, with an occasional pass. In 1959 he tried out for quarterback but was kept at halfback. That year he was named All-Pro. At the

2. The Glory Years (1954–1963)   23

same time, during the '50s he continued with his work in Hollywood and achieved broad celebrity status, appearing on television, modeling swimsuits in Jantzen ads, and trying out, unsuccessfully, for the role of Tarzan in the movies.

With the start of the next decade, Gifford's career took a turn for the worse. During the 1960 season he suffered a concussion after a hit by the Eagle linebacker Chuck Bednarik. The hit, legal, made a crushing sound, described as sounding like Bednarik was wielding a sledgehammer: "They gave Gifford the last rites in the locker room that day, it was that serious."[6] Gifford was hospitalized for ten days and missed the 1961 season as part of a planned retirement. However, he missed playing football enormously—the competition, camaraderie, and roaring appreciation of the fans: "You get the adrenaline rush a bullfighter must get when he enters the arena.... I honestly believe I got more excitement and joy in one day by playing football than most people get in a lifetime."[7]

So, at the age of 31, after receiving many honors and suffering many injuries, Gifford decided to make a comeback for the 1962 season. Allie Sherman now was the head coach and he switched Gifford to flanker from halfback. Initially things did not go well as Gifford was benched in favor of Aaron Thomas, newly acquired from San Francisco. Gifford was shattered inside by the benching as he went from All-Pro running back to second-string wide receiver. He had never felt so down in his life. He also suffered from a bad back for which, he later learned, he was given some cocaine by the doctor of the famed personality Toots Shor. After Thomas was hurt, Gifford returned to the starting lineup. He ended up averaging over twenty yards a reception and went to the Pro Bowl at his third position (defensive back, running back, and flanker). He also was voted the NFL Comeback Player of the Year, a long way from the picture of him as only a glamour boy.

Gifford continued with the Giants in 1963, participating in their third straight title as division champ. His career came to an end with the conclusion of the '64 season, the season the roof fell in on the Giants football team. At this point he had set the Giants' record for most points, most touchdowns, highest rushing average, and most yards receiving. He also was second for total rushing yards and pass catches. In 1971 Gifford began a long career as announcer on Monday Night Football and in 1977 he was inducted into the Pro Football Hall of Fame.

As Gifford describes it, at the time that he began his career as a Giant professional, football "was the ugly duckling of sports. It ranked just a notch above wrestling."[8] In New York, the football Giants played second fiddle to the Yankees, Dodgers, and baseball Giants, led by Mickey Mantle, Duke Snider, and Willie Mays. No reporter was assigned to cover the football

Giants and the team was run as a family business. By the time he ended his career, professional football had become big time and the Giants team had established itself in the hearts of its fans.

Charlie Conerly (1948–1961)

Charlie Conerly had been a star quarterback at the University of Mississippi (Ole Miss) when he was drafted by the Washington Redskins in 1945. However, serving in the Marines in Guam, he was unable to join the NFL at that time. Returning from service to Ole Miss, Conerly became a consensus All-American in 1947. By then the Redskins already had their star quarterback, Sammy Baugh, and traded Conerly to the Giants. Conerly joined the Giants in 1948 when the team used the A formation in which the quarterback was expected to run and block as well as pass. In 1949 the coach, Steve Owen, switched to the T-formation and brought in Allie Sherman to work with Conerly on the change. Conerly credited the change with saving his life as a quarterback.

By the time he retired, Conerly held the Giants' record for passes, touchdown passes, and yards gained. He also was fourth in all-time touchdown passes in the NFL, behind Sammy Baugh, Bobby Lane, and Norm Van Brocklin. He also was in three Pro Bowls (1951, 1952, 1957) and was named the NFL's MVP in 1959.

Sam Huff (1956–1963)

Sam Huff was drafted in the third round out of the University of West Virginia. He grew up in the coal mining area of West Virginia, a world apart from Gifford's California and the Giants' New York. His beginning with the Giants hardly foretold his eventual Hall of Fame career. He was thought to be too small for the defensive line, and too slow to be a linebacker. Then too, as a rookie he felt picked on by the coach, Jim Lee Howell. Lonely, lacking in self-confidence, he, as well as another rookie, kicker Don Chandler, couldn't take it anymore. According to David Maraniss, the biographer of Vince Lombardi, the two rookies were in their dorm room listening to country western music when Huff suggested that the two of them turn in their playbooks and leave. Moving to do so, they bumped into Lombardi and told him they were quitting. Lombardi barked that he would not allow them to quit. The two rookies went back and forth about what to do and then decided to slip away and leave on the next plane out. Lombardi followed them to the airport, "drove up like a truant officer, announced that he would not allow them to leave and escorted them back to training camp."[9] From then on, he considered himself a Lombardi man.

Playing middle linebacker in Tom Landry's 4–3 defense, he became one of the league's most publicized figures, the prototypical player at that position, and focal point of the fans' love for their Giants' defense. Perhaps of greatest renown was his play against the great Cleveland fullback, Jim Brown. Considered by many to have been the greatest runner in NFL history, Brown ran with both power and speed. After being tackled on a play, he would get up slowly as if he could hardly run another play, only to take the handoff on the following play and take right off again. Huff described one of his early contacts with Brown as follows: "Here came Jim Brown through a hole and there I was to meet him. I hit that big sucker head-on and my headgear snapped down and cut my nose and my teeth hit together so hard the enamel popped off. He broke my nose, broke my teeth, and knocked me cold."[10]

Fortunately, other contacts had a better ending. Clearly the key to stopping the powerful Cleveland Browns was stopping Jim Brown, and defenses were especially designed to do this. What the Giants' defensive coach Tom Landry did was to have Huff key on Brown. This did not necessarily mean following Brown on every play, as some have suggested, but rather to diagnose the play based on Brown's movement. For the most part, this appeared to work, as Huff and the others, responding to the fans' chant of "Dee-Fense," often held Jim Brown to limited yards. Particularly noteworthy here was their limiting Brown to eight yards rushing in the 1958 playoff game to decide the conference championship.

Huff fostered the image of himself as mean on the football field, with no nice guys on the opposing team, and the fans loved him for it: "Get the man with the football. This is a man's game and any guy who doesn't want to hit hard doesn't belong in it."[11] He loved the game, what he considered to be America's game. He loved the camaraderie of the defense, describing it as being "like a platoon in the army—you live together, depend on each other. That's what it's all about."[12] His toughness as a player led him to be featured on the cover of *Time* magazine and as the focus of the TV documentary *The Violent World of Sam Huff*. He made the Pro Bowl four straight years and was inducted into the Hall of Fame in 1982. His trade in 1964 to the rival Washington Redskins shocked Giants fans and was part of the precipitous decline that followed the years of glory.

Emlen Tunnell (1948–1958)

Emlen Tunnell walked into the Giant office in 1948 asking for a try-out. He had been a running back at Iowa but, due to eye surgery after his junior year, he did not play in his senior year and went undrafted. He turned out to be quite a free agent acquisition. The first African-American player on the Giants, in the course of his ten years with the Giants he set sixteen team records, including most punt returns (258), most punt return yards (2,214), most interceptions (74), and most interception return yards (1,240). An essential component of the umbrella defense, he was described by Tom Landry as one of the great players of all time.

Not only was Tunnell valuable as a player, but he helped to guide many young African-American players who subsequently joined the team. He was a four-time All-Pro, was the first African-American assistant coach in the NFL, and was inducted into the Hall of Fame in 1967. A few years later he died of a heart attack at age fifty.

Roosevelt (Rosey) Brown (1953–1965)

Roosevelt Brown was drafted out of Morgan State in the twenty-seventh round. Evidently the Giants did not know who to select at that point until someone noticed in a black weekly newspaper that Brown had been named to the black All-American team of 1952. Thus the Giants selected him and he turned out to be "one of the truly great 'sleeper' picks of all time."[13] He signed an initial contract for $2,700.

Brown was taken under the wing of Tunnell and they roomed together. In New York, they roomed in the same hotel as other Giants players. But on the road, Wellington Mara had to make other arrangements: "When we traveled around, we couldn't stay with the white boys. So the Giants would make arrangements for us to stay with a black family. Wellington Mara would check out the people we were going to stay with, and they were always fine people and had very nice homes."[14] Brown describes loving this, being able to party without worrying about coaches checking up on him and the other black players, but the arrangement says something about the times, as did his being picked as late as the twenty-seventh round.

Brown came into the league raw and needed instructions in line play. He once told Ernie Accorsi, later the Giants' general manager, the following story: "I was playing against Len Ford of the Browns and I couldn't block him. He would jump over me. Steve Owen was the head coach then, and he said if you can't block him, we're going to cut you. So I tackled Ford on two straight plays. He said, 'If you do that again, I'm going to kill you.' I said, 'Well, if I don't stop you, I'm going to get cut, so what's the difference if you kill me?'"[15] Nevertheless, he became the Giants' starting left tackle for thirteen years, an All-Pro for eight consecutive years (1956–1963), a Pro Bowler ten times, and was only the second player to be elected to the Football Hall of Fame (1975) for offensive line play.

Y.A. Tittle (1961–1964)

In 1961, the Giants obtained Y.A. Tittle from the 49ers. San Francisco thought that the career of the thirty-five-year-old Tittle was over and traded him for the Giants' 1960 first-round selection, tackle Lou Cordileone. This was to be Conerly's last year with the Giants and the beginning of a storied four years for Tittle with the Giants, leading them to division championships in 1961, 1962, and 1963.

Known as "The Bald Eagle" to all, as Y.A. to many, and as YAT to his teammates, Yelberton Abraham Tittle had a strong, howitzer-like, accurate arm and was an enthusiastic leader in the huddle. With him the term "the bomb" became part of the NFL vocabulary. He was fortunate in that the year he arrived the Giants obtained the talented receiver Del Shofner from the Los Angeles Rams. Tittle and Shofner represented some of the best trades made by the Giants. In a three-year stretch the Tittle-Shofner duo were responsible for 185 receptions, 32 touchdowns, and a total of 3,439 yards. Tittle also was fortunate in having a coach, Allie Sherman, who gave him freedom to play football the way he wanted to play it and didn't second-guess him when things didn't go right.

Tittle had a difficult beginning with the Giants, the players being close to the incumbent Conerly. According to Gifford, he was not asked to go to bars or to dinner by the other players.[16] Gradually, however, he became accepted as the team leader and became the toast of New York. Bald and aging, Y.A. hardly looked like the candidate for such a position. His winning, enthusiasm, dedication to the game, modesty, and commitment to playing through injury endeared him to his teammates and fans. Gifford describes him as radiating exuberance and describes how Tittle once ran along the sideline when the Giants defense picked off a pass until he was nearly garroted by a telephone headset.

In a 1962 rock 'em sock 'em game against Detroit, Tittle hurt his right arm and ended up with a huge contusion. He couldn't throw all week in practice. On game day the following week against the Redskins, coach Sherman asked him to give it a try: "So I threw a few look-ins, short passes; it hurt. But I'd found out in my career that you can be hurting pretty bad, but when they blow the whistle you just forget about it."[17] He ended up throwing for seven touchdowns!

In a 1963 championship game against the Bears, Tittle suffered torn ligaments in his knee near the end of the first half. During intermission he was shot up with the pain killer Novocain and returned for the second half. Barely able to walk, Tittle did what he could but was intercepted often and was unable to lead the Giants to victory.

Tittle's last year, 1964, was the beginning of the decline for the Giants. For the first time in his career with the Giants, Tittle had more interceptions than touchdowns. In a game against the Steelers he was battered, bruised, and bloodied—a "fallen warrior."[18] Now that he was 38, it was time for Tittle to end his career: "In 1964 I got hurt probably the worst of all my seventeen years in pro football.... After that, I knew it was time to quit—especially when I saw our other quarterback, Gary Wood, was wanting to date my daughter."[19]

The Coaches

The year 1953 continued the decline of the Giants, with the team winning only three games and both the offense and defense on the decline. Charlie Conerly, battered and bruised, was planning retirement. Something had to be done. Enter Jim Lee Howell and two assistant coaches, Tom Landry (defense) and Vince Lombardi (offense). The two assistant coaches, both of whom went on to become great head coaches, probably constitute the best duo of assistant coaches in the history of the NFL.

Jim Lee Howell

Jim Lee Howell, a tall 6'6", had been an end for the Giants from 1937 to 1942, and then again during the 1946 and 1947 seasons. In between he served as a Marine drill instructor. Unspectacular as a player, in his eight seasons he had a total of 74 receptions. Prior to his appointment as head coach, he coached at Wagner College (Staten Island, New York) mornings and assisted coaching the Giant ends afternoons. His appointment was a surprise to everyone. The Giants had first offered the job to Earl (Red) Blaik, who turned them down and recommended his assistant, Vince Lombardi, for the job. Speculation turned to Lombardi, with the *New York Daily News* running the headline "Giants boot Owen upstairs, Lombardi seen new coach," but the job went to Howell.

Howell immediately made a number of striking moves. First, he went to Conerly and talked him out of retirement. Meeting with him on Conerly's farm, and listening to the quarterback's complaints about being beaten up behind a weak line, Howell promised Conerly that a bigger and better line would be the first order of business. In fact, the basis for such a line already was there—tackles Rosey Brown and Dick Yelvington, guards Bill Austin and Jack Stroud, and center Ray Wietecha had all been drafted earlier. Second, Howell had the good judgment to appoint Landry and Lombardi as assistant coaches, giving them full responsibility for the defense and offense, respectively. Third, through draft, trade, and signings of returning servicemen, he greatly improved the roster.

There are conflicting views about the extent to which Howell was in charge of things with the Giants. On the one hand, there is the view that he left everything to Landry and Lombardi. He himself quipped that all he had to do was blow up the footballs and Frank Gifford describes him as more a figurehead than a coach.[20] On the other hand, Pat Summerall describes Howell as giving authority to Landry and Lombardi, but as being the one who oversaw everything and coordinated the practices: "He was the glue that held the entire team together.... No one on that team had any doubt who held the ultimate authority, and that was Jim Lee Howell."[21]

In terms of win-loss record, it's hard to tell how much of the coaching success belongs to Howell as head coach. Howell resigned after the 1960 season, a year after Landry left to become head coach at Dallas and two years after Lombardi left for Green Bay. In any case, Howell took a team that had a poor record and was on the decline and led its resurgence. In the course of his seven seasons as head coach the team won one NFL championship, three conference titles, and had an overall record of 53–27–4.

Tom Landry

Tom Landry came from the University of Texas where he initially played first-string defensive back and second-string quarterback, then fullback. He came to the Giants in 1950, age twenty-five, a little old for a rookie. From 1950 to 1955 he played defensive back, and was All-Pro in 1954, the year he also became defensive coach. Overall, he had thirty-one interceptions in seventy games. During this period he also punted over three hundred times, averaging over forty yards a punt. His past experience at quarterback came in handy for two games in 1952 when both Charlie Conerly and the backup quarterback were knocked out of the game. With no one else to play the position, Landry was told he was quarterback: "So I just went in. They didn't send in any plays.... The field was mostly dirt, so I could draw the plays on the ground with my finger. I'd just draw where I wanted the receivers to go and they'd shrug and go off and try to get there."[22] Reflecting back on the experience, Landry noted that Conerly's job never was in jeopardy.

For all of his talent as a defensive back, Landry was a genius as a defensive coach and later as a head coach. When he took over as defensive coach, there weren't any assistants to help and there were relatively few offensive and defensive formations. He took Owen's umbrella defense and refined it.

He developed the 4–3 defense and required special practice sessions of the defense to acquaint them with the new scheme. He developed Sam Huff into the All-Pro middle linebacker he became and developed the scheme for stopping Jim Brown. Landry seemed to have a gift for calling the correct defensive play, although in some of the games against the Cleveland Browns this was based in part on some illicit information. Part of the success of Landry's play-calling was his ability to pick up patterns in the Brown offense. In the critical games where the Giants held the great Jim Brown to limited gains, he instructed Huff about how to key in on Brown so as to recognize how the play was going to be run. In at least one case, however, Landry was able to listen in on the plays being called in on an FM band by the opposing coach, Paul Brown, to the quarterback. Landry then signaled in the defensive alignment to Andy Robustelli, who called the defense in the huddle.

Landry was disciplined, focused, and a perfectionist. For some he was viewed as cold, aloof, almost a robot. Landry, however, had another view of emotion. For him emotion covered up a lot of inadequacies and in the end it got in the way of performance. According to him, an emotional team could not stay that way consistently over a full season or even a few games. The Giants' defense greatly weakened following his departure in 1960 to become the Dallas head coach. He had not planned to follow this path, instead planning to go into industrial engineering. He was talked out of this and into the position of head coach of the newly formed Dallas Cowboys by the new owner, Clint Murchison, and general manager Tex Schramm. In all, Landry coached the Cowboys to twenty consecutive winning seasons (1966–1985), thirteen divisional titles, five conference championships, and two Super Bowl victories. Included, of course, were many victories over his former team, the Giants.

Vince Lombardi

Vince Lombardi became an assistant coach the same year as Landry, but the two were markedly different in background, personality, and style. Whereas one (Lombardi) came from Brooklyn, New York, the other (Landry) came from Mission, Texas; the one was round and the other tall and slender; the one was without experience as an NFL player, the other a former All-Pro; and the one was emotional and the other unemotional. Landry was the more innovative of the two but Lombardi did sell the team on the idea of taking pictures of the opponent's defenses during the game and quickly sending the developed pictures to the bench for instant use. Both were committed to winning and meticulous in their attention to detail. Clearly there is more than one path to becoming a great coach.

2. The Glory Years (1954–1963)   31

Prior to joining the Giants, Lombardi was an assistant coach at West Point. He was scheduled to become head coach of a college team, the Fordham Rams, when the football program was dropped due to its losing money. As already noted, Lombardi was recommended by the West Point coach for the Giants' head coaching position and there was public speculation that he would get the job. He badly wanted that position and was disappointed when it went to Howell. He was prepared to stay at the Point but wanted a raise. When he was told that this was not possible since he already was at the maximum for an assistant, he accepted the Giants' offer to be an assistant coach in charge of the offense. Aside from money, part of the attraction of the job may have been a personal relationship with Wellington Mara, a former classmate at Fordham. Another part may have been the Maras' suggestion that they expected him to become the head coach of the Giants one day.

Lombardi is famous for the saying "Winning isn't everything, it's the only thing," a saying actually first expressed by John Wayne in a 1953 movie. He also is famous for being described by one of his Green Bay players as treating all the players alike—like dogs. His hard-driving style did not win him much initial support with the Giants players. According to Frank Gifford, Lombardi was viewed as loud, arrogant, and a pain in the ass. Players poked fun at him over beers—he seemed comical to them. Then their view of him changed as he spent time with them, solicited their views, and showed compassion for those in need of help. His commitment to preparation and detail was striking from the start. Upon taking the job as assistant coach for offense he brought home films of every Giants game of the past two years and analyzed the movements of all players. He installed Gifford as a flanker back, with the threat of passing as well as running. He introduced the offensive linemen to zone blocking and developed the power sweep, with two pulling guards around the end, for which he became so famous at Green Bay. Gradually he won the respect and commitment of the players.

Lombardi's dream of becoming a head coach was ever-present during his tenure as a Giants assistant. After the 1957 season he was offered the head coaching position of the Philadelphia Eagles, the Giants' rivals, who had had losing seasons the past two years. The problem was the Eagles' management was in disarray and unable to offer a substantial package. Nevertheless Lombardi was prepared to accept the position until he heard from Wellington Mara, who argued that Lombardi never would get along with the management of the Eagles. In addition, Mara offered a raise, making his salary the equivalent of the Eagles' offer ($22,500) and the highest of any assistant in the league, plus an increase in his life insurance policy. Lombardi was torn between his desire to be a head coach with a team that had some potential but problematic management and the positive ties to the Maras and the potential to one day become head coach of the Giants. After much reflection and contemplation, he opted for the latter and remained as the coach of the offense for the 1958 season.

But the burning desire to be a head coach remained, and in 1959 Lombardi left the Giants to become head coach of the Green Bay Packers. During his five years with the Giants the offense averaged seven points more than the year prior to his arrival, a performance capped by the forty-seven points gained in the 1956 championship game. Of course, Lombardi went on to create a dynasty at Green Bay and become one of the great coaches of all time. His dream of becoming head coach of the Giants was not fulfilled, nor was that of the Maras of getting him back at some point in the future. Many Giants fans have wondered about what might have been.

The Games

A season defines a team, but one can select a few games that, for one reason or another, highlight what a team is about. For the Giants of the glory years we can go back to four games—the 1956 NFL championship game against the Chicago Bears, the two 1958 games against the Cleveland Browns that enabled the Giants to reach the championship game, and the 1958 NFL championship game against the Baltimore Colts, considered by many to be the greatest pro football game ever played.

The 1956 NFL Championship Game: The Second Sneakers Game

By 1956 the Giants were showing improvement over the disastrous 1953 record of three wins and nine losses. In addition, the team was bolstered by a good draft (Huff, Katcavage, Chandler) and trades that brought them Robustelli and Modzelewski. However, they still had to face the powerful reigning champs, the Cleveland Browns. Playing their first season at Yankee Stadium, they got off to a fine 6–1 start. Included there was a win against the Browns who, although weakened by the loss of their Hall of Fame quarterback Otto Graham, were still a formidable opponent under the direction of Paul Brown. This was the time when coaches radioed in plays from the sideline to a receiver in the quarterback's helmet. It also was the game when Landry was able to listen in on the play-calling by turning a receiver to the Browns' frequency. Although that only lasted for some plays, the Giants were able to prevail by the score of 21–9.

2. The Glory Years (1954–1963)   33

A few weeks later, after a surprising loss to the then-weak Washington Redskins, the Giants faced the Chicago Bears, the "Monsters of the Midway," who had the top offense of the NFL. After taking a 17–3 lead, the Giants ended up with a 17–17 tie. Part of the reason for the tie was the conservative play of the Giants' offense, with Lombardi telling the quarterback, Charlie Conerly, to kill the clock and not make mistakes. Lombardi vowed to never again follow the conservative strategy of sitting on the ball. Ironically enough, it was around this time that Charlie Conerly was being featured on the cover of *Sports Illustrated* magazine as one of the "old pros who don't make mistakes."

After two more wins and a loss to the Browns, at the end of the season the Giants' record stood at 8–3–1. For the first time since 1950 they were to play in an NFL championship game, in this case against the "Monsters of the Midway" whose record stood at 9–2–1. The Giants, now loaded with talent, were slight favorites. They were being led on offense by Gifford, now the league leader in points scored and among the leaders both in rushing and receiving. And the defense, strengthened through draft and trades, was winning the hearts of the fans. But the Bears were a formidable opponent, led on offense by quarterback Ed Brown, fullback Rick Casares, and end Harlon Hill, and on defense by end Doug Atkins and linebacker Joe Fortunato. The Bears' offense was so strong that at the end of the season it had one hundred more points than that of the Giants. Each team had at least ten players who were named All-Pro that year, split almost evenly between offense and defense.

More than fifty-six thousand fans came out in the bitter cold of a December day to watch the players slug, or slide, it out on a frozen field. It had sleeted all night and the temperature was down to thirteen degrees. Wellington Mara, remembering the 1934 "Sneakers Game," earlier had players test out the field wearing either the standard cleats or basketball shoes. Finding the latter superior, he had Andy Robustelli, who owned a sporting goods store, order four dozen pairs of sneakers, sizes nine to thirteen. Thus this became the second "Sneakers Game." According to Frank Gifford, the Bears also had sneakers, and thus were on an "equal footing," but chose not to wear them.

From the beginning the Giants dominated the Bears. Gene Filipski returned the opening kickoff fifty-three yards and a few plays later Mel Triplett took the ball in for the Giants' first touchdown. Two field goals by Ben Agajanian contributed to a 13–0 lead by the end of the first quarter. Agajanian, who came to the Giants in 1954, was known as "The Toeless Wonder." Earlier, working while a college student, he had four toes sheared off his kicking foot. The operating surgeon squared off the stumps, assuring Agajanian that he would still be able to kick field goals. The two in the first quarter were among the 147 he kicked during his nine-year career, four of them with the Giants.

The Giants' offense typically started with Don Heinrich at quarterback with Charlie Conerly observing the opponents' defense and developing strategy for entering the game, often later in the second half. In this case, Conerly entered the game in the second quarter and directed two touchdowns, both capped off by runs by Alex (Red) Webster. A recovered blocked punt in the end zone gave the Giants another touchdown, their third in the quarter. In the meantime, the defense was holding the Bears' offense to one touchdown, and the Giants led by the end of the half by a score of 34–7. Conerly passed for two touchdowns in the second half and the Giants' defense held firm, blanking the Bears' offense. Thus, a final score of 47–7! As one writer put it, "As some race horses take to mud the Giants in title contention apparently took to ice."[23]

Aside from the dominance of the Giants in winning the championship, the game was noteworthy for its television coverage, for its increased receipts—a then record of a little over a half million dollars, including those from radio and television—and the players' winning shares of almost four thousand dollars apiece.

The 1958 Games Against the Browns

The 1956 season ended on a high note and Giants fans had reason to expect more of the same for the following season. However, three things conspired to operate against such optimism. First, the draft provided no assistance. Part of the reason for this was their low spot in the draft but another part was their having traded draft choices, in this case choices one, four, and twelve, to other teams. The Los Angeles Rams, owners of the Giants' first-round draft choice, selected end Del Shofner with the traded choice. Shofner later became an outstanding receiver for the Giants. Second, their outstanding defensive tackle, Rosey Grier, entered military service. Third, and perhaps the greatest factor, was the great draft of the Cleveland Browns, the former division champions dethroned by the 1956 Giants. Most noteworthy was the first-round selection, number six overall, of the Syracuse running back Jim Brown. Brown gained almost a thousand yards in his first season and went on to become what many consider to be the greatest running back of all time. Brown had size (6'2", 232 pounds), power, and speed. He would get up from the pile after being tackled as if he had no energy left, only to run for gains on play after play. In addition, the Browns obtained a quarterback (Milt Plum) and two linemen (Henry

Jordan and Gene Hickerson) in the draft. Nevertheless, the Giants had nine All-Pros that year, five on offense (Brown, Stroud, Wietecha, Conerly, and Gifford), and four on defense (Robustelli, Modzelewski, Huff, and Tunnell).

The 1958 Giants were helped in the draft by the selection of a running back (Phil King) and tackle (Frank Youso) in the first two rounds, although noteworthy was the loss of their third-round choice to Green Bay, who used it to select the great linebacker Ray Nitschke. In addition, there was the return of Grier from military service and the addition of the kicker Pat Summerall. And the Giants were still loaded with their previous talent. Cleveland remained strong and the basis for a season battle between the two titans had been laid.

The first meeting was in Cleveland, before a record crowd of more than seventy-eight thousand fans. The Giants were having a hard time gaining momentum, losing five of their six exhibition games and coming into the game with a mediocre regular season record of three and two. The Browns, behind the running of Jim Brown, were a strong five victories and no defeats. As usual, there was the keying of Huff on Brown, the mini-battle within the larger battle. Although Brown ran for over one hundred yards, the Giants were victorious with a final score of 21–17.

The last game of the season pitted the Giants and Browns in a rematch. The Giants, with a record of 8–3, were one game behind the Browns. Thus, only a win would enable the Giants to tie the Browns for the division championship. A Cleveland win or tie would end the season for the Giants. The Giants had the home-field advantage but once more the weather was cold and the field at Yankee Stadium was covered with snow. Many figured the game would revolve around the ability of the Giants defense to stop the running of Jim Brown, and thus be a replay of the mini-battle within the greater battle and the basis for the cheers of "Dee-Fense, Dee-Fense."

At first things did not look good for the Giants, with Brown taking a handoff and running for a sixty-five-yard touchdown, eluding Huff's attempted tackle on the way. However, thereafter the defense was able to hold the Browns to a field goal while the offense was able to score ten points, leading to a tie with a little more than five minutes remaining in the game.

The Giants' defense, behind the urging of the fans cheering "Dee-Fense," held the Browns to no first downs for the remainder of the game. It now was up to the offense if the Giants' season was to go on. Again, a tie would be of no value; only a touchdown or at least a field goal would do the job. There could be no mistakes; there was no margin for error. Fortunately, a mistake was made by the Browns, shanking a punt that enabled the Giants to get the ball just inside Browns territory with less than three minutes remaining. The game likely was over if the Browns got the ball again without the Giants' scoring—time would run out. Just earlier Summerall had missed a twenty-five-yard field goal, so movement downfield on the snow-covered field to at least the twenty seemed to be necessary.

Conerly tried three passes, all falling incomplete. What to do now? A punt would seem to end the season, unless there was another Cleveland fumble. It made sense to try another pass and let it all hinge on the arm of the old quarterback, Conerly, the old pro who hopefully would not make a mistake. This was what made sense to Lombardi, still in charge of the offense. But Howell, the head coach, had something else in mind. Despite the blizzard conditions and snow-filled field, and the fact that Summerall had earlier missed a field goal from the twenty-five, Howell called for a field goal. Summerall himself was incredulous. Not only had he never kicked a field goal that far, forty-nine yards, but he was being asked to do so under terrible conditions. Wellington Mara too was incredulous, not believing that Summerall could kick it that far under the best of conditions. But kick it he did—straight-legged, as was the fashion at that time, and dead center, the football just clearing the cross-bar to give the Giants a 13–10 victory.

The fans were delirious. Summerall walked off the field and was greeted by a smiling Lombardi: "You know, you son of a bitch, that you can't kick it that far." At the time of the try, Summerall was so focused on the kick that he had trouble remembering much of what went on: "All I remember about it is that when I got into the huddle, Charlie Conerly, my holder, looked at me and said, 'What the fuck are you doing here?' I said, 'We're going to kick a field goal.' He was in disbelief. But we did it."[24]

So now that the Giants had beaten the Browns twice, could they do it a third time—a trifecta? Luck seemed to be with them as they won the coin toss, giving them the home-field advantage at Yankee Stadium. Over sixty thousand fans again braved the cold to watch their heroes take on the enemy in a battle for the division championship and the right to play the Colts for the NFL championship. Not only could they do it a third time, but the team, in particular the defense, outdid themselves, beating the Browns by a score of 10–0. The key play for the offense was a handoff from Conerly to Webster, who handed off on a reverse to Gifford, who ran the ball to near the goal line. Then, about to be tackled, Gifford lateraled to Conerly, of all people, who ran it in for the touchdown. The defense held Jim Brown to an incredible eight yards on seven carries, and the Browns' offense to a total of eighty-six yards with but seven first downs. As the Cleveland coach, Paul Brown, recognized, his team had been soundly defeated. The Giants' offense gained almost four times the yardage of the Browns and had more than twice the number of first downs. It was time to move on to the Colts!

The 1958 Championship Game Against the Colts: The Greatest Game Ever Played

The Giants were a bruised and battered team after the playoff victory against the Browns. They had played two tough games in two weeks and now had but a week before they were to play for the NFL championship. According to Gifford, they were an exhausted, ripped-up team. Gifford himself had a swollen elbow, two hurting knees, and a hip bruise that had hemorrhaged blood into his legs. True, they had beaten the Colts earlier in the season on a Summerall field goal, but the Colts were without their star quarterback Johnny Unitas, who was sidelined with cracked ribs.

Unitas had taken an interesting route to stardom in the NFL. Originally drafted by the Steelers after an undistinguished college career at Louisville, he was released early on and went to work in construction while playing semipro ball for six dollars a game. On the sandlots he would make up plays for each down, much as in touch football. A call by the Colts for a workout in February of 1956 led to his being signed as a backup. An injury to the Colts' starting quarterback led to a forgettable beginning as an NFL quarterback—three fumbles and an interception. However, by the time of the game against the Giants he was having a second All-Pro season and on his way to the Hall of Fame, recognized as one of the greatest quarterbacks of all time. But Unitas also had a supporting cast of All-Pros, including the fullback Alan ("The Horse") Ameche, running back Lenny Moore, and end Raymond Berry on offense, and linemen Gino Marchetti and Big Daddy Lipscomb on defense. All are considered to be among the greatest players of all time. Berry, who came to play an important role in the championship game, did not have great speed and had weak eyes but had good hands and was an excellent student of the game. He would watch films at length to determine weaknesses in the defensive secondary. Asked whether his new wife was a good cook, he quipped: "I don't know, but she sure can run a projector."[25]

December 28, 1958—game day! Over sixty thousand fans are in the stands at Yankee Stadium. Local television is blacked out so Giants fans without tickets, of which there are thousands, must travel to bars and motels outside the blacked-out area to view the game. These "travel dates" take on a life of their own, with groups sharing the cost of a motel room and tailgate parties being set up in the motel parking lots. Fan fever was reaching a new pitch. Once more the weather was cold and windy but at least there was no snow. The Giants were able to score first on a Summerall field goal. However, the Colts then capitalized on two Gifford fumbles and led at the end of the half by a score of 14–3.

In the third quarter, Unitas led the Colts to the Giants five. With first and goal, and a strong running attack, a Colt touchdown seemed assured. The Giants' defense put up a remarkable goal-line stand and held the Colts for the first three downs. Rather than kick a field goal, the Colts decided to go for the touchdown, running their star fullback, "The Horse" Ameche. Remarkably enough, the Giants dropped Ameche at the five. Never had the calls for "Dee-Fense" been answered better.

The defense had held and now it was up to the offense. The offense was up to the challenge, although at one point the hearts of the fans skipped a beat. A sixty-two-yard pass from Conerly to Rote had the fans cheering—until Rote fumbled the ball at the Colt 25. Fortunately, Webster picked up the ball and ran it to the one. Now it was time for the Colts' defense to turn the tables on the Giants. But the momentum was with the Giants and Triplett scored on the next play. Thus, by the end of the third quarter the Giants had closed the gap but still were behind by the score of 14–10.

The Giants' offense continued to come alive in the fourth quarter, scoring a touchdown on three Conerly passes, two to Schnelker and one to Gifford. The Giants now had the lead, 17–14, with just over two minutes remaining. The Giants' faithful had reason to be optimistic, particularly after the Giants' defense held. Now three incredible things happened, each very different from the other. First, with the Giants' offense on their own forty-three, third down and three yards needed for a first down, Conerly hands the ball off to Gifford. Gifford, running to his right, is tackled by the All-Pro Gino Marchetti. Marchetti's fellow all–Pro, Big Daddy Lipscomb, comes to the play late and falls on Marchetti. Marchetti screams out in pain, his ankle broken. The focus is on Marchetti as he is taken off the field on a stretcher. The referee spots the ball, but where? He forgot to mark the forward advance of the ball. There is no video to go to and check the proper spot. The Giants are convinced Gifford had the first down but the referee spots the ball inches short of the first down. The Giants are forced to do the only sensible thing—punt. Chandler, an excellent punter, does his job and the Colts offense takes the field with the ball on their own fourteen. Under two minutes to go. The Colts need a field goal to tie, a touchdown to win.

And now for the second improbable. The Colts have to go to what today would be called a two-minute offense. In this case, in perhaps a throwback to his sandlot days, Unitas tell his teammates: "Unless the clock is stopped, we won't have time for any more huddles. Stay alert. I'll call the plays at the line of scrimmage."[26] The Giants' defense is asked to once again come up strong, to hold the league-leading offense one more time. A Unitas pass to Moore for eleven yards and one to Berry for twenty-five yards takes the ball to midfield. Time is running out but the Colts are on the move. A pass to Berry brings the ball to the Giants' thirty-five and another to Berry brings the ball to the thirteen. With time running out, the Colts send in their kicker, Steve Myrha, who kicks a twenty-yard field goal. Two weeks ago the Giants were victorious on an improbable Summerall field goal. Today, as time is running out, they are on the short end of a field goal. The score is tied, 17–17.

Overtime—the first in NFL championship history. Sudden death—the first team to score becomes 1958 champions of the NFL. The Giants win the coin toss but are unable to score and have to punt. The Colts take the ball and are on the move when the third improbable thing happens—the television cable is knocked down and there is darkness on the fans' television sets for the next two and a half minutes. Millions of homes with die-hard screaming fans are sitting with a dark screen before them. All they know is what the screen tells them—picture transmission has been temporarily interrupted. If lucky, they can get to a radio; if not, they are lost as the game goes on. How long will the darkness continue? A fan runs onto the field, delaying the game. Later we learn that actually the "fan" was a television employee intentionally giving the television crew time to repair the cable. Fortunately, or perhaps not, the video returns in time for the fans to see a completed pass take the Colts to the Giants' one-yard line. It is too much to ask of the tired Giants' defense to again hold the Colts. Ameche takes the ball in. Unitas has moved his team eighty yards in thirteen plays. The Colts are the winners, 23–17. The conclusion of the best football game ever played and the end of the season. As a writer in the *New York Times* put it: "Time and fortune finally ran out on professional football's Cinderella team, the New York Giants."[27]

The '58 Giants-Colts game was so good that it was replayed twenty years later. The Giants were given a chance to redeem themselves, with Conerly, Gifford, Webster and others again facing Unitas, Ameche, Berry, the now healed Marchetti, and others. This time, instead of the bitter cold, it was a July day with ninety-degree heat. Instead of the Yankee Stadium, it was New York's Central Park. Instead of smash football in the trenches, it was touch football, six to a side. Instead of a live television broadcast, it was filmed to be broadcast later. And, instead of men in their twenties and thirties, it was a game of men in their forties and fifties. Despite trickery and an illegal play for a touchdown on the part of the Giants, the Colts once more were victorious, with Unitas not only hitting Berry for two touchdown passes but also running back an intercepted pass for a winning touchdown. Of course, by now these Giants could hardly be called the Cinderella team.

Throwing for Seven Touchdowns—
Why Not for a Record Eight?

October 28, 1962: With the retirement of Charlie Conerly after the 1961 season, the hopes of the Giants clearly were in the hands of Y.A. Tittle. Now nearing the age of 36, Y.A. was coming off a terrific season in which he led the Giants to the division championship and was named to the all-NFL team. In addition to Shofner and Walton as potential receivers, he also had the option of throwing to Gifford, returning after a year's absence that followed his serious concussion at the end of the 1960 season. The season started poorly for both Tittle and the Giants with a loss to the Browns in which Y.A. was intercepted three times. They righted themselves after that and entered the seventh game of the season with a record of 4–2, following the win against Detroit in which Tittle was injured and forced to sit out much of the first half.

The game today was to be played before over sixty thousand fans at Yankee Stadium against the division leading Washington Redskins who had not lost in six games. The Giants fell behind early but led at the end of the half on three touchdown passes thrown by Tittle. In addition there was a completed bomb to Shofner for 53 yards. But by early in the second half, the Redskin quarterback, Norm Snead, had matched Tittle's passing with three touchdown passes of his own. Although Snead was to pass for over three hundred yards, on this day Y.A. was in a class of his own. At one point he completed twelve passes in a row, nearing the record thirteen set by the Minnesota Viking quarterback Fran Tarkenton. But now another record was in sight—seven touchdown passes in a game. That record had been set by two previous quarterbacks, one of them being the great Sid Luckman of the Chicago Bears. The sixth, a touchdown bomb of 63 yards to Gifford, brought him within sight of the record. The seventh followed shortly thereafter, a short pass to Walton.

Now the question was whether Tittle would go for the eighth and a record to be held by him alone. The game was in hand, the Giants leading 49–34, so how to win was not in the equation. Y.A. was free to call the plays and therefore free to go for the record. The fans cheered for the Bald Eagle to go for it. A favorite with his teammates, Y.A. was urged on by them: "We knew he had a shot at the record. In the huddle we told him, 'Throw the ball.' We said if he didn't pass, we weren't going to play."[28] But Tittle wouldn't do it: "If you're leading by so much, it just doesn't sit right with me to fill the air with footballs. I'm the quarterback. It would be showing off."[29] To Tittle, throwing for the record would have been glory-seeking and that was not what he was about.

Although he didn't go for the record, all in all Y.A. had a great day—27 of 39 completions for a total of 505 yards, with no interceptions! In a hard-fought game of great ferocity, Tittle put on what the great coach Greasy Neale described as "the finest exhibition of pin-point passing I've ever seen."[30] But this was just part of a great season for him. In again leading the Giants to the division championship, Tittle passed for 33 touchdowns and over three thousand yards as he was on his way to being named the year's MVP.

The Glory Years: A Team, a Family, a Sport

The Team

For all of the attention given to individual stars, football is a team game. The Giants of the glory years had their stars but their strength came from their operation as a team. There were rivalries, including some between the offense and defense, but on the whole there were strong bonds among the players. Many of the players had rooms in the same hotel and socialized together during off-hours. As Huff described it: "It's like a platoon in the army—you live together, fight together, depend on each other. That's what it's all about."[31]

It was a team built through craft and luck. Most of the starters came via the draft, including Rote as a number-one bonus pick in 1951, but key players came through other means—Tunnell as a free agent, Landry from the defunct New York Yankees football team, Webster from the Canadian League, Robustelli, Modzelewski, Svare, and Svoboda through trades. Some of these trades involved draft choices given up to other teams, draft choices that might have been used to obtain younger players of equal or greater talent, but that is hard to tell from the uncertainty of the draft. In any case, the Maras were able to put together a blend of players, some younger and some older, and join them with coaches who were able to make maximum use of the talent on hand. Without either the player or coaching talent, they could not have achieved what they did during this time period. But it also is unlikely they could have had these achievements without their sense of cohesion and spirit of determination.

The Giants were a winning team for the remaining five years of these years of glory, 1959–1963. During this period they won three-quarters of their games and were division champs in four of the years. But in all four cases they were unable to proceed to the next level, losing to the Colts, twice to the Packers, and once to the Bears. The team was getting old and for the most part the draft was not supplying them with a new source of talent. In part this was due to losing some draft choices in trades, in part due to poor draft selections, and in part due to competition from the new American Football League (AFL). After the '62 season Rosey Grier said he was retiring to move to the west coast and become a singer. The Giants convinced him to accept a trade to the Los Angeles Rams, thereby enabling him to get his wish while they were able to obtain something of value for him. Some players could be replaced through trades. In 1961 the Giants were able to obtain Y.A. Tittle (the "Bald Eagle") to replace Charlie Conerly and Del Shofner to replace the Kyle Rote. In 1961 Tittle was the MVP and in 1962, at age thirty-five, passed for an NFL record thirty-three touchdowns. In one game against the Redskins he completed seven touchdown passes. But clearly the Giants were an aging team. The seeds of decline were being planted.

In addition to player changes, of equal importance had to be the changes in coaching staff. Lombardi left after the '58 season to become head coach of the Green Bay Packers. There he became one of the all-time great head coaches in the NFL and his Packers beat the Giants in the '61 and '62 championship games. A sidelight note of interest is that the Packers used their 1958 third-round draft choice obtained from the Giants to select Ray Nitschke. Nitschke went on to become a Hall of Fame middle linebacker. Then Landry left after the '59 season to become head coach of the newly formed Dallas Cowboys. Landry too went on to become one of the all-time great coaches and during the next quarter of a century led the Cowboys to many victories over the Giants and NFL championships. Landry proved to be a great innovator not only on defense but on offense as well, using motion and situation substitutions in his offense to confuse the defense and make maximum use of talent. Then, after the 1960 season, Howell retired as head coach to become director of personnel.

When Howell retired as head coach the job was offered to Lombardi. But Lombardi chose to stay in Green Bay, the time for him to coach the Giants having passed. Lombardi felt that he could have done with the Giants what he did with the Packers and it was a great regret for him that he never got the chance.[32] Replacing Howell as head coach was Allie Sherman. Sherman had been the backfield coach under Steve Owen, having been brought in to help Conerly make the transition from the single-wing to the T. At age twenty-six, he was several years younger than Conerly. He had hoped to become head coach when the Maras decided that Owen needed to be replaced and was disappointed when the job went to Howell. After a few seasons as a coach in the Canadian Football League he returned to the Giants as a scout and then became coach of the offense when Lombardi left after the '58 season. He became head coach beginning with the '61 season. He had come a long way responsibility-wise if not distance-wise from his roots at Brooklyn College and backup quarterback for the Eagles. The early years were fine, including selections as coach of the year in 1961 and 1962, but unfortunately Sherman was also at the helm during the period of decline

The Family

During the early years of the NFL many of the franchises were run by the owners with a personal touch. No place was this more true than with the Giants. The family had been owners since the team's inception and the sons increasingly played a role in the team's affairs. What is striking, particularly in terms of how things were to change over time, was the personal trust and fondness that developed between many of the players and the Maras, in particular Wellington Mara. Frank Gifford never signed a contract, always trusting Wellington Mara to honor the terms of their agreement. Sam Huff told the following story at a much later testimonial to Wellington Mara:

> We won the world championship my first year and I made rookie defensive player of the year at middle linebacker. I was making seven thousand, five hundred dollars at the time. When I was here you dealt with Mr. Mara. And I wanted to deal with Jack, his brother. Wellington said, "He deals with the offense, you have to deal with me." I said, "I want to deal with the same guy Charlie Conerly and Frank Gifford deal with." He said, "You're dealing with me." I said, "Yes, sir." He said, "Here's your raise—five hundred dollars." I said, "Five hundred dollars." He said, "Sam, I think you're worth it."[33]

For the Giants as a family enterprise, however, things changed in 1959. In February of that year Tim Mara, the founder of the football team, died of a heart attack at the age of seventy-one. He was survived by his wife of more than fifty years, his two sons, Jack and Wellington, who took over full responsibility for the team, and six grandchildren. Jack and Wellington not only ran the team but played an important role in league meetings and decisions. Wellington in particular was a voice of moderation, reason, and group interest.

The Sport

Professional football underwent tremendous change during the glory years of the Giants. In 1960 there was the arrival of a new commissioner, Pete Rozelle. Rozelle was the surprise choice to be commissioner after the death of Bert Bell in 1959. It took twenty-three ballots of the owners before they settled on him. Rozelle had been general manager of the Rams, and prior to that was involved in public relations with the Rams and a private firm. His experience in public relations served him well both in terms of dealings with the owners and in his sensitivity to the public image of the NFL. During the course of his tenure (1960–1989) the NFL more than doubled in number of teams and negotiated huge television contracts. Also noteworthy were his suspension in 1963 of two star players, Paul Hornung and Alex Karras, for gambling and his introduction of random testing of players for drug and steroid use.

During this period the game became increasingly complex with new offensive formations, new defensive schemes, and increased use of substitutions and role players. During this period the NFL also became more diverse, particularly in terms of the increased participation of black players. For the Giants it wasn't until a year after Jackie Robinson had integrated major league baseball that they had their first black player—Emlen Tunnell. Of course, Paul Brown, then with the AAFC, already had helped to integrate pro football with the great fullback Marion Motley. And in 1946, Dan Reeves of the Los Angeles Rams broke the NFL color barrier by signing two black players. But it wasn't until 1949 that a black college player, George Taliaferro, a running back from Indiana, was selected in the NFL draft. As noted earlier, the Giants waited until the twenty-seventh round of the 1953 draft to select Rosey Brown, and then almost as an afterthought. During the glory years only about ten to twenty percent of the starting Giants were black, a far cry from the case today. If anything, they had an even smaller presence among the reserves.

Frank Gifford defends the NFL against charges of racism during the 1940s and '50s, suggesting that the problem was black players were not competing in big-time college programs, particularly in the racially restricted southeastern and southwestern conferences.[34] While there may be some truth to this, it was still the case that many blacks were starring with integrated college teams. Kenny Washington starred for UCLA but was not selected in the 1940 draft, and it wasn't until 1946 that he was one of the players signed by the Rams to break the NFL color barrier. Clearly professional football was caught up in the racism of the general society. Individual teams, such as the Redskins, had outright discriminatory policies. In 1957 there were pickets protesting the lack of any black players on the Redskins, then the only such team in professional football or baseball. As late as 1961 the owner of the Redskins was saying: "We'll start signing Negroes when the Harlem Globetrotters start signing whites."[35]

In other cases the discrimination was more subtle. And, as noted earlier, in traveling in the South separate rooming arrangements had to be made. Rosey Grier described one incident in Dallas in 1959 where the black Giant players were not permitted to eat at the hotel but were expected to attend a party. He, Brown, and Tunnell told management that they wouldn't go to the party. They relented when they were told that such action might hurt the rookies.[36] A different story involves Paul Brown, who in 1961 refused a Miami hotel manager's requirement that the black players stay elsewhere. Brown's statement that all the players would stay together or the team would fly home led to a capitulation on the part of the manager.[37] Shortly thereafter there were no separate facilities in any city where the NFL played.

As with Jackie Robinson, many players had to withstand racial slurs from fans and players. Opposing players often would be particularly violent in their play against them. At the same time, pro football played a role in increasing contacts and friendships between blacks and whites. Gifford tells the story of how Charlie Conerly, having been raised in a segregationist society, was shocked to be in an integrated world. Conerly liked to sit in the front of the Giants' bus and would be needled by Rosey Grier: "Back of the bus for me once more, right, Charlie?"[38] And on the field, team cohesion and the desire to win overcame racial differences.

Perhaps most dramatic of all was the change in pro football's fortunes as a business and its presence in the national culture. At the beginning of the glory years professional football was not a major national source of interest and entertainment. Gifford describes it when he broke in as "the ugly duckling of sports. It ranked just a notch above wrestling."[39] Many teams were still losing money and for many games attendance was under twenty thousand. Players and coaches had to take jobs during the off-season to make ends meet. Radio and television revenues made up a small proportion of team revenues. There was no players' union and the NFL was of limited national political importance.

All of this changed dramatically during the decade ending in 1963. In 1960 CBS negotiated television rights with individual teams, the Giants receiving a high of $175,000. In 1961, the league agreed to negotiate league TV contracts and to share the revenue equally, something that already was being done by the competing AFL. Wellington Mara was a key figure in this decision. Although initially reluctant to give up the dominant position of the Giants, he ultimately came around to the say, "We should all share, I guess. Or we're going to lose some of the smaller teams down the line."[40] The following year, largely under the influence of Pete Rozelle, the league signed its first national television deal—CBS paid $4.65 million a season for two seasons. Two years later, the three major networks (ABC, CBS, NBC) competed for what by now had become one of television's most valuable properties. The winning bid, by CBS, was for $14.1 million a season for the next two years! Within two years the payment had more than tripled and TV revenues had become a major source of team income.

There are many reasons for the spectacular growth of television revenues during this period of time. Television increasingly was a presence in family households and the technology was improving. Football lent itself to television coverage since, in contrast with baseball, it was fast and viewers could watch most of the players engaged in the action on each play. Also, each team played only once a week as part of a twelve- to fourteen-game schedule. As Pat Summerall has noted, "It's almost as if when the game was invented, it was invented for television.... The field is like a stage on which you see all twenty-two actors, plus the supporting cast on the sidelines."[41] However, many trace the great increase in interest to the 1958 Giants-Colts championship game. Andy Robustelli viewed the '58 game as "a crystallization of what pro football was all about. It brought out a lot of the drama of the game to the public."[42] A later observer views the game as representing a "seismic shift" in the American sports landscape—football was now king and baseball was no longer the national pastime.[43]

With growing television revenues and increased fan attendance, teams were on a better financial footing. In 1955 the Giants were offered a million dollars for the team, an offer Tim Mara turned down with the comment that the horse Nashua went for more than a million. By 1964 the team was worth much more. At the same time, there were problems to be faced. In 1954 the Canadian Football League (CFL) started to raid the NFL. The Giants lost their star tackle Arnie Weinmeister to the CFL that year. Periodically threatened by new leagues, in 1959 they had to face the announcement of the new American Football League (AFL) that would begin playing in 1960. Particularly relevant for the Giants was the competition they would have to face with the New York Titans. The AFL had some wealthy owners and a television deal, and were prepared to compete for players in the draft. Eager to get a jump on the AFL, the NFL held an early secret draft.

In 1956 the owners had to face a players' union—the NFL Players Association. A movement in this direction had begun a few years earlier with a secret meeting of many NFL stars. The meeting was secret because of a fear of being cut or traded if the owners learned of the players participating. The participating players agreed to go back to their teams, recruit members, and start contributing dues. The Giants were represented by Kyle Rote. The initial concerns involved training camp expenses, pension plans, and compensation for injuries. Illustrative demands often were minimal by comparison with later negotiations. For example, there were demands that owners provide football shoes and pay for pre-season games. But the power of players to bargain and negotiate, and to play off one league against the other, was on its way. As big business, management was going to face labor problems.

Nevertheless, the NFL was becoming an important part of the national scene. Important enough, for example, for Congress to get involved in the issue of whether the league should be allowed to sign an exclusive contract with one television station. Was this a violation of antitrust law? After intense lobbying, led by the diplomatic and persuasive Rozelle, and an agreement not to compete on Saturdays with college football games, the league was successful in getting an antitrust exemption. The bill was signed in 1961 by President Kennedy, himself a great football enthusiast, and paved the way for the following lucrative deal with CBS. Football players were beginning to be treated as stars and gained the interest of politicians. Before the 1959 title game Vice-President Nixon visited the Giants' locker room to say hello to the players and indicated some sophistication about the game and players. Of course, all of this was minor compared to what was still ahead in terms of presidential receptions.

Perhaps as much of a statement as anything about the growing national importance of NFL football was the issue of what to do with games following the death of President Kennedy on Friday, November 22, 1963. Rozelle, the commissioner, had less than two days to decide whether the Sunday games should be played. Agonizing over the decision, he consulted with the president's press secretary, Pierre Salinger. Perhaps taking their lead from President Roosevelt's decision that baseball should continue after Pearl Harbor, the two agreed that the president would have wanted the games to go on and that it would be good for the mood of the country. Thus, the decision was made to play the games, although the television networks decided not to broadcast them. The NFL decision to go ahead and play the games was in contrast with the cancellation of many major college games and with that of the AFL, which canceled all of its games. Many felt that Rozelle's decision was misguided and he himself often wondered whether he should have decided otherwise. In any case, the deliberations surrounding the decision reflected just how important the NFL had become to life in the country. Professional football, particularly as represented by the NFL, had indeed become king of sports entertainment.

3

"Fifteen Years of Lousy Football—We've Had Enough" (1964–1978)

On December 10, 1978, during the next-to-the-last game of the season against the St. Louis Cardinals, Giants fans watched a plane fly overhead with a trailing banner saying: "15 Years of Lousy Football—We've Had Enough." The banner expressed the feelings of all Giants fans and the fans at the game responded with the chant: "We've had enough.... We've had enough." No longer was it "*Dee-Fense*," now it was "*We've had enough*." For the third year in a row they were last in their division. Despite the victory that day, Giants fans indeed had had enough for the fifteen years between 1964 and 1978—an overall record of 74 wins, 134 losses, and four ties with but two winning seasons. At the time of the Cardinals game they had lost six straight. During that stretch the opposition had scored 144 points to the Giants' 91. Just three weeks before, the Giants had lost a game to the Eagles on a last-minute fumble blunder. A few weeks later Giants fans had taken to burning their tickets out of disgust with the level of play. According to one observer the "beasts of the East" had become "pussycats."[1] Another described them as having gone "from boom to bust" and as being "the orphans of the NFL."[2]

How are we to account for such a drop in fortunes for such an extended period of time? It is normal for teams to go through periods of rise and decline, but this decline seemed to go on endlessly, with no hope in sight. In fact, in many ways the organization was in chaos for a number of years—chaos in terms of trades, the draft, and the search for a quarterback, chaos in terms of coaches, and chaos in terms of management.

Trades, Drafts and the Search for a Quarterback

> I think that the Jets coming when they did [1964][3] contributed to our bad years, because we tried to do everything for the short term rather than the long haul—we'd trade a draft choice for a player, figuring he'd give

3. "Fifteen Years of Lousy Football—We've Had Enough" (1964–1978)

us one or two good years. We didn't want to accept how the public might react if we had a bad year or two or three.
—Wellington Mara[4]

Ending the 1963 season, the Giants clearly were an aging team. Although they had continued to be productive, the mainstays of the backfield—Tittle, Gifford, and Webster—were 37, 33, and 32 respectively. The defense too had begun to weaken, partly through the loss of Rosey Grier, traded to the Los Angeles Rams because he wanted to start his singing career on the west coast, and partly due to age. Strangely, what the Giants decided to do was trade Huff, not yet thirty, to the Washington Redskins, and Modzelewski to the Cleveland Browns. Huff went on to play for five more years, Modzelewski for three. Each was furious with the Giants for trades that made no sense to them. Huff expressed the following:

> Who did our coach, Allie Sherman, blame [after the loss to the Bears by a score of 14–10 in the 1963 championship game]? The defense. He traded it away the next year.... Guess what happened then? The Giants were 2–10–2 in 1964 and went from first place in the Eastern Conference to last place. I was very ticked off about the trade. I make no bones about it. When you do that—trade away your defense, your strong point, and your team comes up winning only two games after it—you deserve to be fired as a coach."[5]

Huff had received the call letting him know of the trade while sitting with Modzelewski in the latter's restaurant. When Modzelewski let Huff know two weeks later of his being traded as well, Huff jokingly told the rest of the Giants to stay out of Modzelewski's restaurant or they'd also be traded.[6]

Between 1962 and 1964, through trade or retirement, the Giants had lost ten important starters—five on offense (Tittle, Gifford, Webster, Dess, Stroud) and five on defense (Huff, Modzelewski, Grier, Robustelli, Barnes). It would be virtually impossible to replace such All-Pro players. But the Giants' draft selections left much to be desired and not everything could be attributed to the desire to do everything for the short term. Going back to the draft years 1959–1978, many draft picks were given up in trades to get established players, but many represented real duds, and in other cases players were not selected who turned out to be stars. Perhaps best illustrating the former were the selections of Joe Don Looney in the 1964 draft and Rocky Thompson in the 1971 draft, both drafted in the first round. Looney was a big, fast back but he had gone to a number of different colleges and had been dropped by Bud Wilkinson at Oklahoma at the request of his teammates. Frank Gifford describes him as "the most flakey Giant" who didn't like taking signs telling him what to do.[7] He never ran a yard for the Giants! Rocky Thompson was a surprise draft as a running back and possible receiver. He played three years, a total of twenty-nine games, rushed for a total of sixty-eight yards, and had a total of sixteen receptions. In 1965 the Giants selected Tucker Frederickson with the overall number-one draft selection. Frederickson's career unfortunately was shortened by injury. In the year he was drafted number one, Dick Butkus was selected at number three and Gale Sayers at number four by the Chicago Bears.

Perhaps most emblematic of the Giants selection problems is the history of their effort to find a quarterback during this period. We can start here with the year 1959, when the Giants were seeking a successor to the aging Conerly, by then age 38. Drafting in the tenth spot of the first round, the Giants selected Lee Grosscup. Allie Sherman, then a Giants scout, had observed Grosscup play and raved about him. In anticipation of the draft, Wellington Mara had a list of the top college quarterbacks and placed Grosscup at the top of the list. Things went wrong with Grosscup from the start. He had dreams of being a writer and upset his fellow players when he described them as "good drinkers" in a letter to another writer that ended up being published in *Sports Illustrated*. Beyond this, he was isolated from the other players with his long hair (remember, this was 1960) and love of classical music. He also had troubles with Sherman, then coach of the offense.[8]

Grosscup ended up playing a total of eight games over the course of two seasons with the Giants, passing for two touchdowns and having four interceptions. Following one of the touchdown passes Grosscup recalled the experience as follows: "I remember I went over to the bench and just sat there and I was listening to the noise and I started to shake. And then I started crying. The tears just popped into my eyes and I just started crying.... Well, at least I had that. I know what it is to have a standing ovation in Yankee Stadium."[9] This was the high point of his career with the Giants, since soon thereafter he was cut. He was picked up by the Vikings, who also cut him. He then played in eight games for the New York Titans during the 1962 season, following which he had tryouts with various teams, but basically his pro career was over. He was the first in a series of failures to find the replacement for the aging Conerly.[10]

In 1961 the Giants obtained Y.A. Tittle, who led them to division championships in 1961, 1962, and 1963. As in the previous chapter, these were part of the glory years for the Giants. But, as also noted, by 1964 Tittle was on the decline and in the Steelers game he was battered, bruised, and bloodied. In that game he had become the fallen warrior.

Y.A. had had another great year in 1963, again passing for over thirty touchdowns and over three thousand yards, and again leading the Giants to the division championship. But then, as we know, the roof caved in. In his final season, the thirty-eight-year-old Tittle had twice as many interceptions as completions and his quarterback rating was but half of what it had been the previous year, as the Giants fell to a record of 2–10–2.

September 20, 1964: The Giants now were entering the second game of the season after a season-opening thrashing by the not-highly-regarded Eagles. But things were to go no better against the not-terribly-strong Steelers. In fact, for Tittle they got worse. The Giants took an early two-touchdown lead, including a 64-yard touchdown pass from Tittle to Shofner, but ended up losing 27–24. But of greater importance, near the end of the second half Y.A. took a vicious hit by a Steeler defensive end while attempting to throw a screen pass. He was bleeding from the head and his face was etched in pain as he was removed for the rest of the game. Adding insult to injury, the attempted pass was intercepted for a touchdown.

Following the game Tittle was sent to the hospital for X-rays. He was found to have bruised cartilage of three ribs. Doc Sweeny described him as "pretty well beaten up."[11] "He never was able to regain his old form: 'In 1964 I got hurt probably the worst of all my seventeen years in pro football.... It was hard to breathe after that, and every time I got knocked down it was really hard to get up. I played, but I was a sitting duck.... As a result, I had a very poor year.'"[12] He was replaced during the season by the rookie quarterback Gary Wood—the Gary Wood who wanted to date Y.A.'s daughter. Tittle had too much pride to continue as a mediocre quarterback. In all, he played in six Pro Bowls, was named all–NFL three times, was twice named NFL Player of the Year, and in 1971 was enshrined in the NFL Hall of Fame.

When Tittle came to the Giants in 1961 at age 35, clearly he was not the long-term answer to their need for a quarterback. In 1962 the Giants obtained Ralph Guglielmi, who had been drafted by Washington in 1955 with the fourth pick of the first round. He played four undistinguished years for Washington and one for St. Louis before coming to the Giants. With every team, including the Giants, he had more interceptions than touchdowns. Before the end of the 1963 season he was gone.

In the fourth round of the 1962 draft, the Giants picked Glynn Griffing. He completed 16 of 40 passes in 1963, with three touchdowns and four interceptions. That was it for his NFL career. In the 1963 draft the Giants selected Mike Taliaferro in the tenth round. In a separate AFL draft, he was selected in a later round by the New York Titans and chose to play with them. He had an undistinguished four years with them.

In the 1964 draft the Giants selected Gary Wood in the eighth round. This was the year he came in for Tittle after Y.A. had been injured. A rookie who had played Ivy League ball at Cornell, Wood played in twelve games, had but six touchdowns, and completed less than fifty percent of his passes. He played the following two seasons for the Giants. In each season he completed under fifty percent of his passes and threw more interceptions than touchdowns.[13]

The 1965 draft was a defining one for the Giants as well as for their cross-town rivals, the Jets. This was the year that the star Alabama quarterback Joe Namath was available. As early as his junior year, Namath had caught the attention of scouts and coaches, already being tabbed by coach Weeb Ewbank as a quarterback who could take a team to the championship.[14] The Giants wanted to get Namath, but so did other teams. The Giants had the first pick of the draft but were reluctant to select Namath, fearing that the Houston Oilers of the rival AFL would select him; "they were giving people oil wells and gas stations at the time."[15] Also needing a running back, the Giants selected Tucker Frederickson with that pick. When they learned that Houston had traded the rights to Namath to the New York Jets, the Giants tried to trade with the St. Louis Cardinals, who had the NFL rights to Namath after selecting him with the twelfth choice of the first round. The Cardinals thought they could sign Namath but lost out to the Jets. On the very same day that Y.A. Tittle announced his retirement, the Jets introduced Namath as their new quarterback. The Jets had won out with a contract for over four hundred thousand dollars over the course of three years. The contract included yearly salaries of twenty-five thousand dollars for 1965–1967, a bonus of over two hundred thousand dollars, a Lincoln Continental, and salaries as scouts for his two brothers and brother-in-law. It now was a bidding war between the NFL and AFL. The Giants could not get the rights to Namath from the Cardinals but whether they would have been prepared to bid against the Jets for Namath's services is questionable.

The Giants did draft a quarterback in 1965: Bob Timberlake, in the third round. He saw limited duty that year and then was gone. Clearly desperate for a quarterback for the 1965 season, the Giants traded two starters to Detroit for Earl Morrall. Morrall had been selected by San Francisco in the first round of the 1956 draft. He came to Detroit in 1958 and played seven seasons for them. He had a good year in 1963 but dropped off in 1964, when he played in only six games. Morrall played well for a mediocre Giants team in 1965, completing over fifty percent of his passes and throwing for over two thousand yards and twenty-two touchdowns. In that year he began to develop a relationship with a speedy if somewhat erratic and unorthodox receiver, Homer Jones. Jones would often run routes that confounded the quarterback as well as the defenders. Nevertheless, he became the leading Giant receiver in 1966, averaging over twenty yards a reception. In one game that year he and Morrall connected for a 98-yard touchdown. That same year, Morrall fractured his wrist in the second half of the season and was replaced by Wood. He was unable to lead the offense and threw twice as many interceptions as touchdowns.

Which brings us to 1967 and the eighth quarterback on the list—Fran Tarkenton. The year 1966 had been a disaster for the Giants, who had ended the season with a 1–12–1 record. Although the once-powerful defense of the Giants was now largely responsible for their decline, leading the league in points given up, there also was the need for a quarterback to lead the offense. This need became all the more dramatic as the NFL and AFL signed a merger agreement in June of 1966. Now the Jets, with their star quarterback Broadway Joe Namath, would be competing with the Giants in the same league. After initially being one of the holdouts against the merger, Wellington Mara agreed to the merger on the condition that there be a financial indemnity for giving up exclusive territorial rights. In addition, the Giants were to get the first pick in an upcoming draft. The league agreed to this on the condition that the pick be a quarterback. The Giants could also trade that pick but only for a starting quarterback. In a part of the agreement that was not immediately clear, the top pick in a draft was not a bonus pick for the Giants, that is, the top pick *in addition to* their regular pick in the first round, but instead the top pick as a *repositioning of* their place in the draft. The difference between an *addition* as opposed to a *repositioning* may have been key, since the Giants held the second choice in the 1967 draft due to their disastrous 1966 record.

So the question became what the Giants should do as draft time approached in 1967. The Giants had three alternatives. With the second pick in the draft, it hardly made sense to reposition themselves in this draft. With this pick they were in a position to pick a promising quarterback who could be developed while Morrall continued as the first-string quarterback. That would leave them with the top overall pick for the 1968 draft. There were at least three promising quarterbacks available—Steve Spurrier, Bob Griese, and Don Horn. Allie Sherman, a former quarterback himself and former quarterback coach, was impressed with Spurrier. Of course, there was the 1959 first-round choice of Grosscup that turned out to be a dud so, as always, picking a quarterback for the future held some risk. A second alternative would be to pick a top defensive player to bolster the weak defense and then wait until the 1968 draft to use the top pick to select the quarterback of the future—Greg Landry and Ken Stabler would then be available. The third alternative was to trade for a quarterback and say the future is now.

Was a top quarterback available? There were some with potential, for example, Gary Cuozzo of the Colts, but would such a quarterback be a step up from Morrall and bring them to where they wanted to be? Then, a split developed in the camp of the Minnesota Vikings. Tension had been brewing between the Vikings' star quarterback, Fran Tarkenton, and the Vikings coach, Norm Van Brocklin, a former star quarterback himself. Apparently Tarkenton at times rejected the play selected by the coach and called his own selection. Tarkenton also was known to improvise on plays, scrambling to avoid defenders and then either running or buying time to find a receiver. Van Brocklin had been a great classic pocket passer. The team was split between the two, coach and quarterback. Finally, Tarkenton told management that he refused to play for Van Brocklin and that he was quitting the team. Van Brocklin resigned, feeling that the team was so split that if either returned there would never be harmony among the players. Tarkenton now became available.

Wellington Mara moved quickly to obtain Tarkenton and made a trade for him with Minnesota. With the 1967 draft but a month away, the Vikings would get the first- and second-round selections of the Giants in the upcoming draft, the overall top selection of the 1968 draft that was part of the Giants' compensation agreement if they used it to trade for a quarterback, and a second-round pick in 1969. This was quite a bit to give up, but as Allie Sherman noted: "You have to give up a lot to get a lot. We needed a top quarterback and Fran Tarkenton is a top quarterback."[16] Indeed, Tarkenton had starred for six seasons with the Vikings, averaging over fifty percent completions, over two thousand yards and nineteen touchdowns a year in passing, and over three hundred yards a year in rushing. In what was regarded by some as a coup for the Giants, they had obtained a colorful quarterback who could compete with the Jets' Namath for the attention of the fans, one who was still only twenty-seven and thus could be expected to have many successful years ahead of him, and one whose scrambling ability could be expected to help a weak Giant offensive line.

Tarkenton set the stage for scrambling quarterbacks. He rejected the characterization of him as a scrambler, suggesting that he was a pocket passer who only occasionally of necessity moved out of the pocket. However he described himself, there was no question but that in the course of a fourteen-game season with Minnesota he averaged over fifty rushes a season or three a game. This was aside from the times he would scramble out of the pocket but not rush for yardage. In any case, he also was a successful passer, as his record with Minnesota indicated. Between the two he was an exciting player to watch and an exhausting one for defensive linemen to chase.

When he came to the Giants, Tarkenton did not disappoint. In his first season he helped them move from the 1–12–1 record of the previous season to a 7–7 record. The offense averaged a touchdown per game more than the

3. "Fifteen Years of Lousy Football—We've Had Enough" (1964–1978) 55

previous season. Tarkenton threw for over three thousand yards and twenty-nine touchdowns, completed over fifty percent of his passes, and ran for over three hundred yards, averaging seven yards a rush. He continued the successful quarterback-receiver connection with Homer Jones, with Jones making thirteen touchdown receptions and averaging over twenty-four yards a catch. Tarkenton said of Jones: "It's like throwing to a man riding a motorcycle holding a butterfly net."[17]

The next three seasons (1968–1970) also were good seasons for Tarkenton. He averaged over two thousand seven hundred passing yards, twenty touchdown passes and half as many interceptions, forty-six rush attempts with an average gain of just over five yards per rush. For the first two of the seasons the Giants as a team were not able to improve on their 1967 record, but in 1970 they were able to improve to a record of 9–5. That season saw the emergence of Ron Johnson as a thousand-yard rusher, the first in Giants history to do this.

The following season, 1971, started poorly for the Giants and continued on that note throughout. Before their first preseason game Tarkenton announced that he would retire over a salary dispute. He and Wellington Mara had been negotiating for some time and could not come to terms on an agreement. Just before the game he came up to the head coach at the time, Alex Webster, and told him he was leaving. It came as a shock to Webster to then find Tarkenton absent from the locker room. After going home for a few days, Tarkenton decided his move had been hasty and he returned to sign a one-year contract. The writing was on the wall—his remaining time with the Giants was limited.

Even with Tarkenton, the Giants lost their remaining five preseason games and ended up with a 4–10 record. Both the offense and defense regressed, the offense struggling without the injured running backs Johnson and Frederickson. Tarkenton passed for over twenty-five hundred yards but he had twenty-one interceptions as opposed to only eleven touchdowns. His number of rushing attempts, total rushing yardage, and average yards per rush all also declined. He was benched the last game of the year and then was traded back to the Vikings for the veteran Norm Snead, the same quarterback who had dueled Y.A. Tittle in Tittle's 1962 record-tying seven-touchdown game. In addition, the Giants received end Bob Grim, running back Vince Clements, and two draft choices. Grim had been the second-round selection the Vikings obtained from the Giants in the 1967 draft.

In all, then, Tarkenton played five years for the Giants, had some excellent seasons, and then was gone. Although his quarterback-coach difficulties did not rise to the level they did with Van Brocklin at Minnesota, according to Giants coach Alex Webster, he was not easy to deal with: "He knew a lot about the game himself but you ended up constantly arguing with him. He would often ignore plays sent in for one reason or another, and he'd call plays he thought were better. It didn't make for a good relationship. He was never happy. He got to the point where he made it clear he wanted to be traded."[18] Tarkenton went on to play seven more seasons with the Vikings (1972–1978); he threw for over two thousand yards in six of those seasons, including for over three thousand yards in 1978. He led the Vikings to six division and three conference championships. He was inducted into the Hall of Fame in 1986.

Overall, was the trade for Tarkenton a good deal for the Giants, a coup as some initially suggested? There are many ways to look at this. In 1967, the year he came to the Giants, the team could have used their draft choice, number two overall, to draft one of the three highly regarded quarterbacks available in the draft. Steve Spurrier, drafted number three by San Francisco, played nine seasons for them and one for Tampa Bay. His overall record was not outstanding: he threw for over a thousand yards in only three seasons and sixty interceptions as opposed to forty touchdowns. Bob Griese was drafted number four by Miami and played his entire fourteen years there. In half of those years, including his first in 1967, Griese threw for over two thousand yards. In each of another five years he threw for over a thousand yards. Overall he threw for almost two hundred touchdowns, led the Dolphins to three division championships and two Super Bowls, and was inducted into the Hall of Fame in 1990. The third quarterback, Don Horn, was drafted number twenty-five by Green Bay. He played in fifty-seven games for four teams over the course of his eight seasons in the NFL.

So part of the answer to the question of whether the trade for Tarkenton was a good deal for the Giants depends on which of the three available quarterbacks they otherwise might have selected. In addition, there is the question of what they might have done with their other draft choices. For example, they might have used their second round choice in 1967 and the first in 1968 to strengthen their weak defense. Alternatively, the Giants could have drafted the great Alan Page in 1967 to bolster their weak defense and then waited until the 1968 season to draft a quarterback when Greg Landry and Ken Stabler were available.

Another way of looking at the trade is to consider what the Vikings did with their selections. Of course they had different needs but this may in any case be of interest. In 1967 they used the Giants' first-round draft choice to select the running back Clint Jones and the second-round choice to select Bob Grim. Jones played six seasons for Minnesota and never gained seven hundred yards. Grim played five seasons for Minnesota, averaged under twenty catches a season and under twenty yards a catch. He played three

3. "Fifteen Years of Lousy Football—We've Had Enough" (1964–1978)   57

seasons for the Giants, averaged twenty-three receptions a season and fifteen yards a catch. In 1968 the Vikings used their overall first selection to choose offensive tackle Ron Yary. Yary played fourteen seasons for them. He made the Pro Bowl seven consecutive times and is considered one of the all-time great tackles.

To complete the review, Snead played three seasons for the Giants. He started and did well in 1972, along with Ron Johnson returning the Giants to a winning record (8–6). Things did not go as well, however, in 1973, when he threw three times as many interceptions as touchdowns. The back-up quarterback, Randy Johnson, played in nine of the games and started in some. The team ended the season with a 2–11–1 record, being beaten in the final game of the season, 31–7, by the Tarkenton-led Vikings. Clements, the running back traded along with Snead and Grim, played two seasons for the Giants, gaining slightly over two hundred yards each season. With their draft choices from Minnesota, the Giants selected the defensive end Larry Jacobson in 1972 and the linebacker Brad Van Pelt in 1973. Jacobson played three seasons for the Giants, starting in only one. Van Pelt played eleven seasons for the Giants (1973–1983), starting in ten of those seasons and playing excellent defense.

So was it a good trade? A coup? The answer is not clear. The Giants gave up a lot and they got a lot of help for five seasons. Had Tarkenton played for them for the remaining seven years of his career and put up the kind of statistics he did for Minnesota, one could have concluded that it was an excellent trade for the Giants—they gave up a lot and got a lot. On the other hand, had the Giants selected Bob Griese, and had Griese had the career for them that he had for the Dolphins, and had the Giants used their other draft choices wisely, the Giants probably would have been better off not making the trade. We are left with a lot of what-ifs and what might have beens. There is no clear-cut answer. What is clear is that with the departure of Tarkenton after the 1971 season, the search for a quarterback was to again be part of the Giants' picture.

November 26, 1967: Giants 44, Eagles 7. After the disastrous 1966 season the arrival of Fran Tarkenton provided hope for better things ahead for the Giants and he did not disappoint. Although the Giants won only one of their five preseason games, by the end of the tenth week they had a five hundred record, a big improvement over the previous season. In addition, the offense, now led by Tarkenton, was averaging twenty-seven points a game. The Tarkenton-to-Jones combination was clicking as the Giants headed to Yankee Stadium to play the Philadelphia Eagles before over sixty thousand fans. This turned out to be a Giant romp—their best effort of the season and the best offensive effort since 1963 when the Giants, behind Y.A.

Tittle, beat the San Francisco 49ers 48–14. Tarkenton was sharp as he led the offense to scores the first seven times they had the ball. Staying mostly in the pocket, the ordinarily scrambling Tarkenton completed 20 of 31 passes for 261 yards and three touchdowns, two of them to the swift receiver Homer Jones. Tarkenton rushed but twice for twelve yards and Jones had four receptions for a total of 84 yards. This brought the season total for Jones to over a thousand yards on receptions.

After the game an Eagle player was heard to say: "This is a different Giants team. The quarterback makes the difference. We couldn't get to him, he moved so fast. He was sharp." As Allie Sherman, the Giants' head coach, put it: "We put it all together today, offense and defense."[19]

November 11, 1968: *Giants 27, Cowboys 21*. Things were looking up for the Giants as they passed the midpoint mark of the 1968 season. Although the defense continued to be a problem, the offense continued to sparkle. It had been stopped by the powerful Baltimore defense the week before. Could they recoup against the strong Cowboys, who were the division champions the year before and seemed headed toward another championship this season? A difficult task under any circumstances, and in this case in a game to be played at the Cowboys' Cotton Bowl. But Tarkenton and the offense were not to be denied. Tarkenton ran twenty-two yards to score the opening touchdown and passed for two more, one on a sixty-yard completion to Homer Jones. He both scrambled and passed beautifully.

Giants fans had reason to cheer—their team had just pulled off the upset of the year and their most significant victory in five years. The players too were overjoyed and carried Allie Sherman off on their shoulders as if they had just won a division championship or perhaps even the Super Bowl. But these had been difficult years for the Giants and celebration of an improbable victory was understandable. Sherman jubilantly shook his fist in victory and was overcome with emotion: "It was the greatest. I cried."[20] The chants of "Goodbye Allie" after the 1966 season and calls for his firing seemed but a distant memory. Wellington Mara's statement that he expected Sherman to be coach for many years seemed more fitting for the moment.

September 26, 1971: *Redskins 30, Giants 3*. The cause for celebration following the Giants' victory over the Cowboys proved to be short-lived. The Giants lost their last four games that season and their five preseason games in 1969. Sherman was replaced by Alex Webster, the former Giant star running back. The Giants fell to a losing record and Homer Jones, with but one touchdown reception for the season, had played his last games with the Giants.

Things had gone somewhat better in 1970, the offense strengthened by the running of Ron Johnson. But the turmoil surrounding Tarkenton and

3. "Fifteen Years of Lousy Football—We've Had Enough" (1964–1978)

the loss of six preseason games did not bode well for the 1971 season. The Giants opened with a victory over a weak Green Bay team, but the following week were squashed by the Redskins, 30–3. It was a total disaster for a team weakened by the absence of the injured running back Ron Johnson. The team was booed by the fans as Tarkenton was chased all over the field and sacked three times for a loss of thirty-six yards, In addition to being buried by the Redskin pass rush, Tarkenton was intercepted twice, once for a Redskin touchdown, and had a touchdown pass dropped by a receiver—not a good day for the already unhappy quarterback. To make things worse, he had to watch the Redskins' quarterback, Bill Kilmer, in for the injured Sonny Jurgensen, pass for over three hundred yards.

November 29, 1971: Cardinals 24, Giants 7. Things were not going well for the Giants. Not only were they losing to the good teams but in October they had lost to the previously unwinning Eagles, 23–7. In that game there were five fumbles. Tarkenton was intercepted once and while holding for a field goal attempt had let the wet ball squirt through his hands. The blunders that had been typical of the Giants continued in this game against the Cardinals, a weak team they had beaten earlier in the season. On the first play of the game, a halfback option pass was intercepted and a few plays later was followed by a Cardinal touchdown. Later in the game a perfect pass from Tarkenton bounced out of the hands of his tight end and into the hands of the Cardinal defender. With the game less than ten minutes old, another Tarkenton pass was intercepted for a touchdown. With the Giants closing in on a touchdown near the end of the half, another Tarkenton pass was deflected and intercepted, ending a sixty-nine-yard drive that had taken them to the Cardinal six-yard line. A fourth pass was intercepted when there was a miscommunication between Tarkenton and the receiver as to where the receiver was supposed to be. But interceptions were not Tarkenton's only problem. In the first quarter, his halfback fumbled a reception and in the second quarter a long completion, after a long scramble, was called back because the scrambling Tarkenton had stepped just beyond the line of scrimmage. In the same quarter, a completion deep into Cardinal territory was nullified because of a holding penalty. Clearly this was not Tarkenton's day in an altogether losing final season with the Giants.

With the departure of Tarkenton, the saga of the search for a quarterback continued. For the 1972 season the Giants had the newly acquired Norm Snead and Tarkenton's backup, Randy Johnson. Snead was by now much traveled, having played for Washington, Philadelphia, and Minnesota. Snead had ability. In fact, he had dueled Tittle in Y.A.'s record-tying 1962 game. However, he also was not terribly mobile, having also been sacked five times by the Giants in their 1967 victory over the Eagles. Unfortunately, both Snead and Johnson had poor touchdown versus interception records. In his eleven years prior to coming to the Giants, Snead had almost a third more interceptions than touchdowns (201–158). In his four years with Atlanta and one with the Giants, Johnson's record was no better—sixty-five interceptions versus thirty-four touchdowns. In any case, Snead won the competition for the starting job and went on to have a fine season, assisted by the return of running back Ron Johnson, who again ran for over one thousand yards. Snead passed for over two thousand yards, passed for many more touchdowns than interceptions (17–12), helped return the offense to an average of over twenty points a game, and led the Giants to a winning season.

The relative success, however, was short-lived. In 1973, Snead led an offense that averaged under seventeen points a game, passed for under two thousand yards, and had many more interceptions than touchdowns (22–7). The Giants reverted to a losing record, 2–11–1, and head coach Alex Webster was gone.

The Giants could have selected Dan Fouts in the 1973 draft. He was selected in the third round by San Diego and went on to have a Hall of Fame career as one of the great all-time passers. In the meantime, they started the 1974 season with Snead, hoping that a new coach, Bill Arnsbarger, and a revamped offensive line would be of help. Midway into the season it was clear that the offense was in trouble. In its first seven games it averaged under ten points a game. The defense, despite the strong defense skills of Arnsbarger, could not carry the team as it lost six of the first seven. Desperate for help, the Giants obtained Craig Morton, who had been playing in the World Football League, but whose NFL rights were owned by the Dallas Cowboys. With the 1975 first-round draft choice obtained from the Giants, the second selection overall, the Cowboys selected Randy White, who went on to become a Hall of Fame defensive tackle. Also available at that point in the draft was Walter Payton, who was selected number four by the Bears.

Morton led the Giants for the remainder of the 1974 season. He played reasonably well but threw more interceptions than touchdowns and was sacked almost twice a game. The defense remained weak and the team ended with a 2–12 record, thus the number-two selection in the 1975 draft that was traded away to the Cowboys. Things were not much better for Morton or the Giants in the following two seasons. In 1975 Morton passed for over two thousand yards but he again threw more interceptions than touchdowns (16–11) and was sacked on average over three times a game. Things got worse in 1976. Morton passed for under two thousand yards, had twice as many interceptions as touchdowns (20–9), was sacked on average almost

3. "Fifteen Years of Lousy Football—We've Had Enough" (1964–1978) 61

three times a game for an overall loss of almost three hundred yards, and the offense averaged but twelve points a game while losing eleven of fourteen games. After the season Morton was gone in a Giants trade with the Denver Broncos, the Giants receiving quarterback Steve Ramsey in return. Morton started for Denver for five seasons. Ramsey never did play with the Giants. Nor did he play for any other NFL team.

So now, in the thirteen seasons between 1964 and 1976, in addition to many backups, the Giants had gone with five different starting quarterbacks—Tittle, Morrall, Tarkenton, Snead, and Morton. Averaging two and a half seasons a quarterback, one might assume that things had to get better. Hopes for the 1977 season hinged on Joe Pisarcik. Big at 6'4" and 220 pounds, Pisarcik had played three years in the Canadian Football League and was obtained as a free agent by the Giants. He was backed up by Jerry Goldsteyn, a twelfth-round draft choice. Neither was an improvement over the departed Morton. In fact, between them they passed for less yardage than Morton did and had an even worse interception-touchdown record (22–6).

Pisarcik retained the starting quarterback position for the 1978 season and passed for slightly over two thousand yards. But for the second season in a row he threw twice as many interceptions as touchdowns and was sacked an average of twice a game. The Giants ended the season with a 6–10 record and last in their division for the third year in a row. And then, of course, there was the fumble.

November 19, 1978: Giants-Eagles. Entering the twelfth game of the season, things again were not going well for the Giants, what with their having suffered six losses, twice to the division-leading Cowboys. Now it was time to play the Eagles, second to Dallas in the division. In a surprisingly strong effort, the Giants were ahead 17–12 with but thirty-one seconds remaining in the game. The game was in hand; perhaps the season can be salvaged. The clock was running and the Eagles had no time outs remaining. All Pisarcik had to do was take the knee and victory was theirs.

But no! Instead, the play called was a handoff from Pisarcik to fullback Larry Csonka. The quarterback and other players in the huddle couldn't believe it; but that is what the coaches wanted run. So run it was, except that the ball bounced off of Pisarcik's hands and was scooped up by Eagles defensive back Herman Edwards (later to become the head coach of the Jets), who ran it into the end zone for a touchdown—Eagles 19, Giants 17! "I never had control of the ball," claims Pisarcik. "That's the most horrifying ending to a ball game I've ever seen," noted head coach John McVay, whose job now was in danger. Bob Gibson, the offensive coordinator who called the play, was dismissed the following day, the end of a long period of conflict between the coordinator and Pisarcik. Pisarcik described it as being "like when you're with some girl you don't really like. You're not going to be the greatest lover." The players were furious: "Damn, we beat them. Physically we beat them up, only to lose in a horrible, horrible way."[21]

The Giants lost three of the remaining four games. The head coach was gone. Pisarcik no longer was the starting quarterback. A new front office was to be brought in. Thankfully it was the end of fifteen years of lousy football and the end of the search for a quarterback.

The Coaches

The tumult and chaos of the drafts, trades, and search for a quarterback were no less present in the coaching department. As we have seen, Allie Sherman was installed as head coach for the 1961 season and began his career on an upbeat note, leading the aging Giants to the conference championship and being selected Coach of the Year. Although they had lost to Green Bay in a close game earlier in the season, they were crushed by the Packers (37–0) in the NFL championship game.

Things continued to go well for Sherman and the Giants in 1962 and 1963, the tail end of the glory years. The heart of the team remained much the same, in particular with Tittle throwing to Shofner and Gifford on offense, with an established line to protect the quarterback and an established defense. In both seasons the Giants won their division championship and in 1962 Sherman again was selected Coach of the Year. In both seasons, however, they again lost in the championship games, first to Green Bay (16–7) and then to the Chicago Bears (14–10). Clearly the Giants were a strong, competitive team and Sherman seemed headed for a long stay with the Giants.

Suddenly, although probably not unexpectedly, things began to fall apart in 1964. With Tittle, Shofner, Gifford, and Webster all slipping and at the end of their careers, the offense averaged two touchdowns per game less than the previous year. Perhaps even more devastating was the decline in the once-vaunted defense. Gone were Huff and Modzelewski, along with Grier, who left after the 1962 season. On average the defense gave up a touchdown more per game than it had the prior two years. Together with the decline in the offense, for the first time since 1953 opponents scored more points than did the Giants. This pattern continued for the next five years, throughout Sherman's reign as head coach. In 1966 things were so bad that opponents on average outscored the Giants by more than two touchdowns a game. The defense set a league record for points allowed. From the division championship in 1963, the Giants fell to last place in 1964.

3. "Fifteen Years of Lousy Football—We've Had Enough" (1964–1978)

For the remaining years during this period (1965–1978), the Giants were last in their division seven times. The division championships and NFL championship became distant memories.

With the decline of the team, Sherman's star began to fade. By the end of the disastrous 1966 season, with the Giants winning but one game and falling to last in their conference, the fans were calling for Sherman's head. Watching their team fall to the strong Dallas Cowboys, the fans held banners that read "Goodbye Allie" and began to chant the words as well. Pennant hawkers at Yankee Stadium sold over ten thousand flags saying "Goodbye Allie." Perhaps more than most other fans, New York fans do not take losing well, particularly when they have become accustomed to taking pride in their team. Sherman had the backing of Wellington Mara, but even the loyalty of the owner could not protect him after two more mediocre seasons and five preseason losses in 1969. According to Gifford, Sherman was a terrific offensive coach but not a head coach, better as a strategist than as a manager of players, someone who wanted to be one of the guys instead of asserting authority: "He wanted to be loved and that's deadly for a coach."[22] In fairness to Sherman, however, Gifford also notes that there was the problem of older players being gone before new, younger players were ready to take their place.

Altogether, Sherman lasted eight seasons with the Giants, far more than the average tenure of the coaches during the remainder of this period. After the preseason losses in 1969, Alex Webster, the running back "Big Red" of the Giants from 1955 through 1964 and assistant under Sherman for two years, was appointed head coach. Webster began to bring the team back in 1968. In 1970 he led them to a winning season, the first in six years. But 1970, the year in which Webster was selected Coach of the Year, was the apex of his career as a coach. The Giants were last in their division for two of the remaining three years during which he was head coach. Overall, Webster had a record of 29–40–1. He proved to be a better player than head coach. In his own words, he really wasn't ready to be a head coach when he became one: "The head-coaching job was not something I really wanted—it was something I didn't feel prepared for. I felt it was like going from a salesperson one day to the president of the company the next.... I'd enjoyed the hell out of coaching as an assistant, but head-coaching was another thing."[23] An offer of a two-year contract at fifty thousand dollars a year, almost tripling his salary as an assistant coach, was enough to remove his doubts about taking the job, but it was an unfortunate ending to a career with the Giants.

With the team reeling after a 2–11–1 record in 1973, and with criticism for poor trades and drafts, the Giants brought in Andy Robustelli, their star defensive end from the glory years, to be director of operations. Robustelli, who had experience as a businessman but not as a football executive, brought in Bill Arnsbarger to be head coach. This seemed like an incredibly good selection. Arnsbarger was considered to be a genius as he coached the strong Miami Dolphins defense to championship seasons and Super Bowl victories under head coach Don Shula. Arnsbarger had never played in the NFL but he had been an assistant under a number of outstanding coaches, serving under the great Shula from 1964 until he left to become head coach of the Giants. As was to be observed by the Giants and other teams on many subsequent occasions, being a head coach is a vastly different job from being an assistant coach or defensive or offensive coordinator. The Giants again were last in Arnsbarger's first season, winning but two games. They improved in 1975 but in 1976 again were last in their division, winning but three games. Midway through the season, after a string of seven losses, including a loss to the Vikings led by Tarkenton, Arnsbarger was gone, replaced by his assistant John McVay. Over the course of less than three years Arnsbarger had achieved a record of 7–28.

McVay had experience as a head coach, leading the World Football League's (WFL) Memphis Southern to winning seasons. He was particularly successful in his work with the offense and the Giants' brain trust hoped that he could jump-start the anemic offense. But McVay was hardly able to improve the offense much, only slightly increasing their average points per game from ten to thirteen. At least part of the problem was that the offense was being led by two aging, immobile quarterbacks—Craig Morton age 33, and Norm Snead, age 37. Another part of the problem was that Larry Csonka, who had starred for Miami for seven seasons and was obtained by the Giants after the demise of the Memphis team in the WFL, was injured much of the season.

Things did not go much better for the Giants in 1977 or 1978, their being last in their division both years. And, of course, in 1978 there was Pisarcik and The Fumble. With a record of 14–23 over the course of two and a half years, McVay too was gone. In addition to six starting quarterbacks, the Giants now had gone through four coaches in the course of eighteen years.

The Family and the Search for a Home

After Tim Mara died in 1959, responsibility for the team fell completely into the hands of his two sons, Jack and Wellington. In 1965, shortly after the beginning of the decline and Tittle's retirement, Jack Mara died. Jack

Mara had served as team president for thirty-one years. His son, Tim, became co-owner and vice president, with Wellington becoming president and chairman of the board of directors. Whereas Jack and Wellington had a harmonious relationship, this was not true for the uncle and nephew. According to Frank Gifford, the two were total opposites: "Wellington Mara lives the perfect spiritual life. I never heard him utter a swear word. He goes to mass almost every day and has put all of his eleven children through Catholic colleges. That's Well's life: his family, his church, and his Giants."[24] In contrast with this, Tim was described as charming, extroverted, fun-loving, a man-about-town with two ex-wives.[25] Although Gifford's characterization may be biased by his strong bond with Wellington Mara, the dissimilarity between the two was clear, as was the split between them. The two had very different views as to how the team should be run and things got so bad that at times the two did not speak to one another and the owner's box had a partition between them. This was no way to run a football team.

At the same time that the family was split and divisive in running the team, the Giants found themselves without a stadium to call home for their games. In August of 1971 Wellington Mara and Governor Cahill of New Jersey announced the signing of a thirty-one-year lease, beginning in 1975, of a stadium to be built by the New Jersey Sports and Exposition Authority on the Meadowlands across the river from New York. Heresy—the New York Giants were moving to New Jersey. The announced move created a political storm as well as a fan storm. Mayor Lindsay of New York made plans for a suit in federal court challenging football's exemption from antitrust laws, sought a congressional investigation, and threatened to prevent the Giants from playing in Yankee Stadium while the new stadium was being built: "The Giant management crossed the line that distinguishes a sport from a business.... We made them a successful operation and now they want to leave. If they want to play in a swamp, let them play in a swamp right now."[26]

Ground was broken for the new stadium in November of 1972, but things were not about to go smoothly. First, the Giants were evicted from Yankee Stadium after the first two games of the 1973 season. The presumed reason was the renovation of Yankee Stadium, but there was suspicion that it was a retaliatory move on the part of the city. This left the Giants scurrying to find a place to play the next two seasons until the new stadium was ready in 1975. First, they thought they had an agreement to use the Yale Bowl in New Haven, Connecticut. But, of all things, a snag was hit in relation to a blackout television ruling. The NFL rule concerning television broadcasting of games would have prevented the local station from broadcasting

Giants games. The deal to use the Yale Bowl fell through. The Giants sought to use Princeton University's Palmer Stadium but were turned down.

At the time of the announcement of the NFL's announcement of the 1973 schedule, the Giants were without a home—"the orphans of the NFL."[27] With both the Giants and the NFL now desperate, the move was made to waive the blackout rule for the Giants so as to permit them to play in the Yale Bowl. The plan first ran into congressional resistance, but finally legislation that lifted blackouts if a game was sold out three days before kickoff was passed and signed into law by President Nixon. Once more there was evidence that professional football had become a major part of the social, cultural, and political scene of the nation.

The dire situation seemed resolved when new problems arose. In the summer of 1973 the New Jersey Sports and Exposition Authority found itself having problems selling bonds for the development of the Meadowlands. The problem led to a political battle between the outgoing Democratic governor and the incoming Republican governor. Thrown into the mix was an effort on the part of the New York governor to force the Giants to stay in New York. Things on the political front were resolved, only to be followed by cost overruns and delays in the construction of the stadium. Now the question was where the Giants would play in 1975—the season they thought they would be playing in their own stadium. Arrangements finally were made for them to play that season in Shea Stadium, home of the rival Jets since completion of its construction in 1964.

The Giants finally were able to move into their home for the 1976 season. No longer nomads, they still were a weak team. The opening game at the stadium was against the strong Dallas Cowboys and the Giants lost by a score of 24–14. A banner read "Brand New Stadium—Same Old Giants." The journey for a home had been long and difficult; that for a winning team was to be equally long and difficult.

The NFL

The years 1964 through 1978 were a disaster for the Giants. They were years of tremendous popularity and success for the NFL. But along with this increased popularity and prosperity there were new problems to be faced— competition and threats from rival leagues, threats from players organizing themselves, and questions concerning the status of professional football as free from antitrust action. Professional football no longer was just entertainment, it was business—big business, and it was part of the national and local political scene.

The NFL, the AFL, and TV

Rival leagues have periodically been pitted against the NFL, in part due to the glamour of the enterprise and in part to the potential financial gain, the latter increasingly so as franchises have made more money and been sold for increasing amounts. Meetings to begin a rival league, the American Football League (AFL), began in 1959 when a number of wealthy businessmen found themselves unable to obtain NFL franchises. The new league began with eight franchises, some in rival NFL cities, and held its first draft in 1960. The teams were not in great organizational shape, many without complete front office and coaching staffs, but went ahead with the draft. The draft had a unique element to it—a territorial pick for each team. In order to build local support, each team was allowed to draft one star player from the local region to build fan support. For example, Houston picked the star running back and Heisman Trophy winner Billy Cannon from LSU and the Dallas Texans the star quarterback Don Meredith from SMU. In the meantime, the NFL held an early secret draft to get a jump on its new competition. The rivalry had begun with the AFL outbidding the NFL for many stars and teams making draft decisions partly on the basis of their optimism concerning their ability to outbid a team from the rival league. In some cases players signed with both leagues and courts had to settle the question of which was the valid contract.

The AFL brought some innovations to the game (e.g., player names on jerseys, a one- or two-point conversion after a touchdown) and emphasized an exciting, wide-open passing game. It developed its own stars, some from the draft of college graduates and some from players who had not been able to be stars in the NFL. At the same time, the new league struggled financially for many years, with the NFL doing what it could to undermine its success; at the same time, occasional feelers would go out about a possible merger. Then two major events unfolded that gave the AFL important credibility. First, in 1964 it signed a television contract with NBC for thirty-six million dollars over five years, dividing the revenue equally among the teams.[28] This rivaled the NFL contract with CBS in terms of revenue for each team, gave the new league a tremendous financial boost, and brought into play the ability of television to influence the dynamics of the game. Second, in 1965 the New York Jets were able to outbid their rivals for the services of the star Alabama quarterback, Joe Namath. Not only did the contract make Namath one of the highest-paid players in team sports, it included a Lincoln Continental and salaries for his brothers and brother-in-law as scouts. The Jets now not only had a new home, Shea Stadium, and were developing a strong fan base, but they had the star quarterback the rival Giants had been so eager to obtain.

By now some owners of NFL teams were thinking seriously about a merger. One of the opponents was the Giants' Wellington Mara. On the AFL side, too, there were some interested in a merger at the same time that the newly elected commissioner, Al Davis, vowed to take the fight to the NFL. Then, an unexpected turn of events changed the course of negotiations. During the six years of competition between the leagues there was an unwritten agreement that they would compete for the signing of rookies in the draft but not raid one another's veterans. To the surprise of all, in May of 1966 the Giants, desperate for a field goal kicker, signed the soccer-style kicker Pete Gogolak of the AFL's Buffalo Bills. Vince Lombardi, sitting at the meeting where the signing was announced by Pete Rozelle, the NFL commissioner, was outraged by what had been done by his old friend: "This is a disgrace! Wellington, I can't believe that you would do something like this, to put us all into jeopardy!" Carroll Rosenbloom, the owner of the Baltimore Colts, fumed at Mara: "Goddamit, if you'd wanted a kicker, why didn't you just ask me? I'd have given you one."[29]

The Gogolak signing set the stage for generations of soccer-style field goal kickers. It also set the stage for the NFL–AFL merger. War was otherwise about to break out, with the AFL teams targeting NFL players they would attempt to sign—good for the players but not for the owners. Among the NFL owners there remained but a few, including Mara, who wanted to hold out and fight the AFL. Mara, of course, was particularly concerned about the competition of the Jets in his backyard. The San Francisco 49ers were in a similar position concerning the Oakland Raiders. There were thoughts of trying to get the Jets and Raiders to move as part of a merger but the teams were too popular with their fans for this to be feasible: "If I try to get the Jets to move I'd be crucified," noted Mara.[30] The matter was settled by the Giants' and 49ers' getting indemnity payments for the teams entering their area of territorial exclusivity, and the Giants' getting the first pick in the draft on the condition that it be a quarterback. Or the draft pick could be traded for a quarterback—the one that led to the trade for Tarkenton. A common draft would begin in 1967 and a championship game between the two leagues, the Super Bowl, would be held after the 1966 season. The merger settlement changed the course of history for the NFL. The trade probably changed the course of history for the Giants for the next decade.

Television revenue played a role in the survival of the AFL and it increasingly played a role in the financial well-being of the NFL.[31] In 1964 CBS paid the NFL fourteen million dollars annually, each team receiving slightly under one million dollars. By 1977, a four-year contract was signed for $576 million, the biggest deal in television history. Each team's annual television revenue now was over five million dollars—more than was brought in from ticket sales.

Fans could not get enough of it. In 1967, Super Bowl I, broadcast by both NBC and CBS, was watched by somewhere between sixty-five and eighty-five million fans, the largest audience ever to watch a sporting event in the U.S. In one 1968 game between the Jets and the Oakland Raiders, television fans were enraged because NBC switched from the game to the movie *Heidi*, leaving the fans unable to view Oakland's two touchdowns in the final minute of the game. In 1970, ABC agreed to produce *Monday Night Football* after plans for it were rejected by the rival NBC and CBS networks that had popular Monday evening programs. It immediately became a hit with the team of Howard Cosell, Dandy Don Meredith, and Frank Gifford becoming the well-known voices of the program for many years.[32] More fans watched the fourth Super Bowl (1970) than watched Neil Armstrong walk on the moon, and by the time of the eighth Super Bowl (1974) the popular minister Norman Vincent Peale was saying, "If Jesus Christ was alive today he'd be at the Super Bowl."[33] Sunday afternoons and Monday evenings had taken on their own holy quality among diehard football fans.

Player Unrest: Unions and Strikes

With the merger of the leagues, a common draft, and big money coming in from television, it's not surprising that the players began to organize and make their own demands. In 1968 a strike by the Players Association was avoided just days before the opening of training camps. In 1970 the players threatened to sit out the season unless their pension fund was supported. They received increased funding.

In 1974 things began to heat up between the players and the owners. There had been growing demands for free agency and now the players were ready to strike for it. During the summer of 1974 they went on strike and picketed the training camps wearing T-shirts that read "No Freedom, No Football." The players were seeking the end of the draft and the end of the "Rozelle Rule" that if a team signed a player from another team it was due compensation, both of which were deterrents to higher salaries and sacrosanct as far as the owners were concerned. But with the players returning to camp after a federal mediator ordered a two-week cooling-off period, and the upstart World Football League folding under the weight of red ink, the players had lost the battle.

Things went somewhat better for the players in 1977 when the Players

Association and the NFL signed a new labor agreement. The college draft was preserved but free agency was modified—the team losing a free agent would be given a specific set of draft choices depending on the player's salary. Progress had been made but this could hardly be called freedom. Things would get more heated and contentious in the years ahead.

The NFL and the National Scene

With the rapid growth of the NFL, the issues surrounding it became more complex and matters started to involve Congress, the courts, and local politicians. Should the NFL be held to the same antitrust regulations as other businesses or was there an exception to be made? Could a team move its franchise at will or did the NFL have a responsibility to the fans of a city with an established team? How was the cost of a new stadium to be funded and how were revenues to be distributed? Was the draft legal and would the courts support the player demands for free agency?

Two major issues dominated American society during much of the period 1964–1978—the Vietnam War and race relations. The NFL was surprisingly untouched by the Vietnam War. One rarely heard of a team suffering the loss of a player to the military draft. When the Giants' field goal kicker, Pete Gogolak, was inducted into the Army in 1967, the Giants were in trouble. They had acquired him just the year before, an acquisition that partly led to the NFL–AFL merger, and now he was to be unavailable. However, a "deal" was worked out whereby Gogolak would receive weekend passes that allowed him to play in Sunday games. How many other such "deals" were worked out, of one kind or another, is unknown.

Although the matter of race relations was far more present as a part of NFL activity, there was nothing comparable to the demonstrations and riots that were occurring in the broader society. Sports, with its emphasis on teamwork and team spirit, tends to bring people of different backgrounds and views together—players and fans alike. This is one of the beautiful aspects of sports. At the same time, the racism that was present in the broader society could still be felt in the NFL. Racial epithets and slurs could still be heard at games and, as at dining halls at public schools and colleges, black and white players often chose to eat at separate tables. In dorm rooms, players were paired by race and if there was an uneven number, a black or white player would be given a single room.[34] Black players often felt that they were supposed to act as if they were part of one happy family but couldn't help but notice that often they were not invited to "family" occasions. Talent was supposed to be the great equalizer but race appeared to play a role in which positions blacks played. Noticeably lacking were black quarterbacks and middle linebackers, positions of leadership where other players were expected to take orders from the leader.[35] Marlin Briscoe played quarterback for Denver in 1968 but then was traded to Buffalo, where he became a wide receiver. It wasn't until 1967 that a black middle linebacker, Willie Lanier of Kansas City, was allowed to star at that position and not until 1978 that a black quarterback, Doug Williams of Tampa Bay, was allowed to start a game.[36] In addition, there was a disparity in black and white salaries and, despite the fact that by 1973 nearly fifty percent of the players were black, there was an absence of black head coaches and black participation in management.[37] There was variation among teams, with the Giants and Kansas City Chiefs considered among the less racist teams, but the problem was there in one form or another among all.

Summing It Up

The fifteen years 1964–1978 were a disaster for the Giants and a success for the NFL. For the Giants it was a tsunami combination of an aging team, bad trades, bad drafts, and poor management due in part to divisions within the Mara family. Whereas other teams, such as the Dallas Cowboys, were developing their scouting operation and making use of more sophisticated schemes for selecting players in the draft, the Giants were comparatively running a "Mom and Pop" or "Uncle and Nephew" operation. At times appointments were based more on familiarity and loyalty than on experience and a proven record of success.

In contrast, this was a period of prosperity and management skill for the NFL. By 1964 almost all of the NFL teams were profitable. Television revenue skyrocketed as Sunday games and then *Monday Night Football* became a part of the new national pastime. Wives were considered to be Sunday afternoon widows until many of them became as enthusiastic fans as their husbands. The league, under the skillful leadership of the commissioner, Pete Rozelle, weaved its way through the labyrinthine halls of Congress. With teams in major cities spread throughout the country, and a solid base of fan support, politicians were only too eager to facilitate the growth of the league. Many politicians were captivated by the glamour and political payoff of being associated with football stars. Presidents now would call to congratulate winners of the Super Bowl.

The league also was skillful in managing the entertainment value of the game. Rules were changed to make the game more exciting. For example, a sudden-death overtime period was added to decrease the likelihood of ties, the field goal posts were moved to the back of the end zone to discourage field goal attempts, the bumps to wide receivers were limited to increase passing. Developments in technology, such as instant replay, were used to make the game more accessible to the viewing fans. Of not the least significance was the early recognition of the value of parity. Thus, television revenue was split evenly among the teams, the draft order gave the losing teams priority, and the game schedule was organized so that weaker teams had a softer schedule than stronger teams. More than was true for any other sport, the owners recognized the entertainment value of competition where fans could always hold out hope that their team would make the playoffs this year—and, if not, then the next year.

The emphasis on parity and competitiveness made the Giants' history of failure all the more pointed. Something needed to be done.

4

George Young, Bill Parcells, and the March to Two Super Bowls (1979–1990)

As the 1979 draft approached, the Giants were left without a director of operations, since Andy Robustelli had resigned, and without a coach, since John McVay had been fired. Wellington Mara and Tim Mara, uncle and nephew, continued to feud. Unable to agree on a general manager, Wellington Mara indicated that, as president, he would go ahead and appoint a new coach. Considering such high-profile coaches as Joe Paterno, John Robinson, and Bill Walsh, he was worried that he would be unable to hire a top-flight coach in time for the draft and the season if he waited for agreement on a general manager. Of course, one possibility would have been to hire Walsh as head coach and general manager, as the 49ers did—Walsh went on to establish an '80s dynasty with them. However, Tim Mara disagreed with the approach of first hiring a coach, and he and Wellington were at loggerheads.

How long could the feud go on and what would be necessary to bring an end to it? Along with the other family members of the Giants, the NFL was concerned that one of its oldest and most established teams was in management disarray. Earlier, Commissioner Pete Rozelle had tried to step in and help solve the problem. Rozelle asked each of the Maras to select a list of acceptable candidates. An executive of the NFL, Jan Van Duser, was a name common to both lists and seemed to be a reasonable choice for general manager. The problem was Van Duser wanted nothing to do with working for a feuding family. Now, with the family feud dragging on and becoming public, Rozelle again stepped in and recommended George Young, at the time director of pro scouting for the Miami Dolphins and someone he had earlier proposed to Wellington Mara. The elder Mara liked the choice of Young but thought this would be enough to make Young unacceptable to his nephew. In any case, whether the uncle had misread his nephew, or Rozelle now was more persuasive, or out of desperation, the two Maras agreed to offer the job of general manager to Young. After two meetings with the Maras, Young called his wife on Valentine's Day to get her permission to accept the job: "This was a flagship franchise, a very special job and a terrific opportunity for me. I was very aware of the Giants, I knew the tradition of the team, and I was excited about working there."[1]

George Young's early career history hardly would have projected a position as general manager of the Giants. Born and raised in Baltimore, Young played defensive tackle at Bucknell, a small college in Pennsylvania, earning honors as a Little All-American. Drafted in 1952 by the Dallas Texans (later Dallas Cowboys), he was a late preseason cut and returned to Baltimore to teach political science and coach football at a local high school. He was a successful coach and in 1968 Don Shula, then with the Baltimore Colts, hired him as a personnel aide and assistant coach. When Shula took the head coaching job with the Dolphins in 1970, he brought Young along with him as director of pro scouting: "If Don Shula didn't come along, I'd still be a teacher and still be with people who discuss books and ideas all the time."[2]

With the '79 draft less than three months away, Young had to move quickly to hire a coach and prepare a list of draft selections. For the head coaching position he interviewed Ray Perkins, then a successful offensive coordinator with the San Diego Chargers, and Dan Reeves, then an offensive assistant with Tom Landry's Dallas Cowboys. He felt that both would be good coaches but selected Perkins because he knew him better, the two having been with the Colts at the same time. Then there was the draft, with the Giants holding the number seven pick. Clearly the Giants needed a quarterback. A few were available in the draft, among them Phil Simms. Simms was big, 6'3" and 215 pounds, with a big arm. However, he came from a school, Morehead State, that was not part of big-time college football and used an offense that did not emphasize passing. But the scouts were aware of Simms's ability, and Perkins worked him out and liked him a lot, so Young selected him as the Giants quarterback of the future. Giants fans were not impressed, fearing another Rocky Thompson selection. An interesting footnote to the '79 draft, one which again brings home the difficulty in selecting quarterbacks, is that in addition to Simms two other quarterbacks were selected in the early rounds. On the one hand, the Cincinnati Bengals, with the number-three pick, selected Jack Thompson, from Washington State, who went on to have a limited and undistinguished NFL career. On the other hand, in the third round, the San Francisco 49ers, with their new general manager and head coach Bill Walsh, selected Joe Montana from Notre Dame. Interestingly enough, Walsh, who did not have a pick in the first round, later said that he would have selected Simms in the first round had he been available to him.

This being before the time of free-agent signings, Young had to build through the draft, which meant slowly. With the exception of the newly drafted players, the team roster would be pretty much as it was the previous season when the team was last in its division, with a record of six wins and ten losses, and the defense gave up more points than the offense gained. Things immediately began on a bad note. In June of '79, Troy Archer, their defensive lineman selected in the first round of the 1976 draft, was killed in an auto accident. Then, although the team won its preseason opener against Cleveland, the victory was followed by three preseason losses, with the offense scoring a total of twelve points. The season began with five straight losses, with the offense, led by Joe (The Fumble) Pisarcik, averaging just ten points a game while the defense gave up an average of more than twenty points a game.

After a brief appearance in the fifth game, Simms was inserted into the starting lineup and led the team to four straight wins. During this period the offense clearly picked up, doubling its earlier average per game, and the defense showed a slight improvement. But optimism proved to be short-lived as the team went on from there to a 2–5 record and a 6–10 record for the season—the same as the previous season. Although once more the team gave up more points than it scored, there was at least some grounds for hope for the future—Simms came in second to Ottis Anderson in voting for the Rookie of the Year, Anderson having been drafted by the Cardinals right after Simms, and another rookie, wide receiver Ernest Gray, drafted in the second round, also was named to the All-NFL rookie team. And, for the second year in a row, linebackers Brad Van Pelt and Harry Carson, as well as punter Dave Jennings, made the Pro Bowl.

But the hopes for the immediate future were not to be realized, with the team losing twice the number of games won over the next three years (1980–1982). The 1981 season suggested things might be turning around with the team having a winning record (9–7) for the first time in nine years, points scored exceeding points allowed for the first time during the same period, and the team making the playoffs. In addition, this was the year that the great linebacker Lawrence Taylor was selected with the second choice in the first round. Taylor, who would go on to revolutionize the outside linebacker position, was voted Rookie of the Year and, by the Associated Press, Defensive Player of the Year. But then, in a strike-shortened 1982 season, the team fell to a 4–5 record. The offense, at times led by Simms and at times by Scott Brunner when Simms was injured, which was frequently, hardly showed much progress. Despite the draft of a promising running back, Butch Woolfolk, in the first round of the 1982 draft, the Giants still were without a thousand-yard gainer. The offensive line just could not compare with that of the conference-winning Redskins, known as The Hogs. Large for the time, The Hogs averaged 6'5" and 274 pounds, two inches and almost twenty pounds more than the line of the Giants.[3] And the defense, despite Pro Bowlers such as Carson, Taylor, and the cornerback Mark Haynes, selected in the first round of the 1980 draft, continued to give up points.

What was the problem? Could it be the coach? Washington, led by Joe Gibbs, by 1982 was coming on strong, and Dallas, still led by Tom Landry, was a continued powerhouse. Perkins's job did not seem to be in jeopardy, the Giants organization liking continuity and having already gone through a series of coaching changes. But then, three games before the end of the 1982 season, Perkins announced his resignation to become head coach at the University of Alabama. Certainly it was unusual for an NFL head coach to leave for a college head coaching position, but this one had some special significance associated with it. Alabama was Perkins's alma mater, his having been an All-American end there in 1966. His coach there was the legendary Paul "Bear" Bryant, the winningest coach in the history of college football. Bryant's announcement that he would retire was immediately followed by the announcement from Perkins that he was returning to his alma mater, something that had been a dream for him.

So now George Young was faced with a second coaching selection. He immediately decided upon the defensive coordinator, Bill Parcells. In 1979, Parcells had been contacted by Perkins and offered the job of linebackers coach. At the time Parcells was head coach at the Air Force Academy but working in a weak program. He was excited about the offer to come to the Giants but his wife was not. She was happy in Colorado and concerned about another move for the children. Choosing family over job, he stayed put. Unhappily working for a while in real estate ("dying inside"), going to Bronco games and missing football coaching, within six months Parcells was back in touch with Perkins. Although no job was available with the Giants, Perkins first helped him get a job as a coach of the defense at Stanford and then as linebackers coach with the Patriots. While there he got the name "Tuna." The Patriot players played a practical joke on him and he quipped: "Who do you think I am, Charlie the Tuna?"[4] The players then established a weekly "Tuna Award" for the player praised most by Parcells. In 1981 Perkins brought him to the Giants as the defensive coordinator and in less than two years he was the new head coach.

Given his defense coaching background, it is not surprising that Parcells emphasized a strong defense as key to a winning program. The nucleus of a strong defense appeared to be in order—it included linebackers Brad Van Pelt (five-time Pro Bowl selection and All-NFC), Harry Carson (four-time Pro Bowl selection and four-time all–NFL), Lawrence Taylor (All-NFL and Defensive Player of the Year in his first two seasons), cornerback Mark Haynes (one-time Pro Bowl selection and two-time All-NFL), and safety Terry Kinard, their first-round selection in the 1983 draft. The punter, Dave Jennings, was a Pro-Bowl selection four times and All-NFL selection five times. In addition, Parcells promoted Bill Belichick to be defensive coordinator and linebackers coach. Belichick, who later went on to be considered a defensive genius and head coach of the Super Bowl champion New England Patriots, had been brought to the Giants by Ray Perkins as a defensive assistant and special teams coach and then promoted to linebackers coach. In sum, one had reason to be optimistic about the defense.

In addition to his emphasis on a strong defense, Parcells emphasized a strong running game, something that appeared to be key for the snow and windy conditions often present late in the season at Giants stadium. Here there were reasons to be concerned, since in the previous season the two main runners, Butch Woolfolk and Rob Carpenter, between them gained less than seven hundred yards and scored but three touchdowns in the strike-shortened nine-game season. Perhaps there was hope that Simms might yet fulfill his promise, but the fact that he had been injured much of the past three seasons gave cause for additional concern. Finally, during the past two seasons, the offensive line had given up an average of between two and three sacks a game. Of particular note was the fact that Simms, when he did play, was sacked an average of about once every ten pass attempts. He was not one of the more mobile quarterbacks. In sum, one had reason to be concerned about the offense.

As it turned out, Parcells's first season as head coach was pretty much a disaster. With a 3–12–1 record, the Giants came in last in their division. The team was beset with injuries both on offense and defense. On average, the defense gave up more points and the offense scored fewer points than the previous season. Of small consolation was the appearance of Ali Haji-Sheikh ("The Sheikh") as an All-NFL place kicker.

What accounted for such a poor performance, in many ways even poorer than that of the previous year? Many factors entered into this. First, once more there was a quarterback problem. Parcells selected Scott Brunner to start over Simms. Brunner had more than twice as many interceptions as touchdowns as the Giants lost three of their first five games. Then Simms replaced Brunner, only to suffer a season-ending injury—the fourth year in a row in which he suffered a serious injury. Their replacement, Jeff Rutledge, completed just fifty percent of his passes and, like Brunner, had more than twice as many interceptions as touchdowns. Once more the offensive line was a problem, giving up an average of three sacks a game. Second, Parcells's backfield coach died of a stroke, his father had open-heart surgery, his mother had cancer and died, and the former running back Doug Kotar died after a long fight with brain cancer. Third, some of the players were aging. Fourth, Parcells had perhaps been too easy with the team, too eager to be well-liked. Fifth, and as significant as anything, there was little team unity and a big problem with drugs. All in all, a tough first year: "What was supposed to be the best year of my life turned out to be the worst."[5] To top it all off, now there was reason to believe that his job might be on the line, with rumors that Young was considering a coaching change.

The next two years, 1984 and 1985, were years of improvement for the Giants. Parcells took hold of the team and began to shape the team to the form he wanted. This included a strong stand on drugs and getting rid of some players he considered not part of the program, whether because of age or because of personality. For 1984, the starting defense had five new starters, including defensive linemen Jim Burt and Leonard Marshall. Special teams continued to be led by the punting of Dave Jennings and the place kicking of "The Sheikh." The new punt and kick returner, Phil McConkey, added excitement to this part of the game. On offense, a revamped offensive line had four new starters. In addition, Simms began to fulfill his promise, throwing for over four thousand yards and twenty-two touchdowns. At the same time, however, he was sacked on average three times a game and once every ten pass attempts. Finally, there was the beginning emergence of Joe Morris as a star running back. Morris, another in a line of great Syracuse running backs, had been selected in the second round of the 1982 draft. A far cry from the earlier Giants emphasis on big running backs ("Baby Bulls"), Morris was a small 5'7" and 195 pounds—small in stature but, as it turned out, big as a runner. He was the first of what turned out to be a number of such running backs for the Giants.

The Giants ended the 1984 season with a 9–7 record, second to the Redskins in their division. They beat the Los Angeles Rams in the wild card playoff game but then lost the conference playoff game to the 49ers, the team that went on to win the Super Bowl.

Aside from signs of progress, the season is noteworthy for what began to be a tradition, the dousing of Parcells with a bucket of Gatorade after a victory. The tradition started when Jim Burt doused Parcells after a big victory against the Redskins. Parcells had been riding Burt all week long, which Parcells was prone to do with him. While tough on Burt, Parcells also had an affection for him, Burt being his type of blue-collar player who through determination would achieve beyond what was expected of him on a pure talent basis. Near the end of the game, with Burt performing well, Parcells commented to him: "I got you ready for the game, didn't I?" So Burt went and got a bucket of Gatorade and dumped it on Parcells. The other players on the team couldn't believe what Burt had done but Parcells accepted it. A week later, Carson called on the players to do it again and it then became a Carson-led tradition.

In 1985, the starting defense remained pretty stable. The starting offense had four new players, led by the tight end Mark Bavaro. Bavaro, out of Notre Dame, was selected in the fourth round of the 1985 draft. Big at 6'4" and 245 pounds, he was a strong blocker, had excellent hands, and was a powerful runner with the ball. To the delight of Giants fans and his fellow teammates, he would often be seen dragging multiple would-be tacklers for yardage after making a catch. Simms continued to shine at quarterback, setting a team record with forty completions and 513 yards gained passing in one game.[6] In addition, he was voted the MVP in the Pro Bowl. And Morris truly came into his own, setting team records with 1,336 rushing yards (average of 4.5 yards a carry) and twenty-one touchdowns. The last Giants runner to gain over a thousand yards in a season was Ron Johnson in 1972! The Giants ended the 1985 season with a slightly improved 10–6 record, again second in their division, this time to the Dallas Cowboys.

1985 NFC Wild Card Playoff Game: Giants 17, 49ers 3

December 29, 1985: The Giants and 49ers entered the wild card playoff game with identical 10–6 records. The Giants were eager to make up for their playoff loss the previous year to the 49ers, 21–10. The 49ers, reigning NFL champs, were eager to show that they still were championship caliber, despite their slippage from the previous year's 15–1 record. The 49ers still had a potent offense, led by the future Hall of Fame quarterback Joe Montana and the future Hall of Fame receiver Jerry Rice. The Giants continued to have a strong defense, leading the league this year in sacks of opposing quarterbacks. The two teams seemed evenly matched, not only in terms of won-loss records but in terms of points gained and points allowed. The game, the first playoff at home since 1962, was being watched by more than seventy-five thousand fans at Giants stadium.

The Giants took the lead in the first half on a field goal and a Simms-to-Bavaro touchdown pass following a Giants interception of a Montana pass. On the play, Bavaro made a sensational one-handed catch. The Giants' defense bent but did not break, holding the 49ers to a first-half field goal.

On the opening series of the second half, Joe Morris led the Giants on a seventy-seven-yard touchdown drive, capped off by a pass from Simms to tight end Don Hasselbeck, making the score 17–3. Hasselbeck had only played in seven games for the Giants that season, his only one with the team, and had only a few catches but made a clutch play in this game.[7] Both defenses were strong during the remainder of the game, each holding the opposition scoreless.

The win against the 49ers suggested that the Giants were beginning to be a power to be reckoned with. The Giants' defense sacked the mobile Montana four times, held him to a net loss of twenty-eight rushing yards, and intercepted him once. It also stopped the 49ers' running game and at one point held them to a field goal from the three-yard line. On offense, Simms passed for two touchdowns and Morris ran for 141 yards on twenty-eight carries—an average of five yards a carry. After being beaten by the 49ers five straight times over the previous five years, including in playoff games in 1981 and 1984, things seemed to be turning around for the Giants. The fans could look for excitement from the offense as well as once more scream "Dee-Fense."

After defeating the reigning Super Bowl champion 49ers in the wild card playoff game, the Giants were soundly beaten by the Chicago Bears, 21–0, in the conference playoff game. Once more the Giants had lost to the impending Super Bowl champs. Disappointed about once more not making it to the Super Bowl, Parcells promised two of his aging players, Harry Carson and George Martin, both now thirty-two, that next year the team would win the Super Bowl for them.

The 1986 Giants starting offensive and defensive teams differed little from those of the previous season. The strong defense now was bolstered by the additions of linebacker Carl Banks, their first-round selection in the 1984 draft, and Mark Collins at cornerback, their second-round selection in the 1986 draft. Collins replaced cornerback Elvis Patterson who often would make excellent plays but also periodically would be burned badly, thus his nickname "Toast." The offense was strengthened by the additions of wide receiver Stacy Robinson, taken in the second round of the 1985 draft; free-agent fullback Maurice Carthon, a devastating blocker for Morris; and the place-kicker Raul Allegre, a newly acquired free agent who previously had played with the Indianapolis Colts.

The Giants entered the 1986 season full of expectation coming on the heels of their success the previous year and three straight pre-season wins. There was some concern about Lawrence Taylor, who had entered drug rehabilitation treatment during the off-season, but there remained optimism that he would be his usual devastating self. The team had a rude awakening the first game of the season, a loss to the Cowboys by a 31–28 score. The Cowboys' winning touchdown with little more than a minute to go was scored by Herschel Walker, obtained from the defunct upstart United States Football League (USFL). The Giants righted themselves and went on to win eight of their next nine games, including wins over all of their division rivals (Redskins, Cowboys, Cardinals, and Eagles). The defense was particularly outstanding against the Cardinals—ten tackles and two sacks for Banks, six tackles and two sacks each for Taylor and Marshall, while holding the opposition offense to six points. The lone defeat during this period (17–12) was to the not-overly-powerful Seattle Seahawks, and was a game in which Simms was sacked seven times and intercepted four times.

The eleventh game of the season was against the Minnesota Vikings, a strong contender from the Central Division that earlier barely lost to the Redskins by a score of 44–38 in overtime. In an exciting game that Parcells and others called the turning point in the season, the Giants prevailed by the close score of 22–20. Although Morris was held in check by the Vikings, Simms passed for over three hundred yards. The star of the game for the Giants, however, was the place-kicker Allegre who made five field goals. Allegre was the hero again the following week in a tense struggle against the Western Division leading Denver Broncos. With the score tied and the Giants deep in their own territory, the offense was able to mount a drive that was capped off by a winning Allegre field goal (19–16) with just six seconds remaining on the clock. It was Allegre's fourth field goal of the day. The lone Giants touchdown was scored by one of the "old men" Parcells promised a Super Bowl victory, defensive end George Martin, who intercepted a John Elway pass and ran seventy-eight yards for the score. The modest Martin, a respected team leader, commented: "When I caught the ball, it was a bright sunny day. By the time I got to the end zone it was partly cloudy."[8]

So at that point the Giants had won their last four games by a total of eleven points—three each against Dallas, Philadelphia, and Denver, and two against Minnesota. The Giants were not dominating but they were winning. The next game against San Francisco not only continued the pattern of winning close games, in this case by the score of 21–17, but provided a game highlight when the tight end Bavaro carried four 49ers for a post-reception extra twenty yards. Bavaro was known as the "bionic man" for all of the repairs to his body, and this feat, characteristic of Bavaro's fight and determination, provided inspiration for the rest of the team.

The Giants went on to win their remaining three games, capped off by a rout of the once-mighty Green Bay Packers by the score of 55–24. The Giants concluded 1986 with a division-winning 14–2 season and all kinds of records: Morris's rushing record of 1,516 yards gained, Simms's four games of over three hundred yards passing, Bavaro's most tight-end receptions in a season (66) and most tight end receiving yards in a season (1001), Taylor's most quarterback sacks in a season (20½), and Martin's most career touchdowns by a defensive lineman (6). In addition, Parcells was named NFL Coach of the Year and Taylor NFL Defensive MVP. In addition to many others, the punter Sean Landeta was named to the Pro Bowl. After nine straight victories it was time for a march to the Super Bowl, beginning with a playoff game against the winners of the Western Division and arch rivals, the San Francisco 49ers.

The Road to Super Bowl XXI

Division Playoff, Giants vs. 49ers, January 4, 1987. Once more the Giants were to face the 49ers in a playoff game, having lost to them in 1984 but beating them in 1985. Although winning the latter game by the score of 17–3, the Giant defense gave up 362 yards to the potent San Francisco offense. In addition, the Giants were fortunate in having a strong running performance by Joe Morris—141 yards. Would the Giants be able to repeat that performance? They were a stronger team this year, had a better won-lost record, had beaten the 49ers earlier in the season at San Francisco by a score of 21–17, and had a home-field advantage. At the same time, there was little difference between the two teams in points scored and points allowed, the 49ers remained one of dominant teams of the NFL, and they continued to be led by a great coach, Bill Walsh, and a strong offense that still included Joe Montana at quarterback, Roger Craig at running back, and Jerry Rice at wide receiver.

Over seventy-six thousand fans cheered as before the game it was announced that Taylor had been selected by the Associated Press as the NFL Player of the Year. The game began on a strange note that could have been an ominous one for the Giants. On the first 49er drive, Montana hit Rice on a short pass and Rice was headed for a fifty-yard touchdown when suddenly he dropped the ball as he approached the goal line. The Giants' defense, badly burned on an early play, was in hot pursuit of Rice and was able to recover the Rice fumble in their own end zone. Blessed by this good fortune, the Giants were able to mount an eighty-yard touchdown drive, capped by a Simms-to-Bavaro pass. Rather than being down by a touchdown, they now were up by one. Holding the 49ers to a field goal, the Giants led at the end of the quarter by a score of 7–3.

The second quarter was a remarkable performance by the Giants. Not only did the defense hold the 49ers scoreless, but the team was able to put twenty-one points on the scoreboard. First, Morris scored on a forty-five-yard run. Then, Simms hit Johnson for a touchdown. And, then, near the end of the first half, Taylor intercepted a Montana pass intended for Rice and ran it back thirty-four yards for a touchdown—a 28–3 Giants lead at the half. On that same play, Montana was knocked unconscious after being knocked to the turf on a hit by Jim Burt. Not only was Montana knocked out of the game, the fourth quarterback to have been knocked out of a game by the Giants defense during the season, but he had double vision and headaches for hours afterwards. The 49er offense was unable to do much with Montana in the lead and even less without him, being held scoreless in the second half. In the meantime, the Giants offense scored three touchdowns, two on passes by Simms and one a run by Morris.

The final score was 49–3, and the game ended with the traditional dousing of Parcells with a bucket of Gatorade. There was joy in New York and New Jersey that night. Walsh said the Giants "played a perfect game. We were shattered by a great team." And Belichick said it was "our best defensive game of the year—the aggressiveness, the intensity, the effectiveness, not letting up even for one play."[9] Parcells was a bit more understated, describing it only as pretty close to a perfect game. Dave Anderson, the *Times* sportswriter, commented: "If it was a fight, the referee would have stopped it."[10] Now on to play the division rival Washington Redskins, who the day before had beaten the Bears by a score of 27–13.

Conference Championship Game, Giants vs. Redskins, January 11, 1987: Fresh from their impressive playoff win, the Giants were ready for the Redskins, who had come in second to them in the division. The Giants had already bested their division rivals twice during the season (27–20 and 24–14) and thus would have appeared to be heavy favorites. But the Redskins were coming off an impressive win over the Bears, a team that far and away had the best league defense record in terms of points allowed. The Redskins still had some "Hogs" on the offensive line (Russ Grimm, Joe Jacoby, and Mark May), a powerful runner in George Adams, and the great Art Monk at wide receiver. Although not as strong as the Giants' defense, the Washington defense was competent and included the sensational defensive back Darrell Green—teams often avoided throwing in his direction altogether. And, the Redskins were led by another great coach, Joe Gibbs, who would go on to win three Super Bowls with three different quarterbacks and be inducted into the Pro Football Hall of Fame. Another tough Giants-Redskins game could be expected.

As was not unusual for that time of year, there was a stiff wind blowing at Giants Stadium. Thus the Giants, winning the coin toss, decided kick off with the wind at their back during the opening quarter. Taking note of the wind, punter Sean Landeta commented before the game, "The wind will be a bigger factor than LT."—a comment about the significance of both the wind and Lawrence Taylor.[11] "The decision to go with the wind was a wise one and Landeta's comment proved to be prophetic. In the first quarter the Redskins had difficulty passing and punting into the wind. In two cases in that quarter, Redskins punts left the Giants in Redskins territory, in one case leading to a Giants field goal and in the other to a Giants touchdown on a Simms pass to Lionel Manuel. In all the Redskins punts went for 23, 27, and 24 yards during the quarter and they were forced to run on two-thirds of their plays. In contrast, the Giants were able to pass on two-thirds of their plays.

But clearly the wind was not the only factor in the game since the Giants were able to hold the Redskins scoreless in every quarter—whether the Redskins had the wind at their back or in their face. Another opposition quarterback was knocked out of the game, in this case Jay Schroeder. In the meantime, with the wind in their face during the second quarter, the Giants were able to score on a Morris run. Both teams were scoreless in the second half—final score 17–0, Giants. Once more there was the ritualistic Gatorade dousing of Parcells by Carson. Parcells was alert to what was about to happen and tried to turn the tables, or in this case the bucket, on Carson. But the stronger Carson prevailed. In the meantime, Burt, ever the prankster, spilled a bucket on both Parcells and Carson. Confetti rained down from the stands as the over seventy-six thousand fans cheered their team that was headed to the Super Bowl against the Denver Broncos—on to Pasadena!

But all was not one hundred percent well. In the third quarter LT suffered a sprain as he collided with Carson. Ironically, it was Carson who had suggested that LT wear an S on his jersey for Superman. Suddenly it appeared that he was not made of steel and was not invincible, although he did return near the end of the third quarter, unable to tolerate watching the game from the bench. Although he was less of a factor than the wind in this game, the Giants were sure to count on LT in the game against the Broncos.

Super Bowl XXI, Giants vs. Broncos, January 25, 1987, Rose Bowl, Pasadena, CA: For the Giants, this was their first Super Bowl appearance. The Broncos had been there once previously, losing to the Cowboys in the 1977 season Super Bowl XII. The Giants and Broncos had played earlier in the season, with the Giants winning at home but only by a field goal with six seconds left to play. The Giants had reason to be optimistic—the offense was holding its own, and the defense, widely considered the best or second-best in the league, was coming off holding the opposition without a touchdown in two playoff games. The Broncos offense could be expected to be a challenge, however, being led by the All-NFL quarterback John Elway. Now in his fourth year, Elway had established himself as among the elite, dangerous with his scrambling ability as well as with his rifle arm. This was a potent offense designed by the head coach, Dan Reeves. The coach and quarterback had interesting relevance to past and future Giants teams. Reeves had been considered by George Young for the head coaching position in 1979 and later would become the head coach of the Giants. Elway had been selected by the then Baltimore Colts in the first round of the 1983 draft but refused to sign with them, threatening to sign a baseball contract instead. He got what he wanted: a trade to the Broncos. This move later was seen as precedent for Eli Manning's force of a trade from the San Diego Chargers to the Giants in the 2004 draft, but more about that later.

The game was to be played before over one hundred thousand fans in sunny Pasadena, a far cry from the wind and cold of Giants Stadium or the rarefied atmosphere of Mile-High Stadium in Denver. The Broncos won the coin toss and chose to receive. Elway immediately led his team to an opening field goal. The Giants immediately pulled ahead with a touchdown pass from Simms to tight end Zeke Mowatt. Elway in turn led the Broncos on a touchdown drive, capped off by his running a quarterback draw—Broncos 10, Giants 7. Elway was on fire, completing thirteen of twenty passes for 187 yards in the first half alone. Before the end of the half, however, Elway was dropped in the end zone by defensive end George Martin, his nemesis from the earlier game, for a safety, leaving the score 10–9 at the half.

Perhaps Parcells had something to say to the team during the halftime break because they came out storming. A key play occurred early in the third quarter. The Giants had a fourth and one at their own forty-six yard line. The Giants lined up to punt, a reasonable decision given the close score and their field position. Suddenly the Giants shifted out of punt position and Jeff Rutledge, the reserve quarterback, set himself under the center. Clearly the Giants would seem to have had in mind an effort to draw the Broncos offsides, leading to a first down and the opportunity to continue the drive. But, surprise of surprises, Parcells was up to his old tricks: "Jeff could take a delay or run. He looked at me, I nodded my head and he went for it."[12] Rutledge ran for two yards and the first down, followed by four completed passes by Simms, the last a touchdown strike to Bavaro. The Giants now had the lead and the faked punt appeared to have turned the tide.

The Giants' defense stiffened in the third quarter, holding the Broncos without a first down. In the meantime, the Giants' offense scored thirty points in the second half, more than enough to offset the Broncos' ten points in the fourth quarter—final score 39–20 Giants!

Although Elway passed for over three hundred yards and led the Broncos in rushing with twenty-seven yards, he could not lead his team to victory. In the meantime, his counterpart Simms, who this year also had gained All-NFL status, set two Super Bowl records—most consecutive completed passes (10), and highest pass completion percentage (22 of 25, 88 percent). For his record-setting performance, Simms was voted MVP of the game. He had come a long way from the 1979 draft, when fans groaned at the selection of the unknown quarterback from Morehead State and the injury-plagued early years. The Giants' defense held strong, most notably in holding the Broncos to a total of fifty-two yards rushing, more than half of them gained by Elway. The Broncos, seeking to stay away from Taylor, had run into the grasp of the other outside linebacker, Carl Banks. Banks, the 1984 first-round draft choice, had ten tackles and frequently could be seen chasing Elway: "It's a game I've dreaming of playing since I was a kid. Five minutes before the game, I must have had a million butterflies."[13]

So Parcells received the traditional Gatorade dousing, happy to have fulfilled his promise to Carson and Martin. Then he was carried off on the shoulders of members of the offensive line. Jim Burt reached up into the stands, grabbed his son and put him on his shoulders as he paraded around the field. Over a hundred million fans worldwide had watched the Giants win their first Super Bowl. Once more there was pride in the team and hopes that the glory years had returned.

Not to be left out of the picture of the Super Bowl victory was the accomplishment of George Young, the general manager who came to the team in 1979 when the team and front office were in disarray. How had George done it? With skill in draft and free agent selection and perhaps no small bit of good fortune in not having replaced his head coach after the dismal first season.

How George Young Did It—The 1986 Giants

Offense

WR	Bobbie Johnson	1984 free agent
LT	Brad Benson*	1977 free agent
LG	Billy Ard	1981 draft (Round 8)
C	Bart Oates	1985 free agent
RG	Chris Godfrey	1984 free agent
RT	Karl Nelson	1983 draft (Round 3)
TE	Mark Bavaro	1985 draft (Round 4)
WR	Stacy Robinson	1985 draft (Round 2)

QB	Phil Simms	1979 draft (Round 1)
RB	Joe Morris	1982 draft (Round 2)
FB	Maurice Carthon	1985 free agent

Defense

LE	George Martin*	1975 draft (Round 11)
NT	Jim Burt	1981 free agent
RE	Leonard Marshall	1983 draft (Round 2)
OLB	Carl Banks	1984 draft (Round 1)
ILB	Gary Reasons	1984 draft (Round 4)
ILB	Harry Carson*	1976 draft (Round 4)
OLB	Lawrence Taylor	1981 draft (Round 1)
CB	Mark Collins	1986 draft (Round 2)
CB	Perry Williams	1983 draft (Round 7)
FS	Kenny Hill	1984 trade
SS	Terry Kinard	1983 draft (Round 1)

Special Teams

K	Raul Allegre	1986 free agent
P	Sean Landeta	1985 free agent

Totals: 15 draft, 9 free agent
*Players not selected by Young

The Giants had reason to be optimistic about the future—they were coming off a fantastic season, there was good spirit on the team, and most of the key players were returning. There was the unfortunate loss of their tackle Karl Nelson to Hodgkin's disease, but their 1984 first-round draft choice, William Roberts, held promise as a replacement. In addition, they had George Adams, their 1985 first-round draft choice available at running back, a promising linebacker in Pepper Johnson from the 1986 draft, and a crew of new wide receivers selected in the 1987 draft.

As it turned out, the 1987 season was a total disappointment, with the team falling to last place in its division with a 6–9 record. The season began with two losses and then there was a league players' strike that lasted over three weeks. One week of play was canceled and then there were three games played by replacement players. By the end of the strike the Giants had a record of no wins and five losses. Although they had a winning record the rest of the way, there were injuries to many key players, including Taylor.

The 1988 season was a mixed bag for the Giants. On the positive side, Simms and Morris again had good seasons. Simms passed for twenty-one touchdowns and over three thousand yards. Morris again ran for over one thousand yards and became the Giants' career rushing leader, surpassing Alex (Red) Webster. The offensive line appeared to be improved for the present and the future by the addition of their first two selections in the draft, Eric Moore and John (Jumbo) Elliot. Moore weighed in at just under, and Elliot at just over, three hundred pounds, putting them in the same category as The Hogs of the previous year's division champion Washington Redskins. Although Taylor missed the first four games because of a drug suspension, with the Giants losing two of those games, he went on to make fifteen sacks in the remaining twelve games. He was voted to his eighth straight Pro Bowl and eighth straight All-NFL team. At the same time, Banks held out at the beginning of the season and Carson missed the last four due to injury. Altogether the defense had slipped some. Entering the last game of the season, the Giants had won three straight and looked like they were headed toward the division championship. However, they lost the last game to the Jets, who barely had a winning record, and were left not only without a division championship but without a playoff berth.

Gradually the Giants were changing since their 1986 Super Bowl victory. For the 1989 season some of the stars remained, for example Simms and Bavaro on offense, and Taylor, Banks, and Marshall on defense. But only Oates remained from the starting line and on defense Carson had retired and Burt had moved on to San Francisco. Carson had been with the team for thirteen seasons and was the leader of the defense. He had been selected to nine Pro Bowls, seven straight between 1981 and 1987, and five times was All-NFL. It was impossible to replace him. Also gone was the exciting punt returner and occasional wide receiver Phil McConkey. Here, however, the Giants found a new star in their fifth round draft choice, Dave Meggett. Meggett, another small back (5'7") who played big, proved to be an exciting punt and kick returner as well as a third-down back who could rush or receive out of the backfield. As a rookie he made the Pro Bowl. Finally, missing from the Giants was Joe Morris, their career rushing leader, who had injured his knee in an exhibition game. He was replaced by Ottis Anderson, who had come to the Giants in 1986 after seven seasons with the Cardinals. Anderson, of course, was the running back picked after Simms in the 1979 draft who then beat out Simms for rookie of the year. Anderson had five seasons with the Cards during which he ran for over one thousand yards but was tailing off when he was traded to the Giants in 1986. Between then and 1988 he saw limited action with the Giants but in 1989, at the age of thirty-two, he was able to again rush for over one thousand yards.

In 1989 the Giants improved to a 12–4 record and won their division championship, but they lost their playoff game to the Rams, 19–13, in overtime. The Rams, wild-card qualifiers, had earlier beaten the Eagles behind the passing of Jim Everett. In this game, in which the Giants were favored, Everett passed for over three hundred yards and completed twenty-five of forty-four attempts, including the winning touchdown pass in overtime. The Rams then lost to the 49ers, who went on to win the Super Bowl for the second year in a row.

Bill Parcells's Favorite Game

September 11, 1989, Giants vs. Redskins: With all of their playoff games and a Super Bowl victory, one might have expected Parcells to pick one of these games as his favorite. Instead, he picked the Giants-Redskins game of September 11, 1989.[14] Why this game? It was against their long-time rivals; it was against Joe Gibbs, a coach greatly admired by Parcells; and, as we shall see, it had a dramatic quality to it.

The Giants entered the 1989 season with much of their team intact and reason to look forward to a good season. The defense, despite the loss of Carson, was largely intact and the offense, despite the loss of Morris, had most of its key players returning. The 1989 draft looked like a good one with strength added to the offensive line and an exciting surprise in the kick returner and running back Dave Meggett. The preseason seemed to confirm that promise with three victories, including one over the Jets, and only one close loss to the Steelers.

The opening game for the Giants was against the Redskins at Washington's RFK Stadium. The Redskins, winners of the 1987 Super Bowl, remained a strong team with much of their Hogs offensive line remaining in front of Doug Williams, the 1987 Super Bowl MVP, and the great receiver Art Monk for him to throw to. The defense too was strong and included the great cornerback Darrell Green as well as the pass-rushing defensive end Dexter Manley. The Giants pulled to a 21–10 lead on the basis of two Simms touchdown passes, one a long one to Meggett, and a touchdown run by Ottis Anderson. But the Redskins, under the leadership of quarterback Mark Rypien, came storming back. First, Rypien passed to Monk for a touchdown. Then, Simms, who generally was having a terrific game, was intercepted. The interception was run back for a touchdown—Redskins 24, Giants 21. With but a little over two minutes left in the game, the Giants' field goal kicker, Raul Allegre, kicked a 32-yard field goal—score tied, 21–21.

With millions watching on *Monday Night Football*, the game was on the line with but two minutes left to play. The Giants kicked off to the Redskins and the game now depended on the ability of the defense to hold. The defense was up to the challenge and the Redskins were forced to punt. The Giants took over on their own twenty-nine yard line with but forty-four seconds left to play. Now it was up to the offense. The offense drove to the Redskins' thirty-five when, with but six seconds left on the game clock, Parcells called on Allegre to attempt a fifty-yard field goal. The snap was good, the placement down was good, and the kick was true, the ball just clearing the crossbar as time expired—Giants 27, Redskins 24! Lawrence Taylor, who was used as a blocker on the field goal, described events as follows: "As soon as he hit the ball I knew it was solid perfect. It was just like a great golf shot off the tee." Bavaro, who unlike Taylor closed his eyes and prayed, said: "I didn't watch it. Raul is a Mexican and I said a Hail Mary to Our Lady of Guadalupe. My eyes were down. Then I could hear our guys scream and I knew it was good."[15]

It was a game that many players called the biggest win since the earlier Super Bowl victory. Parcells, who had run onto the field to embrace his players, had particular praise for the often maligned Simms, now age 33, calling him perhaps the best quarterback in Giants history. Taylor, who at half-time needed two liters of intravenous fluid, had his usual game—two forced fumbles, one sack, and frequent chases of Rypien out of the pocket, along with his blocking on the winning field goal: "I hadn't eaten since Sunday afternoon. I got a little nervous. I had no appetite. It was a big game—well worth the price of admission."[16]

So the Giants had a good 1989 season but could not be satisfied with the overtime loss to the Rams in the conference playoff game. For the 1990 season they were able to retain much of their defense. The '86 draft had been particularly good in this area and four players from that draft now were contributing significantly: Erik Howard and Eric Dorsey on the line, Pepper Johnson at linebacker, and Mark Collins at cornerback. The offense was even more stable and now was strengthened by the addition of their first-round draft choice Rodney Hampton. Hampton, from Georgia, was a bigger back than Morris and Meggett and would turn out to be adept at both running and receiving out of the backfield. Meggett in the meantime continued his all-purpose contributions—punt and kick returns, rushing, and receiving. Allegre was lost early in the season but was replaced by an experienced kicker, Matt Bahr.

Preseason went well for the Giants. They won all four games, including one against the Jets, with the defense giving up an average of eight points a game. The winning streak continued over the next ten regular season games, including wins over all of their division rivals. The team was clicking on all cylinders with the offense averaging almost twenty-five points a game and the defense holding the opposition to an average of eleven points a game. During this period the offense had not scored fewer than twenty points and the defense had held the opposition to seven points or less in five games.

The ten-game winning streak was broken by an away loss to the Eagles and then another away loss to the 49ers in a hard-fought defensive struggle (49ers 7, Giants 3). The Giants were able to win three of the remaining four games, the one loss being to a strong Buffalo Bills team led by their great quarterback, Jim Kelly. But a significant problem had arisen for the Giants as they headed toward the playoffs. Simms, who had been having a magnificent year, with fifteen touchdowns and only four interceptions, was hurt in the Buffalo game and was not available to them for the remainder of the season. Replacing him was Jeff ("Hos") Hostetler, who had been with them since 1984 when he was drafted out of West Virginia in the third round. Despite the years of service with the Giants, Hostetler had attempted but fifty passes before the 1990 season and had led the team to but two victories before he was to lead them into the playoffs. Hostetler was more mobile than Simms, but Simms had for years been the leader of the offense. How far would "Hos" be able to take them?

The Road to Super Bowl XXV

Division playoff, Giants vs. Bears, January 13, 1991: The Giants were coming into their first playoff game of the 1990 season as the Eastern Division champs and a home-field advantage. Their opponents, the Chicago Bears, were coming in after a playoff victory against the Saints in which their defense held the Saints to sixty-five yards rushing and but two field goals. In addition, the Bears' offense gained over three hundred yards, led by running back Neal Anderson's 166 rushing yards. The Monsters of the Midway, led by a strong defensive line (Trace Armstrong, Dan Hampton, Steve McMichael, and William "The Refrigerator" Perry) as well as the stellar linebacker Mike Singletary, could be expected to be formidable opponents.

Talk before the game focused on the tricky wind conditions at Giants Stadium, expected to be between 25 and 30 miles per hour. Although always an unknown factor at the stadium, if anything it could be expected to play as an advantage to the Giants' kickers, who were more familiar with the uncertainties of the wind conditions. Noted Sean Landeta, the Giants' punter: "I know this place. I know the wind. I can just feel it, know what it's doing. All my perceptions, my antenna, are alive."[17] This, despite his whiff on an attempted punt in 1986 at Chicago's windy Soldier Field. Aside from the wind, the big uncertainty for the Giants was the likely play of Hostetler, filling in for the injured Simms. Hostetler, who had been aching for more action, proclaimed confidence. But this was the playoffs, with a notable increase in pressure, and this was his first start in a playoff game.

The Giants started off on the right foot, with a long field goal by Bahr and then a touchdown pass from Hostetler to the speedy Stephen Baker ("Touchdown Maker"). Holding the Bears scoreless in the first quarter, they led by the score of 10–0. A critical point then occurred in the second quarter. The Bears, still trailing 10–0, had a first down at the six yard line of the Giants. Could the defense of the Giants, for the game switched by defensive coordinator Bill Belichick from their usual 3-4 defense to a 4-3, hold? A first-down run by the Bears' Anderson resulted in a two-yard gain—now second down and four to go for a touchdown. An incomplete pass was followed by a Bears draw play to the fullback that resulted in a three-yard gain—fourth down and one yard to go. After a time out, Bears coach Mike Ditka decided to go for it. The Giants sent in their goal-line defense. Giants fans again were shouting the familiar chant of "Dee-Fense." The Bears' fullback Brad Muster was given the ball for a straight-ahead charge behind the all–NFL tackle Jim Covert. But the defense was up to the task and defensive end John Washington stopped him for a one-yard loss. The momentum now clearly was with the Giants, who then scored a touchdown in each of the remaining three quarters. Hostetler accounted for two of them, one on a pass to tight end Howard Cross, better known for his blocking than his pass catching, and one on a short run. Final score: Giants 31, Bears 3.

So Hostetler had held up under pressure, completing 10 of 17 passes for 112 yards and two touchdowns while also gaining 43 yards and a touchdown running. And the defense had once more established itself as a force to be reckoned with, holding Anderson, who the week before had rushed for 166 yards, to but nineteen yards on twelve carries. But the news was not all good. Bahr, the field goal kicker in for Raul Allegre, who was on injured reserve since early in the season, suffered a neck injury while tackling on a kickoff return. And running back Rodney Hampton, their second leading rusher, had broken his leg. These were in addition to the injured Simms, who still had a cast on his sprained right foot. The Giants would not be completely healthy for their upcoming conference championship game against the 49ers, champions of the Western Division.

Conference championship, Giants vs. 49ers, January 20, 1991: As division playoff winners, the Giants now were headed to San Francisco to play the Western division champion 49ers. The 49ers had the best regular season record in the NFL (14–2) and were coming off a decisive 28–10 victory over the Redskins. Led by the combination of quarterback Joe Montana, the

4. Young, Parcells, and the March to Two Super Bowls (1979–1990)

third-round 49er draft choice in the year Simms was picked in the first round by the Giants, and the great receiver Jerry Rice, a 1985 first-round draft selection, the 49ers were coming off two Super Bowl victories—a 20–16 victory over Cincinnati in Super Bowl XXIII and a 55–10 victory over Denver in Super Bowl XXIV. In the latter game Montana was named Super Bowl MVP for the third time, setting a Super Bowl record five touchdowns. Included in those touchdowns were two receptions by Rice. In that game the 49ers not only were strong on offense but, led by defensive back Ronnie Lott and pass-rushing specialist Charles Haley, they were strong on defense, holding the Broncos to under one hundred yards rushing and just over one hundred yards passing. Clearly the Giants had their work cut out for them. San Francisco was favored to win and move on to a third straight Super Bowl victory.

In the first quarter both teams were held to field goals. The same was true for the second quarter, leaving the teams tied 6–6 at the half. Although the score was tied, the Giants were showing a strong running attack as well as a strong pass defense. Giants fans retained reasons to be optimistic. Then, in the third quarter the 49ers pulled ahead on a long touchdown pass by Montana: 49ers 13, Giants 6. Behind the passing of Hostetler and the running of the aging Ottis Anderson, now 34, the Giants offense was able to move on the 49ers. However, they were not able to punch through to the end zone and were forced to settle for a Bahr field goal: 49ers 13, Giants 9. Bahr, playing with a neck injury from the previous game against the Bears, was keeping the Giants close.

The hitting was hard. In the fourth quarter Montana was knocked out of the game altogether and Hostetler briefly. Montana's injury, a broken bone in his right hand and a bruised sternum, occurred during a sack by Leonard Marshall. Hostetler's injury, a hyperextended knee that kept him on the ground for four minutes and out of the game for three plays, was caused by a hit from his former teammate Jim Burt. With under six minutes left to play, the Giants had the ball on their own forty-six with a fourth down and two yards to go. Ordinarily a clear punting situation, Parcells made one of his not-infrequent gambles. With the Giants lined up in punt formation, the ball was snapped to the blocking back Gary Reasons, who ran for thirty yards. Again unable to score a touchdown, the Giants had to settle for another Bahr field goal: 49ers 13, Giants 12.

With the game progressing, the 49ers had the ball with two minutes left to play and a one-point lead. The ball was handed off to the reliable 49er running back Roger Craig, who was hit hard by the Giants' nose tackle Erik Howard. Fumble! Taylor recovered the ball at the Giants' forty-three yard line with just over two minutes left to play. Could the Giants' offense mount one more drive, needing only a field goal to pull ahead, and take enough time off the clock so as to leave the 49ers without an opportunity to mount their own final comeback? As the clock ran down, Hostetler first completed a pass to Bavaro and then, as he was about to be sacked, completed a pass to Baker to the San Francisco twenty-four yard line. With just over a minute left to play, the Giants ran some time off the clock with some safe running plays. With but four seconds left to play, the game now was in the hands, or foot, of Bahr to make a forty-two-yard field goal. The Giants held hands on the sidelines with the season on the line in the final play of the game. Some players prayed, others not, some kept their eyes closed, others their eyes open as the ball was snapped and placed down for the field goal attempt. Bahr was up to the task, making his fifth field goal in six attempts: Giants 15, 49ers 13! For Bahr it seemed like an eternity until the ball sailed through the bars after starting to drift. As Taylor put it: "We've played eighteen weeks. There's been a lot of blood, sweat, and tears. But this is what we came here for."[18] The Giants again were on their way to the Super bowl.

Super Bowl XXV, Giants vs. Bills, January 27, 1991: The Buffalo Bills were coming to the Super Bowl favored to beat the Giants. They were coming off a 44–34 victory over the Miami Dolphins and then a 51–3 rout of the Los Angeles Raiders in the AFC championship game. The scores were indicative of the high-octane Bills offense led by the quarterback-receivers team of Jim Kelly to Andre Reed and James Lofton, as well as the strong running of Thurman Thomas. Featured was the "No-Huddle Offense," which prevented teams from substituting defensive players between downs. Thus, the Bills offense was able to pick the play that best fit the defensive players on the field at the time. Other teams, of course, had used the "Hurry-up" or "Two-Minute Offense," which had the same features. But the Bills were the first to feature this as a standard part of their offense.

As usual, there was excitement in the air as Super Bowl time approached. The tension level was elevated by uncertainty over Parcells's plans for the future—would he continue to coach or retire? Would it depend on whether the Giants won or lost? The years of stress as a head coach were taking their toll on Parcells but, at the same time, he continued to get a charge out of the game: "This is even better than Christmas morning."[19] Part of the handling of the stress was his superstitious behavior, in this case insisting that the same pilot who flew them to victory in Super Bowl XXI fly them to Tampa for Super Bowl XXV. Another part was confidence in his team. Asked if he would concede the Bills twenty-one points—less than their season average and far less than the 44 and 51 points scored in their two postseason games–Parcells responded: "Concede 'em twenty-one points? Doesn't it say 0–0 when we start the game? Or, have they got twenty-one up there? If they do, I'm not going." Asked if he feared Kelly, the Bills' quarterback, he responded: "Let me tell you what I'm scared of: spiders, snakes, and the IRS."[20]

In addition to interest in the battle between a strong offense and a strong defense, and uncertainty over Parcells's future, there were a number of sidelights to the game. Hostetler would continue to be the quarterback for the Giants, Simms's foot having been hurt in the December 17–13 loss to the Bills. In the earlier days of the AFL, the Giants had signed the Bills' kicker Pete Gogolak, setting off the feud that ended eventually in the merger of the two leagues. Now there was rivalry between two great players, Taylor of the Giants and defensive end Bruce Smith of the Bills, as to who was the best defensive player in the league.

Our troops were fighting in the Persian Gulf War, but that did not prevent many of them from watching the game on television in the desert. Asked about whether the game should be canceled, one soldier echoed Parcells: "You wouldn't cancel Christmas, would you? The Super Bowl is a tradition just like Christmas."[21] At the same time, the Giants' center Bart Oates was able to offer another perspective: "This is not the most important thing happening in the world right now. More important things are happening in the Persian Gulf. This is a game, a nice game, but it's still a game."[22]

The game started slowly with each team scoring on a field goal in the first quarter. In the second quarter the Bills pulled ahead by nine points on a touchdown and a safety, the latter on Smith's tackling of Hostetler in the end zone. Before the end of the half the Giants were able to come back with a Hostetler-to-Baker touchdown pass, leaving the score 12–10 in favor of the Bills. Although trailing, the Giants' strategy of using extra backs on defense and using up the clock with a running game on offense appeared to be working.

The third quarter was a gem for the Giants. Continuing with their strategy, the Giants featured the running of the aging Ottis Anderson, now thirty-four. In their first drive of the quarter the Giants held the ball for over nine minutes, a Super Bowl record. The stretch included fourteen plays and a gain of seventy-five yards, barely giving the Bills' offense time to show off its wares. Thus, in the third quarter the Giants were able to hold the Bills scoreless while scoring on a run by Anderson, taking the lead by a score of 17–12. But the Bills were not done yet. In the fourth quarter they came back to take the lead on a long run by Thomas: Bills 19, Giants 17. Then the Giants retook the lead on a field goal by Bahr: Giants 20, Bills 19. With little time remaining, the Bills were able to drive into Giants territory, ending up with a Thomas rush to the Giants' twenty-nine yard line. With but seconds left in the game, Kelly quickly downed the ball. Now, with but four seconds left to play, the Bills called upon their kicker, Scott Norwood, to win the game for them—a forty-seven-yard field goal. Norwood was capable of such a kick, but in this case the ball sailed wide to the right. Final score: Giants 20, Bills 19!

There were many heroes for the Giants. Hostetler completed 20 of 32 passes, one for a touchdown, while often under pressure from Smith. After years of frustration as a back-up to Simms, Hostetler could take joy in his accomplishment and continued self-confidence. The defense, under the direction of coordinator Belichick, held the NFL's highest-scoring team to nineteen points. In the three postseason games the defense had given up a total of thirty-five points. But the MVP of the game was Ottis Anderson, who ran for over one hundred yards and kept the offense on the field at critical moments. In winning, Parcells could retain his title as the great motivator. With grit and determination, he called upon the same from his players and was able to lead them once more to victory.

With the end of the 1990 season the Giants had their second Super Bowl victory in five years. But big changes were in store for them—in players, in coaches, and in ownership. George Young once more had worked his magic to build a team that a great coach could take to victory. Would he be able to continue to do this under the changes that lay ahead?

Heroes of the Period: Taylor, Simms, and Parcells

Given the two Super Bowls during the period, there are many heroes to choose from, individual as well as groups such as offensive and defensive lines. On offense, in addition to Phil Simms, there were Joe Morris at running back, Mark Bavaro at tight end, Dave Meggett at kick returns and receiving, Jeff Hostetler producing leadership at quarterback as a substitute for Simms, Raul Allegre and Matt Bahr producing critical field goals, as well as many others. On defense, in addition to Lawrence Taylor, there were Harry Carson and Carl Banks at linebacker, and Mark Collins at cornerback. And, of course, there was the coaching staff, led by Bill Parcells and including Bill Belichick, who would go on to win Super Bowls as head coach of the New England Patriots. Whatever the contributions of the many players and coaches who were part of the Giants teams during this period, three stand out: Lawrence Taylor on defense, Phil Simms on offense, and Bill Parcells as head coach.

Lawrence Taylor—LT

It is hard to exaggerate the greatness and contributions of Lawrence Taylor, known as LT, during his career as a Giant (1981–1993). People emphasize LT's strength and speed, and these certainly were noteworthy. But there were two additional features that made him stand out—his determination or intensity, and his ability to excel while enduring pain and injury. For him it was not enough to sack the quarterback or tackle the runner, the goal was to cause a fumble while sacking or tackling the opponent: "Stripping the ball. I brought that to the NFL."[23] Virtually all observers would agree that he was one of the great linebackers of all time. Many would argue as well that he was one of the greatest professional football players of all time—perhaps *the* greatest. This may seem like a bit of hype but the fact of the matter is that LT made offenses completely change their designs to account for him and he revolutionized the position of linebacker:

> *Harry Carson:* "LT revolutionized the position of linebacker.... Lawrence is the most gifted linebacker I've ever seen."[24]
>
> *Bill Parcells:* "If you look back, things began to turn around when L.T. showed up.... What he really did was change the way other teams looked at the Giants' defense. He scared them.... By the end of the 1981 season, coaches were drawing up game plans around Lawrence. Their top priority was dealing with this number fifty-six who just seemed to be everywhere."[25] And: "He was the major reason for our winning.... without question he is the best player I ever had the good fortune to coach.... Above all, Lawrence changed the way the game is played."[26]
>
> *John Madden:* "LT was the most dominating defensive player who's ever played."[27]
>
> *Total Football II:* "Lawrence Taylor is the standard by which all future outside linebackers will be judged. In effect, he reinvented the position."[28]

LT has given an account of his life growing up and his time with the Giants in his books *LT: Living on the Edge* and *LT: Over the Edge*.[29] He was born in Williamsburg, Virginia, in 1959. The middle of three boys, as a youngster he was not the gregarious Superman he came to be known as, describing himself then as a runt of a kid and spending a lot of time alone. Although close to his parents who were disciplinarians, as a youth he tested and violated the rules, for example forging a check of his mother's and stealing his father's truck. This pattern, described by him as living on the edge, was to continue in his later years of fame and glory, both on and off the field.

Baseball was LT's first love and he didn't start playing football until his sophomore year in high school. At the time he was not big for his age and was somewhat roly-poly. However, between his junior and senior years in high school he hit a growth spurt, going from 5'8" and 180 pounds to 6'1" and 205 pounds. By this time he was reading books by great linebackers such as Ray Nitschke, Jack Ham, and Sam Huff, and thinking about football the way other kids (i.e., white kids) thought about careers in law or medicine.

Strange as it may seem to those whose image of him is based on his years as a Giant, LT was anxious about playing at the University of North Carolina, feeling intimidated by the size of the players and calling his mother almost every night. Nevertheless he persevered, grew to 6'3" and 230 pounds while also becoming faster, was a consensus All-American, and caught the attention of the pro scouts. Three other aspects of his time at UNC are noteworthy. First, his living on the edge continued there as he went to bars, got into fights, frequently was taken to the police station, almost got kicked out of college, and argued with coaches while doing his own thing. Second, he met his future wife, Linda, waiting for her calls for hours and curtailing his misbehavior for her. Third, he assessed the college football season as follows: "College football is to the pros what minor league baseball is to the majors. The players are there to make the NFL and the colleges want to make money. The NFL gets a free ride. The NCAA and colleges are part of a corrupt system that winks and nods at violations.... The system is a total fraud."[30]

The Giants had the second selection in the 1981 draft, following the New Orleans Saints. The Giants needed a running back and George Rogers might be available unless selected by the Saints. At 6'2" and 228 pounds, he was the kind of big back they often looked for. But the Giants also had their eyes on Taylor, his having been scouted by both Parcells and Belichick. With the first pick the Saints selected Rogers, leaving the Giants with the player they hoped to get, LT. Things did not start off well. First, LT had wanted to be drafted by the Dallas Cowboys. Second, after the draft he was taken around Giants Stadium and was unimpressed. At the time he knew nothing about the history and tradition of the Giants. Third, and most upsetting, he heard rumors that Giants players were resentful that he would be earning more than they did. If this was the case, he didn't want to join the team. Reassured that this was not the case, and befriended by Carson, he joined the team.

As soon as training camp started, a number of things were clear. First, the Giants knew that they had an exceptional player. LT was raw but his strength, speed, aggressiveness, and talent were evident. As described by Wellington Mara:

> When Lawrence Taylor first came to us early in training, I was standing on the sideline watching the workout with Harry Carson and Brian Kelley, our

two best linebackers at the time. Taylor was in the scrimmage. He came flying through on defense, and a big, strong-blocking fullback came at him from the blindside and hit him, just flattened him, upended him. And I remember Kelley and Carson laughing, and Kelley hollered out, "Welcome to the NFL, Lawrence." Something like that had never happened to Taylor before. But he just got up, and on the next play he came in even harder, beat everybody. And the next play was the same. Kelley turned to me and said, "Oh, man, we got something here."[31]

LT hardly needed extra motivation to play the way he did. But, in fact, he had dedicated his rookie season to his friend, Steve Streater, who had broken his neck in an auto accident.

Second, LT early developed a love-hate relationship with Parcells, increasingly over time more love than hate. Parcells, at the time defensive coordinator, as was his wont, would ride LT. But LT would have none of it, telling Parcells: "I've had enough. You either cut me or trade me but you better get the fuck off my back." This hardly was the typical response of a player to Parcells, particularly a rookie, number one pick or otherwise. But Parcells said nothing to LT and instead said to the older players: "I like that LT. That mother-fucker's got a mean streak."[32] LT was arrogant and defiant but was willing to learn, and there was something there that created a bond with Parcells, something beyond the evident talent. During his rookie season, in a game against the Cardinals, Taylor rushed and forced a fumble when he was supposed to drop back in pass coverage. He did this a second time. When Parcells told him that what he did wasn't what he was assigned to do and wasn't in the play book, LT responded: "Well, coach, we better put it in on Monday 'cause it's a dandy."[33] Did LT get special treatment as time went on? According to him: "Yeah, I got special treatment. If I didn't feel like running at the end of practice, I didn't run."[34] Some players resented the special treatment he received, but they and Parcells knew that come game time no one would be more determined or give more than LT.

Third, there were beginning to be signs of LT's enjoyment of living on the edge, not only on the field but off it. At first he was amazed with the New York scene: "Live sex shows. Try that one on if you come from Lightfoot, Virginia."[35] But he quickly was able to adapt to it. Impressed with the speed of the pro game, he also enjoyed the speed of cars. By the end of the season he had almost been killed in an auto crash. George Young told the trainer of the Giants that he didn't expect LT to live past age thirty and took out a two-million-dollar life insurance policy on him. Young already had seen the Giants lose a star player in an auto accident, this having happened in 1979 to Troy Archer, their 1976 first-round draft choice.

There are two intertwined strands to LT's career. The first involves his incredible performance on the field. The second involves his history of drug abuse that continued beyond his career with the Giants and almost wrecked his football career and his life. Although he had not yet fully learned the defensive play book or his position generally, LT already was a force in his rookie year. In a critical game against the Cowboys, with a playoff spot on the line, he again played a crucial role in the Giants' victory. On a cold, windy day at Giants Stadium, the last game of the season, the Giants and Cowboys were locked in a defensive battle. The Giants were dominating but they were unable to score, the kicker Danelo having missed two short field goal attempts under the windy conditions. Late in the game the Giants scored a touchdown and took a 7–0 lead. Then the Cowboys quickly came back with a touchdown to tie the game. After intercepting a pass, the Cowboys made a field goal to take the lead, 10–7. With two minutes left in the game, the Giants recovered a fumble by the Cowboys' running back, Tony Dorsett. With time running out, Danelo kicked a field goal to tie the game, 10–10.

In overtime, Dorsett again fumbled and thought he recovered the ball only to discover that a Giants player had jumped on his back and taken the ball from him: "It was a great play by whoever came down on top of me. I had my hand on the ball and he came down and just took it away."[36] Dorsett should have known who it would be—LT. Later Danelo tried a field goal to win the game for the Giants but at the last minute the ball curved and hit the upright, falling back on the field. The score remained tied at 10–10, Cowboys' ball, with a chance to win the game. A few plays later the Cowboys quarterback, under pressure from LT, was forced to scramble. His pass was intercepted and the Giants were able to move the ball deep into Cowboys territory from where Danelo kicked the winning field goal—13–10 Giants. LT's constant pressure and recovered fumble had been key to the victory and the progress on to the playoffs. This was just one game in a season in which LT was named Rookie of the Year and Defensive Player of the Year. But this also was the year in which LT began to use drugs.[37]

The next season, 1982, the Giants started with two losses, followed by a players' strike that resulted in the cancellation of eight games. This was a difficult time for LT, both financially and emotionally, and he considered returning before the strike was settled. However, he held out and returned with the other players late in November. He was not the LT of his rookie year in the first game back, hampered by a sprained knee that limited his mobility. In the next game, against the Lions, LT did not start because of a sprained foot and knee. Parcells wanted him to sit out the game because of the injuries but, unable to stand not playing, LT grabbed his helmet and ran out onto the field, "like Tom Mix riding to the rescue in a vintage western. The game became increasingly complex with new offensive formations, new defensive schemes, and increased use of substitutions and role players."[38] On one play LT forced the great Lions running back Billy Sims to fumble. On another play, deep in Giants territory, LT intercepted a pass and, despite the sprained foot and knee, returned it ninety-three yards for the winning touchdown. His teammate Brad Benson commented: "There should be a law against linebackers running that fast."[39] LT made the Pro Bowl and again was named Defensive Player of the Year, but the strike-shortened season was a disappointment—the Giants had a losing record and did not make the playoffs. It was also a season of increased use of cocaine by LT and awareness of his use by some of his teammates.

The 1983 season was the first full season with Parcells as head coach, his having taken over late in the 1982 season after Ray Perkins resigned to succeed the legendary Paul Bryant at his alma mater, the University of Alabama. Although LT continued to be a force, being selected to his third straight Pro Bowl, things did not go well for the Giants as they ended the season with a 3–12–1 record. LT hated losing and started to take liberties, coming late for meetings and refusing to do laps in practice. Before the season, LT asked to renegotiate his contract and held out for three weeks. The Giants agreed to revise his contract at the end of the year and, desperately missing football, LT returned. Near the end of the season LT received an incredible offer from Donald Trump of the New Jersey Generals of the fledgling USFL—a million-dollar interest-free loan to be paid back in twenty-five years and a four-year deal starting at six hundred thousand dollars and rising to seven hundred and fifty thousand dollars. He would be the defensive star of a team led on the offense by Heisman Trophy winner Herschel Walker. A million dollars was deposited in LT's bank account and he agreed to play for the Generals starting after the 1984 season. The Giants, threatened with the loss of their superstar, bought out the contract from Trump and gave LT a new six-year contract for more than the Generals had offered. In addition, he was allowed to keep the million dollars as a loan!

After the disappointing 1983 season Parcells cleaned house of players he knew to be using drugs and those who were not prepared to commit in the way he wanted. There is reason to believe that the Giants knew of LT's drug abuse and that they spoke to him about it. But LT felt he was too good to be touched—they wouldn't stop him as long as he continued to perform as a star. And this he did, collecting eleven and a half sacks and another Pro Bowl selection in 1984. But LT also was becoming increasingly addicted to cocaine. Before the 1985 season he had a dirty urine sample and Parcells tried to help him get treatment. LT insisted he didn't have a problem and focused on beating the system by using someone else's urine, an old trick of drug abusers. Despite his continued drug abuse, including moving on to crack cocaine to get an even more intense high, he continued to be a Pro Bowl player and recorded thirteen and a half sacks. LT was everywhere on the field, confusing the offense by lining up at different places and generally wrecking plays despite being double teamed. In his mind he could live on the edge both on the field and off of it: "For me, crazy as it seems, there is a real relationship between being wild, reckless, and abandoned off the field and being that way on the field."[40]

One other noteworthy event of the '85 season occurred in a game against the rival Redskins. The Redskins quarterback at the time was Joe Theisman, later to become a football commentator on ESPN. On one play in the game the Redskins tried a flea-flicker, with Theisman first handing the ball off to the fullback Riggins who in turn pitched it back to Theisman. Unable to find a receiver, Theisman was hit by Taylor. Due to the way they fell, Theisman's leg was broken: "You could hear it.... The pain was unbelievable. It snapped like a breadstick. It sounded like two muzzled gunshots off my left shoulder. Pow, pow!"[41] Taylor's response was shock and then a frantic waving for help for the injured Theisman. He had a clear look of concern as Theisman was administered to. LT was a ferocious hitter but he never was out to injure a player.

After the 1985 season LT finally agreed to go for treatment—his wife had had it with him and his mother was informed of the problem. Despite brief treatment with a fancy room in a non-drug rehab program, LT appeared eager to play drug-free for the 1986 season and he had the best season of his career—twenty and a half sacks, another Pro Bowl, and being named both NFL Player of the Year and Most Valuable Player. But his personal achievements and those of the Super Bowl–winning Giants had a downside to them—there was nothing left to achieve: "I'd won every award—I felt deflated.... The thrill is the chase to get to the top, and when you're finally there and the game is over, then there's nothing."[42]

In 1987 there was a players' strike for six games. LT considered abandoning the strike and showed up at one practice of the replacement players. He was losing over fifty thousand dollars a week and felt that he needed football to maintain his sanity. Finally he did cross the strike line and returned to the team the day before the strike ended. A few weeks later LT played in one of those games that made his toughness legendary. In a November game against the Eagles, LT pulled his hamstring while chasing down the fleet quarterback Randall Cunningham. Unable to walk, he had to be helped to the Giants bench. With an injury that typically takes weeks to heal, and requiring assistance to walk up stairs, LT was an unlikely player the following week. Nevertheless, risking injury, he played some in the following game—his 106th consecutive game. The streak ended the following week when he finally was forced to sit out a game due to the severity of the hamstring injury.

But the Superman of the football field was no match for the draw of drugs. Despite protection and support from the Giants, in particular from Parcells and Wellington Mara, LT flunked a drug test in 1987 and again in 1988. He was suspended for the first four games of the 1988 season. He went home and cried continuously. A third offense and he would be barred from the NFL. The threat of the ban from football led to a change: "Football was more important than any drug that I could take.... I didn't want to lose it all."[43] Sent for treatment to the Giants' psychologist, Joel Goldberg, and then to a drug rehabilitation program, LT committed himself to staying clean, something he was to do for the rest of his career with the Giants.

In the meantime, in a 1988 game against the Saints, he added to his legend of playing with pain and injury. Playing with a torn pectoral muscle, coming out of the game for a play or two to recover if only temporarily from the pain, LT led the Giants to a 13–12 victory with seven tackles and three sacks. Writing in the *Times*, Dave Anderson described the effort as follows: "Seldom does one defensive player ever dominate an NFL game, much less win it. But if a defensive player ever won a game virtually by himself, this twenty-nine year old outside linebacker did Sunday night.... And it was not only a one-man show, it was a one-arm show.... He keeps playing with an injury that would prevent some people from combing their hair." In contrast, asked how the torn muscle affected him, LT replied: "It slows down my golf backswing."[44]

By the time of the 1990 Super Bowl season, LT had been an all–NFL and Pro Bowl selection for nine straight years. Before the season, he held out for over a month until he obtained a three-year contract for over seven million dollars. He again led the team in sacks. He had the high of the NFC championship game against the 49ers and the Super Bowl game against the Bills: "There was no bigger high than running out of that tunnel and onto the field every Sunday at one, with seventy thousand Giants fans screaming LT! LT! LT!... The PA announcer would say my name and I'd go running out there, and the crowd would go crazy."[45]

In mid-season 1992, LT tore his Achilles tendon, and he retired after the 1993 season. He left an incredible record: 184 games over 13 seasons, 142 sacks, 10 Pro Bowl and All-NFL selections, and selection to the NFL's 75th Anniversary All-Time team. In 1994 his number was retired from the Giants. In 1999 he was inducted into the NFL Hall of Fame. Many described him as the best player they had ever seen. Unfortunately, as soon as his football career was over, he started to think about returning to drugs. He accumulated business losses, went into bankruptcy in 1998 and was divorced in 1996. He had gone from living on the edge to living over the edge: "I was young, I was dumb, I was in the biggest candy store in America and I didn't know how to handle it."[46] In 2003 he appeared to be getting his life back on track: "LT died a long time ago, and I don't miss him at all."[47]

Phil Simms

In the first round of the 1979 draft, Commissioner Pete Rozelle announced that with the seventh choice the New York Giants selected quarterback Phil Simms of Morehead State College (Kentucky). The announcement was greeted with a chorus of boos from Giants fans. When Rozelle repeated the announcement it again was greeted with a chorus of boos. Phil who? From where? Is this another Rocky Thompson selection? What about running back Ottis Anderson? Tight end Kellen Winslow? The fans didn't know that the Giants had worked Simms out at length and that Ray Perkins, who knew something about quarterbacks from his time in San Diego, was sold on Simms. They also didn't know that Bill Walsh, coach of the 49ers who selected Joe Montana in the third round, said that he would have selected Simms in the first round. Actually, Simms wasn't too happy about the selection himself: "All I was thinking was which teams I would rather play for—the Green Bay Packers, the Kansas City Chiefs, San Diego, San Francisco.... At the time, I just thought, Oh, I don't want to go to New York."[48] Clearly neither the fans nor Simms had any idea of what lay ahead.

As with many rookies, Simms was in awe of some of the players he would be playing against. Recalling his first preseason game against the Steelers, he said: "I was going to get to play against the guys I had watched on television when I was growing up.... To play on the same field, in the same game, with Terry Bradshaw. I couldn't even comprehend it. To walk up to the line of scrimmage and see staring back at you Mean Joe Greene, Jack Ham, Jack Lambert, Mel Blount. I mean, I was going, 'Hell, I want to get some autographs.'"[49] In need of a quarterback, the Giants rushed Simms into service. He played reasonably well that season, passing for thirteen touchdowns and coming in second to Ottis Anderson for Rookie of the Year honors. The next season was a disappointing one for the Giants, ending with a record of 6–10. Although he passed for over two thousand yards, for the second year in a row Simms threw more interceptions (19) than touchdowns (15) and was sacked over thirty times. In addition, he was out the last three games with a shoulder injury.

The shoulder injury was the first of a number that were to limit his play during the next three seasons and to call his career into question. In the eleventh game of the '81 season, Simms suffered a separated shoulder in a game against the Redskins and was out for the remainder of the season, including two playoff games. In preseason '82, Simms tore ligaments in his knee and was out for the season. Once more he was replaced by Scott Brunner, a 1980 sixth-round choice out of Delaware. Although the Giants had a losing record, Brunner actually played pretty well, completing over fifty percent of his passes and throwing more touchdowns than interceptions.

Enter the 1983 season and a period of stress for Simms and his relationship with the new head coach, Bill Parcells. Simms thought that the starting quarterback job would be his, but Parcells picked Brunner. By the end of the fifth game, Simms was fit to be tied and asked to be traded. In the next game he seemingly had an opportunity to reclaim his job. He came in for Brunner and brought the offense to life, only to suffer a season-ending dislocated right thumb—the fourth year in a row in which he suffered a major injury. This was the disastrous first season as head coach for Parcells and neither Brunner nor Jeff Rutledge, the other quarterback, excelled. The quarterback of the future for the Giants remained uncertain.

The injury during the 1983 season had one positive outcome for Simms. Ron Ehrhardt, the offense coordinator, got him to watch films, something he did little of in college and early in his career. Preparing for the '84 season, Simms began to understand the complexities of the game—the various formations, the use of the shotgun, how to read the defense and call out the offensive line protections or change the play at the line of scrimmage. He came to see that there was a game within the game. Perhaps most important of all, he worked out with the new strength coach, Johnny Parker, and was able to remain healthy for the entire season. He began to fulfill the promise of being a first-round selection, passing for over four thousand yards and for over twenty touchdowns. The one negative remained a sack problem, his being sacked over fifty times. But things were looking up for Simms and for the Giants as they made their way to the second round of the playoffs.

Simms and the Giants showed further progress in the 1985 season. He again remained healthy for the entire season and, although sacks remained a problem, he completed more than twenty touchdowns and threw for almost four thousand yards. A key game this year was the October game against the Bengals. In this game Simms completed forty of sixty-two passes, including twelve to tight end Mark Bavaro, and at one point had thirteen consecutive completions. His passing for 513 yards was the second highest for any quarterback in the history of the NFL, second only to the great Norm Van Brocklin of the Los Angeles Rams, who in a 1951 game passed for 554 yards. To cap off the season, for the first time he was elected to the Pro Bowl. Things were beginning to come together.

Perhaps it is the 1986 season that is most memorable for Simms and Giants fans who have followed his career. This is the year, of course, that he took the Giants to the Super Bowl and the NFL championship. During the regular season Simms led the Giants to a 14–2 record and a division championship. In the divisional playoff game against the 49ers, Simms threw four touchdown passes to four different receivers. In the NFC championship game against the Redskins, Simms completed a touchdown pass as the Giants' defense held the Redskins scoreless. Finally, there was the Super Bowl game against the Broncos in which he was matched against John Elway. Elway did not disappoint Broncos fans, throwing for one touchdown and running for another. But it was Simms who stole the honors, completing twenty-two of twenty-five passes for 268 yards and three touchdowns to three different receivers. His completion percentage was a Super Bowl record and he was voted MVP of the game. In addition, he was voted All-NFL for the season.

Simms performed well during the next two seasons, '87 and '88. Particularly noteworthy was his throwing for almost twice the number of touchdowns as interceptions. Sacks continued to be a problem, reaching fifty-three in 1988. His statistics were down somewhat for the '89 season and although he led the team to the division championship, he did not have a good game in the playoff loss to the Rams. With the end of the '89 season Parcells indicated that Jeff Hostetler, a backup for six years, would challenge Simms for the starting job. Parcells said that he was not unhappy with Simms but that he had to be thinking about the future—Simms now was thirty-four: "Someday, when there's another quarterback here, you'll be saying 'He's pretty good, but he's no Phil Simms.'"[50] Also, Hostetler was much more mobile than Simms, as he demonstrated in a game during the '89 season when he ran for two touchdowns. Eager to start and frustrated with his backup, Hostetler, like Simms earlier, had asked to be traded. Simms won the job for the '90 season and was the top-rated passer in the league, throwing for fifteen touchdowns and but four interceptions and only twenty sacks. Unfortunately for Simms, injury again reared its ugly head and he was unable to play in the playoffs. Hostetler made the most of his opportunity, passing for two touchdowns and running for one in the divisional playoff victory over the Bears. "Hos" then led the Giants to a victory over the 49ers in the conference championship game and then the Super Bowl championship over the Bills. In the latter, he completed twenty of thirty-two attempts and threw for over two hundred yards with no interceptions. Competition for the starting quarterback job was heating up.

4. Young, Parcells, and the March to Two Super Bowls (1979–1990)   107

The following two years were not easy for Simms. In 1991, the first year for the new head coach Ray Handley, Hostetler replaced Simms as the starting quarterback. Simms got into only six games but with eight touchdown passes was able to break Charlie Conerly's career mark. The following year, 1992, Hostetler continued as a starter. In addition, the Giants selected quarterback Dave Brown from Duke in the first round of the supplemental draft as the heir apparent. Simms, now approaching age 37, appeared to be nearing the end of his career. Simms took over when Hostetler was injured. However, the injury bug returned and Simms appeared in only four games. In those four games he was able to pass for almost a thousand yards, bringing him to a career mark of over thirty thousand yards, only the fourteenth quarterback in NFL history to do so.

Things seemed different heading into the 1993 season. Hostetler signed with the Los Angeles Raiders and Simms signed a two-year contract with the Giants. The year was a good one for Simms, playing under the new head coach Dan Reeves. He played in all sixteen games, leading the Giants to an 11–5 record in the regular season and a wild card playoff game victory over the Vikings. Despite a generally poor offensive showing in the conference playoff game against the 49ers, Simms could look back upon a season in which the passed for over three thousand yards and fifteen touchdowns. He also had a career-high completion percentage and threw 173 passes over the last six games without an interception. He could look forward to the second year of the contract.

Or so he thought. With a new salary cap agreement in place, the Giants announced the release of Simms. According to Reeves: "That never would have happened under the old system. We needed some money to sign players and if we didn't have the 2.5 million dollars that was earmarked for Phil, I don't know where we would have come up with it.... We were also looking at Phil's age.... I didn't like having to make the decision, I would have loved it if we could have gone some other way. But that was what we had to do."[51] According to GM George Young: "You cannot divided the football and the financial anymore."[52] After fifteen years as a Giant, including seven playoff years and two Super Bowl championship years, Simms was shocked to find that his career with the team was over. Teary-eyed and disappointed, Simms remained positive about the organization. Wellington Mara called it "a day of overwhelming sadness."

Blond-haired and soft-spoken, Simms had a toughness about him on the football field and a macho view of the game: "It's about your manhood. It's what the game is about. How tough are you? How tough are we?... The harshest, most insulting comment you could have made to me when I was a player was 'Simms, you don't have the courage to stand in the pocket when the rush was getting close.' ... It's like someone spitting on you. It's like being slapped and pushed to the ground. It's degrading.... It's the ultimate macho thing for men. It's testing your manhood, what you're made of."[53] As with all highly competitive athletes, he experienced the highs of winning and the heartache of defeat. He was respected by his teammates for his cockiness, courage, and dedication. He had what Wellington Mara described as a love-hate relationship with Parcells. As was the case with many players, Parcells would needle Simms: "So what do you think, Simms? Are we going to complete a pass today or, hell, am I going to have another sleepless night? I need my rest."[54] But Simms, along with Taylor and perhaps a few other players, was able to come back at Parcells when he felt he was right. And, Parcells respected him for this, as well as for his overall toughness and his ability to take the heat: "Simms is a star quarterback who has the personality of an offensive lineman."[55]

Parcells felt that although often criticized, Simms would be the standard by which future Giants quarterbacks would be measured. And, the record he left would be a difficult one to surpass—the career records for Giants quarterbacks in total completions, completions in a game, most straight completions, most completions without an interception, total passing yards, total touchdowns, and most seasons as an active player. After considering playing for other teams, he decided to retire as a Giant. Today he is a featured analyst on NFL games televised by CBS.

Bill Parcells

Bill Parcells, considered one of the great coaches in NFL history, will long be remembered for the eight years (1983–1990) he was head coach of the Giants, during which time they won two Super Bowl championships. His teams had a regular season record of 77–49–1, including the disastrous '83 first season and '87 strike season. They were 8–3 in the playoffs, including the Super Bowl victories.

Parcells was born in 1941, in New Jersey, and named Duane Charles. His father, a lawyer, had been a track and football star at Georgetown. When he was in school a teacher mistook his name for that of a girl, he decided to change his name. When he later moved and people confused him with a guy named Bill, he adopted that name. He grew up a Giants fan, living five miles from Giants Stadium. He went to Giants games at the Polo Grounds and listened to games on the radio, his emotions rising and falling with the fortunes of the team. Of particular importance was the '58 classic game against the Colts. He went ice skating with some friends but stayed in the car to listen to their heartbreaking defeat while the others were on the ice.

4. Young, Parcells, and the March to Two Super Bowls (1979–1990)   109

After graduating from high school, Parcells went to Colgate. Upset that his fellow football players didn't seem to want to win, he quit and transferred to Wichita State. Upon graduation he was drafted by the Lions but was cut by them before the season began. He did what he could to stay in football, finding a job as defensive line coach and working with linebackers at his alma mater Wichita State. The staff was fired after the '66 season whereupon, at age 25, he landed a coaching position at West Point. During his three seasons there he met Bob Knight, who became a lifelong friend, Jon Mackovic, who later became head coach of the Chiefs, and Al Groh and Ray Handley, who later joined him as coaches.

After positions at Florida State, Vanderbilt, and Texas Tech, he took the position of head coach at the Air Force Academy. He was miserable there, hating the poor program and college recruiting. However, his family was enjoying life in Colorado Springs with hopes of staying put for a while. As already described, in 1979, Ray Perkins, newly hired as the Giants head coach, called Parcells and offered him the job of linebackers coach. He was excited about the job and accepted it, only to find his wife cool to the idea of another move that would be disruptive for the children. He chose family over career, but now was without a coaching job. He got into real estate and was successful in it but was miserable. He would die inside as he watched the Denver Broncos play and realize how much he missed football.

After a period outside of football, Parcells called Ray Perkins who, although he could no longer offer him a job, referred him to Stanford where he got a position as coach of the defense. Then Perkins helped him get a position as linebackers coach with the Patriots, finally bringing him to the Giants in 1981 as defensive coordinator. When Perkins left for Alabama, George Young immediately turned to Parcells: "Picking a coach is like picking a wife, you only get one pick. You can't take two or three, unless you're in Saudi Arabia."[56] But 1983 was a bad year for Parcells and the Giants, one that almost cost him his job. In addition to the deaths of his mother and father, and the deaths of an assistant coach and former running back, the team was decimated by injuries. Although Young denied it, Parcells was convinced that Young tried to get Howard Schnellenberger to be the coach of the Giants.[57] Young knew Schnellenberger from their days with the Colts and now he was a successful coach with the University of Miami, winning the national championship and beating Nebraska in the Orange Bowl. Schnellenberger turned down the job, leaving Parcells with the opportunity to redeem the team and himself. Perhaps another element was the strong backing Parcells received from LT.

After the '83 season Parcells decided to take hold of the team, getting rid of those he felt were not his kind of player. In all, half the '83 team was gone. He brought in Johnny Parker as strength coach and put a greater emphasis on training to reduce injuries. He emphasized what for him has been the key to winning—a sound running game, a strong defense, a desire to win, discipline and consistency. Talent was fine but could not alone produce wins.

So, with the 1984 season, things were looking up with the play of Simms and running back Joe Morris on offense, as well as the outstanding play of Carson and Taylor on defense. In addition, Parcells was gaining confidence as he felt more in charge. While clearly a tough coach and strict disciplinarian, he used events such as the Gatorade shower to demonstrate that he also was one of the guys: "The showers showed I was one of them. They weren't planned, contrived, or staged; mostly they were just fun, and I went along with it because I'm one of them.... You can't ever have enough Gatorade."[58] From there things continued to improve, culminating in the 1986 and 1990 championships.

What was it that made Parcells so successful? In general, this is difficult to figure out, which is why so many errors are made in the selection of head coaches. Clearly there's more than one way to be a successful head coach. As Parcells said, Gatorade wasn't for Papa Bear Halas, Vince Lombardi, or Tom Landry, but it worked for him. All successful head coaches have to know the Xs and Os, have to know how to prepare for games, and have to know how to select players. Parcells, as with all other successful coaches, had a great desire to compete and win. There is joy in victory: "How do you measure the levels of elation exactly? It's never final. Every time you do it. You want to do it again."[59] And: "All of us are competitors, or else we wouldn't be in this business.... There's something about the game that is addictive. It becomes a way of life. It's in your blood.... We come from all kinds of backgrounds and difficulties, but when it comes to competing, there are no differences."[60] But the joy is matched, if not exceeded, by the pain of defeat: "No matter how much you win or what you've won, it's winning now that counts. If you're not winning, you think you suck and that you are a loser as a coach."[61] As wonderful as the feeling of winning was, and for Parcells there was no feeling like it, the feeling of losing was ten times as bad. Yet, with each defeat one had to move on and seek the joy of another victory. The successful coach must not only be competitive but must manage the highs and lows of the game, both for himself and for the players.

Perhaps the key element of being a successful head coach is the ability to motivate the players, to be tough and demand excellence while also communicating care. According to Simms, being called a real player's coach is the worst label you could ever attach to a coach—it means he's soft. Like

Parcells, you have to be able to drive players to places they don't want to go and to do it in a way that may be tailored to the individual. In general, Parcells was a master motivator and used different techniques with different players. Players were not uniformly positive in their response to Parcells, but generally they were strongly bonded to him and prepared to play hard and disciplined for him. Of course, LT was one of his strongest supporters as there was a strong bond between them. Parcells cut him more slack than other players, but he also knew LT always showed up to play. He also protected LT's privacy when it came to the drug problem, telling reporters it was none of their "goddamn business." LT remained grateful to him for this as well as for all his efforts to help him with his drug problem.

Harry Carson describes Parcells as emotional at games but generally even-tempered. According to him Parcells's strength was his ability to be tough, threatening to release players if they did not perform, but also to communicate with the players. For Simms, it was Parcells's ability to pressure the players during the week, including berating and humiliating them, but then encouraging them before the game. According to Simms, Parcells demonstrated that he cared about the players—otherwise his approach would not have worked. He yelled at players but also let them know he had a heart and could be compassionate. Jim Burt's view of Parcells was that "the guy can piss the brass balls off a monkey but he's also a great friend.... When people ask him about me, he begins by explaining that football is not a game for well-adjusted people. He's also fond of saying that I'm a few quarts low. Bill, who is close to empty himself."[62] One of the things Burt may have been referring to was Parcells's superstitions. Among the many were the following: before the coin toss he always had to stand on the fifty yard line with the same person on his left, he would always start practice with the ball on the twenty-eight yard line, he would refuse to call the coin toss before the game, he would never pick up a penny that was tails up, he had a "lucky sweatshirt," and specific players had to be the first and last to attend team meetings.

To round out the players' views of Parcells, there is that of Hostetler and Bob Kratch. Hostetler often felt ignored by Parcells and after a certain point he felt that Parcells had lost him as a player. He felt that Parcells mostly emphasized the negative, was not much of an encourager, and would not let players ride a high for very long.[63] Clearly this is at odds with the more general picture of Parcells, but one can see where his approach would rub some players the wrong way. Parcells could make biting comments to players and this could extend to his coaches as well, including defensive coordinator Bill Belichick. This created an enduring tension with Belichick despite their years of successful collaboration.⁶⁴ Kratch, who played guard for Parcells both with the Giants and Patriots, described the two sides of Parcells: "You win with him but he could be the nastiest person you ever met. He can be loyal, brilliant, passionate, caring, and uncomplicated.... But the same Parcells can be bullying, manipulative, nasty, and humiliating."⁶⁵

The two aspects of Parcells, tough but concerned and caring, came out in his treatment of the issue of drug abuse. When, early on in his career as head coach of the Giants, Parcells recognized that there was a drug problem, he decided he had to take action: "Is substance abuse a problem for me? You bet your ass it is, and it can get me fired if I don't get off my ass and learn something about it and do something about it."⁶⁶ One of the things he did was to become an outpatient at a drug rehabilitation program to learn about the problem and how it might be treated. Parcells cared about players and attempted to get them help but would not tolerate it if it continued to be a problem. In his first three years as head coach he asked between twenty and thirty players to leave because of drugs. This was after, in many cases, calling their mothers: "I swear, sometimes they're more scared about mamma finding out they were sniffing than they were about losing their job."⁶⁷ He could cry with a player who had slipped after efforts to help him but he would not alter his decision.

So why did Parcells resign after the '90 season? At the time Parcells claimed that it was for health reasons, but this was met with skepticism on the part of many. LT claimed that had George Young offered more money Parcells would have stayed. There was much speculation of a rift between Parcells and Young, but Parcells claimed that they were able to work well together despite some disagreements concerning personnel decisions. Ultimately Parcells stood by his claim that he resigned for health reasons, in particular because of concerns about heart trouble.

After leaving the Giants, Parcells tried broadcasting. But it was like being in real estate all over again. He missed football, and a coach was what he felt he was as a person. In 1993 he became head coach of the New England Patriots and in 1996 took them to the Super Bowl, where they lost to the Packers. Within two years he had taken a 2–14 team to the playoffs and within four years to the Super Bowl. After battling with the Patriots' owner, Parcells moved on to the Jets in 1997. The Jets had won but four games in the previous two seasons. Once again he worked his magic, taking them first to a 9–7 record and then to a 12–4 record with a trip to the conference championship game.

After he had again departed football, saying that he would not coach again, the bug returned and the owner of the Dallas Cowboys, Jerry Jones, was able to convince Parcells to become head coach in 2003. In 2004 he took them to the playoffs. He retired from the Cowboys after the 2006 season, in which he was able to take the team to the playoffs but was disappointed that they were not able to progress past the first round. In 2008 he joined the Miami Dolphins as vice-president with responsibility for all aspects of the team. Overall, Parcells has over 180 career victories (ninth most in NFL history), is the only NFL coach to lead four different teams to the playoffs, and is listed in *Total Football* as one of the thirty greatest coaches.[68]

The Family

One of the amazing things about Wellington Mara was his ability to retain the respect and love of the players despite problems that might exist on the field, in the clubhouse, between players and the general manager, or between the players' association and the league. Equally amazing was that these feelings existed without exception. Harry Carson, who often was frustrated with the losing Giants teams in his early years and his low salary relative to others throughout his career, retained a fondness for the organization and Wellington Mara in particular: "The Giants' organization cares about its players more than most teams in the NFL. This stems from the top. The Maras are family men and Wellington, especially, has sought to cultivate a family atmosphere in the team.... If any NFL owner deserves a championship, it is Mara."[69]

Although some believed that Wellington Mara didn't care about winning, Carson said that he and the players knew that Wellington lived and died with each win and loss. Bill Parcells admired Wellington's love for the Giants and his demonstrated interest in the players: "The Giants are Wellington Mara's whole life, they have been his whole life. He's at the office every day, he's at practice very day, he loves hanging around the locker room and getting to know the players."[70] And LT, whose lifestyle of living on the edge was the antithesis of that of Wellington Mara, had this to say: "Nobody did more for me than Wellington Mara. He didn't have to save me, he didn't have to keep helping me to find help.... And he never lectured me. I could tell he disapproved but he never lectured me."[71]

Unfortunately, the bond between players and owners was not there between the owners themselves. Although George Young served as a buffer between them and they were joined in their desire to field a winning team, the tensions remained. Thus, after the '90 season Tim Mara sold his half of the team to Preston Robert Tisch, a successful businessman, for a reported seventy-five million dollars.[72] Tisch had been told of the opportunity to buy half the Giants by Art Modell, owner of the Cleveland Browns. Modell told him that half the Giants was worth more than one hundred percent of any other team. Wellington Mara recalled that when Tisch bought his half of the team he told Wellington that he was looking for ten years of fun. Wellington told his new partner that he'd have to stay in the game for thirty years if he wanted ten years of fun.[73]

The NFL: Prosperity, Strife, and Competition

The decade of the 1980s was one of continued prosperity for the owners of the NFL teams. Teams were being bought for prices far beyond what one ever could have anticipated in the founding years of the NFL—the Chargers for forty million dollars in 1984, the Eagles for sixty-five million dollars in 1985, the Patriots for ninety-five million dollars in 1987, and the Cowboys for one hundred and forty million dollars in 1989, after having been bought for eighty million in 1984. Fans just could not get enough of the NFL. In 1981 a five-year television contract was signed for 420 million dollars a year. In 1987, a new three-year contract was signed for 473 million dollars a year. In 1990, a new four-year contract for 900 million dollars a year! Networks felt that they had to have NFL football to maintain their standing, even if it meant losing money on the contract. And since all teams shared in the revenue, they all prospered. If ever there was a question about whether professional football had become big business, these sales and revenue figures provided an answer.

But along with prosperity came strife. Players were unhappy with the disparity in salaries among them and the disparity between the new wealth of the owners and the relative lack of it on the part of the players. Players wanted free agency and a greater share of the wealth, leading to the eight-game strike in 1982. The owners relented some in terms of more money for the players, but were not prepared to accept radical changes in terms of free agency. With the ending of the 1982 player-owner agreement in 1987, tensions and disagreements were renewed, culminating in the strike by players and the signing of replacement players by the owners. Although the games with replacement players were hardly of NFL caliber, the games did go on and the television revenue continued to come in. The players were in a weak bargaining position. After three weeks the players decided to return to the field, seeking free agency through an antitrust suit against the NFL in the federal courts. In 1989 limited free agency, known as Plan B, was instituted. Under Plan B, teams could protect two-thirds of their roster, leaving the remainder open to free agency. Of course, teams protected their

4. Young, Parcells, and the March to Two Super Bowls (1979–1990)   115

best players and the only ones to benefit were the marginal players. From the standpoint of the players, free agency was a farce. The issue would remain, to be dealt with again in the future.

Not only was there strife between players and management, but there was strife among the owners. In 1978 the Los Angeles Rams moved from the Los Angeles Coliseum to Anaheim. In 1980, Al Davis, seeing future revenues in pay TV and not getting the offer from the city of Oakland that he desired, signed an agreement to move to the now vacant Los Angeles Coliseum. In addition to the larger stadium, Los Angeles would provide a much larger pay-TV market than Oakland. Not only did Davis do this without the approval of the league owners, but he joined with the Coliseum in their charge that the NFL's rules limiting team movements were an illegal restraint of free trade. In 1982 a jury ruled in favor of Davis and the Coliseum, finding the NFL in violation of free trade. The Raiders were free to move to Los Angeles, followed in ensuing years by other teams to other locations.

In addition to strife, there was competition from yet another new league—the USFL (United States Football League). In 1982 the USFL announced that beginning in 1983 it would play during a February–July season, thus adding to, rather than competing with, the NFL. Although not competing in terms of schedule, backed by revenue from television they ultimately decided to compete for some star college players. The offer that gained NFL and national attention was the signing of Heisman Trophy winner Herschel Walker by the New Jersey Generals. Not only was Walker signed for a contract double that of Walter Payton, the star running back of the Bears, but he was only a junior. The USFL began to sign other outstanding rookies, thereby raising the price of rookie contracts. Then it began to sign star NFL players, such as Steve Young, to outsized contracts. Finally, there was the incredible contract with LT that necessitated a huge expenditure on the part of the Giants. Although initially attendance and television ratings were good, these began to decline and most teams ended up losing money in the first season and even more money in the second season (1984).

After the 1984 season the USFL announced that after one more season it would, in 1986, go to a fall schedule and compete against the NFL. The USFL claimed that the change was because of greater fan interest in fall football, but others suspected another motive when the league soon filed a 1.7-billion-dollar antitrust suit against the NFL. With a poor 1985 season, escalating losses, and many of its star players crossing over to the NFL, the USFL found its fortunes depending on the decision of the courts concerning the antitrust case. Prior to the 1986 season the USFL argued in federal court that the NFL was a monopoly and had pressured the major television networks to avoid contracts with the competing league. Some advised the NFL to settle with the USFL, but the owners, led by Wellington Mara among others, decided to fight the case, fearing that they would continuously be held hostage to start-up leagues. The case was not settled until the summer of 1986, when the jury found in favor of the USFL concerning the monopoly power of the NFL but against the USFL in terms of its claim that the NFL had used this power to prevent television networks from signing contracts with the new league. The jury awarded the USFL a dollar in damages, trebled to three dollars. The fate of the rival league was sealed and the power of the NFL over professional football remained.

Returning to the NFL itself, progress occurred on one front but new problems emerged on another. In terms of the former, progress was made in terms of race. By the decade of the '80s more than fifty percent of the players were black. Black players such as Harry Carson were playing middle linebacker and leading their teams on defense. Doug Williams had led his team to the Super Bowl. Art Shell had become head coach of the Raiders, and Dennis Green, Ray Rhodes, and Tony Dungy were gaining attention as respected assistant coaches. Things weren't the way they should be—many owners still seemed reluctant to hire a black head coach and there were no black owners, but more progress was being made than in most other elements of society.

The problem that was emerging was that of drugs. Drug abuse was becoming an increasing problem throughout American society and the NFL was not immune to it. With more money, there was more to be spent on expensive drugs such as cocaine. Some owners and coaches tried to ignore the problem while others tried to deal with it. The careers of players were threatened, as was the image of the NFL. LT's troubles were perhaps more noteworthy for his stardom than for the drug abuse itself. Despite player protest, the league was moving toward a policy of testing for substance abuse and suspensions for repeated offenses. Parcells, whose efforts to come to grips with the problem were noteworthy, was a strong proponent of testing and rejected the claim of some players that it was an invasion of their privacy: "There are no easy answers. Mandatory testing isn't an easy answer, it's just the best one."[74] In his eight years with the Giants he did all he could to help players get treatment, but he also had to get rid of many who either refused treatment or relapsed after treatment. Twenty years later, with the problem of steroid abuse making headlines in other sports, baseball owners were looking to learn from the NFL about the problem of handling player drug abuse.

Conclusion

On the whole, the decade of the '80s was a winning period for the NFL generally and the Giants in particular. There were many components to the winning Giants team—a talented general manager who had the skills and patience to build a team and to work as a buffer between feuding owners, an owner who showed strong allegiance to the players as individuals, a coach who knew how to motivate players and build team chemistry, and a few stars who were able to blend with a greater number of "blue-collar" players to attain what their talents warranted and at times to go beyond that.

5

The Times They Are A-Changin'[1] (1991–2003)

The 1990 season ended on a high note for the Giants—Super Bowl champs in a dramatic final game, a terrific season on the part of Simms and the emergence of Hostetler as a capable quarterback, the promise of the new running back Rodney Hampton, the special teams play of the punter Sean Landeta and punt and kickoff returner Dave Meggett, and a defense that allowed the opposition an average of under fourteen points a game. There seemed to be much to look forward to in 1991. Although questions had been raised about the return of Parcells, such concern seemed unnecessary as he rearranged his coaching staff in plans for the '91 season: Al Groh, the linebackers coach, was moved up to defensive coordinator to replace Bill Belichick, who became head coach of the Cleveland Browns; Ray Handley continued as running backs coach and also became the offensive coordinator; and Jim Fassel was hired as the quarterbacks coach. In addition to Belichick's leaving, the wide receivers coach Tom Coughlin left to become head coach at Boston College.

The Coaches Carousel

Known as an organization that prides itself on stability and loyalty, the Giants in the '90s found themselves dealing with a carousel of coaches.

Ray Handley (1991–1992)

Alas, a repeat of the 1990 season was not to be. As we have seen, in May it was announced that Parcells was resigning for health reasons and that the new head coach would be Ray Handley.[2] Prior to his 1984 appointment as running backs coach with the Giants, he had NFL experience neither as a player nor as a coach. As a college player, he was an All-American running back in 1964, setting an all-time record at Stanford. Although he had no experience as a head coach, Handley had plenty of coaching experience and was thought to be a terrific head coach prospect. He had been an assistant coach at West Point, the Air Force Academy, and Stanford, learning Bill Walsh's west coast offense at the latter. He was considered brilliant—a Stanford graduate, banned from Las Vegas casinos as a card counter, and admitted to law school before Parcells convinced him to stay with the Giants as offensive coordinator. As part of his appointment announcement, Handley indicated that he planned to open up the offense and have open competition for all positions, including that of quarterback between Simms and Hostetler.

Unfortunately for Handley and the Giants, his two-year reign (1991–1992) as head coach turned out to be a mini-disaster. From a 13–3 record in their Super Bowl year, they fell to 8–8 in 1991 and 6–10 in 1992. In both years the offense generated fewer points and the defense gave up more points than in 1990. By the end of the second season the earlier chants of "Allie [Sherman] must go." had been replaced by "Ray must go." Indeed, at some points these chants got so loud that the offense had to ask for quiet so as to hear the signals—at their home playing field!

The reasons for Handley's failure are many and point to the complexity of being a successful coach in the NFL. First, Parcells was a hard act to follow. Handley's style was completely different from that of Parcells. Whereas Parcells was emotional and close to many players, Handley was more cerebral and remote. As the sportswriter Gerald Eskenazi quipped: "Are the Giants going from baloney to quiche?"[3] Partly due to stylistic differences and partly due to differences in personnel decisions, there developed a "Camp Parcells" and a "Camp Handley."

Second, Handley was without the defensive coaching genius of Belichick. Third, Handley took over an aging team, one that also suffered from many injuries during his reign. Fourth, and probably of the greatest significance, Handley just could not gain the trust, respect, and dedication of his players. As soon as he became head coach, he was faced with the controversy concerning starting quarterback—Simms or Hostetler. Often the Giants appeared lethargic and unmotivated. Handley's view that motivation came from players, not coaches, did nothing to help the situation. Inconsistent play became the defining characteristic of the team and, with embarrassing losses becoming more frequent, division between players and coaches became a problem. Shouting matches between coaches and players occurred—a sure sign that leadership and discipline had broken down.

As an organization, the Giants pride themselves on loyalty and continuity. These values, however, were not sufficient to override Handley's problems—business still is business. Thus, as 1992 came to a close, the dismissal of Handley was announced by General Manager George Young.

Who to turn to as the new head coach? Who could be counted on to return the Giants to their days of glory? The name of Dave Wannstedt came up. Wannstedt had been an assistant to Jimmy Johnson, first at the University of Miami and then with the Dallas Cowboys (1989–1992).[4] Another person considered was Tom Coughlin, formerly an assistant under Parcells with the Giants and then head coach at Boston College. As we will see, Coughlin went on to become head coach of the Jacksonville Jaguars and then the Giants. There also was the possibility that Parcells would return. He was the favorite of the fans, as well as of LT, who felt that his old coach could return and bring back a championship to the Giants. For two years Parcells had been a television commentator, a job not all to his liking. In 1992 he had a handshake agreement to become head coach of the Tampa Bay Buccaneers. At the last minute he backed out, leaving the owner of the Bucs feeling like he had been jilted at the altar. Then, in 1993, for reasons not altogether clear, rather than returning to the Giants he became head coach of the New England Patriots. There were rumors that he and George Young did not get along, just as there were at the time of his retirement from the Giants in 1990, but whatever the reason in this case, switching teams became part of a pattern, with his going from the Patriots to the Jets and then, after a few years off, to the Dallas Cowboys.

Dan Reeves (1993–1996)

While George Young was considering possible head coaches, Dan Reeves became available. Reeves had been a successful player with the Cowboys both in terms of rushing and receiving. Following this he became running backs coach and then offensive coordinator under Tom Landry. Then he went on to be a highly successful vice president and head coach with the Denver Broncos (1981–1992), except for two problems—in three appearances he never won the Super Bowl, and he had a stormy relationship with his star quarterback, John Elway. Although there were concerns about whether Reeves would want more control of the team than Young and the Giants might be prepared to give him, Reeves was a known entity as a successful head coach. Young flew out to meet Reeves and signed him to a contract to become head coach of the Giants. Once more things were looking up for the Giants.

Reeves had his work cut out for him—there were players in revolt against Handley, a quarterback controversy between Simms and Hostetler, a declining LT and more generally an aging team. He began with major changes. First, he selected Simms as his quarterback, and Hostetler moved on to a successful career with the Raiders. Second, those players noted for public controversy with Handley either moved on to other teams—Carl Banks to the Redskins, for example—or went to backup positions—such as linebacker Steve Deossie and guard Eric Moore. Third, and of great significance, he brought with him players from the Broncos, most notably the linebacker Michael Brooks. This not only was significant in and of itself but led to disgruntlement on the part of players such as linebacker Pepper Johnson, who referred to the team as the New Jersey Broncos. Johnson was released and joined his old coach Belichick with the Cleveland Browns. In all, the '93 starters represented an almost new team. The offense still had Simms and the talented running back Rodney Hampton, but the receiving corps had all new faces. The changes were even more striking on defense, where, except for LT, the entire front seven was new. Although Dave Meggett remained as punt and kickoff returner, the punter and place kicker were new.

Reeves was able to work some magic in his first year. From a 6–10 record the team went to 11–5. On offense, Simms and Hampton had good years. The defense on average gave up ten fewer points a game. Reeves became the first Giants head coach since 1963 to lead the team to the playoffs in his first year and was named Coach of the Year. George Young was Executive of the Year for the fourth time.

During the '93 season the Giants' offense was led by Rodney Hampton and Dave Meggett—running backs different in size and style of play but both exceptional in talent. Hampton came to the Giants in 1990. The Giants, often playing at home in cold and windy conditions, had always liked the idea of a big, durable running back. For ten years (1955–1964) Alex Webster (6'3", 225 pounds) filled that role. With Webster retiring, in 1964 the Giants used their first-round pick to select Joe Don Looney. Looney was both big (6'1", 230 pounds) and fast. Unfortunately, he also was undisciplined and troubled. The Giants gambled on him and lost—he never played for them. In 1965 the Giants again used their first-round pick to draft a big running back—Tucker Frederickson (6'2", 220 pounds). Frederickson, talented but injury-plagued, was with the Giants for six seasons but never gained over a thousand yards. Hampton, 5'11" and 221 pounds, represented their third effort to use a first-round selection to draft the big running back they wanted. Fortunately this one turned out far better than the earlier two.

Hampton played for eight seasons with the Giants, running for over a thousand yards in five of them. Somehow Hampton was able to gain yardage in situations where other Giants running backs were unable to do so—either the line blocked better for him or he knew how to hit the hole better. In the course of his career with the Giants he gained almost seven thousand yards and scored forty-nine rushing touchdowns, both records for the Giants at the time that he retired.

Dave Meggett, 5'7" and 190 pounds, was one of a line of smallish Giants running backs, going from Joe Morris to Tiki Barber, although he was more of a special situations player than either of the other two. He provided plenty of excitement whether returning punts and kickoffs, or taking handoffs or receiving passes out of the backfield. In the course of his six years with the Giants he averaged over twenty yards on kickoff returns and ten yards on punt returns, scoring seven touchdowns on the latter. He averaged almost forty catches and ten yards per reception during this period. When he left the Giants he held their records for most career punt return yards and most punt return touchdowns. In 1995 he left the Giants to join his old coach, Bill Parcells, with the Patriots.

A highlight of the 1993 season was the playoff game against the Minnesota Vikings at Giants Stadium. The Vikings were a formidable opponent with an offense led by quarterback Jim McMahon and receiver Chris Carter, and a defense ranked at the top of the league. There were freezing temperatures, flurries, and gusting winds that would play havoc with passes and punts or kickoffs. At the end of the half, the Vikings led by a score of 10–3 on a McMahon-to-Carter pass.

Both the defense and the offense of the Giants came alive in the second half. They were led by veterans such as LT, who screamed at the team to get its act together—they were not ready to go home. On the second play of the half, McMahon was knocked hard to the ground, leaving his body numb for what seemed to be minutes, and his teammates worried that he had broken his neck. McMahon was helped off the field only to return on the next Vikings series. Minutes later he again was hit and fell on a shoulder that had been separated earlier in the season. A pinched nerve resulted in a loss of sensation in parts of his body. After again leaving the game, the tough 34-year-old returned and looked forward to the next season, saying that he was having too much fun to get out of the game! In the meantime, the Giants' offense was able to score two touchdowns, led by the running of Hampton (both touchdowns and a total of 161 yards for the game). In a game in which all points were scored with the gusting wind, the Giants prevailed: 17–10!

The win over the Vikings was followed by a bad loss to the San Francisco 49ers, 44–3, in the divisional playoff game. The 49er offense, led by the passing of Steve Young to Jerry Rice and the running of Ricky Watters (NFL postseason record five touchdowns), was too much for the Giants defense and their offense could do no better. According to Reeves, "they all looked like they were on some fast ponies and we were on some slow mules."[5] Unfortunately, this probably was a harbinger of what was yet to come. The new free agency and salary cap presented special problems for the Giants—they had twenty-six restricted or unrestricted free agents and little salary cap room. As noted earlier, the salary cap problem led to the cutting of Phil Simms and the problem of finding a new quarterback. In addition, LT decided to retire. A year after recovering from a torn Achilles tendon and signing a two-year contract, he'd decided that, after thirteen years, it was time for him to go.

Thus, for the 1994 season the Giants were without their leaders on offense and defense. Could individual players or collections of players take their places? At quarterback their hopes rested on the arm of Dave Brown. Brown was selected in the 1992 supplemental draft, the Giants thereby giving up their pick in the 1993 first round. He was out of Duke, not a football powerhouse, but neither was Morehead State where Simms came out of. Brown had limited playing time in his first two years, playing in only three games and attempting only seven passes, none in 1993. Despite his limited NFL experience, he was expected to take over in 1994 and be the Giants' quarterback hopefully for the next decade. He would be playing with a new wide receiver, a new tight end, and two new linemen.

Although things did not look promising during the preseason, the season began well with three victories. However, this was followed by seven straight losses with Brown being benched after the sixth, a 38–10 loss to Dallas. Against the Cowboys the Giants looked overmatched with no one to compete with Troy Aikman, the Cowboys' quarterback. Brown had been replaced by Kent Graham, an eighth-round 1992 selection. Graham's first pass of the game, also his first of the season, was an interception. In the next loss the Giants' offense was without a touchdown.

Heading into the eleventh game of the season, things looked bleak for the Giants. Was the season already over? LT, now retired but still feeling a part of the team, went to Houston to be with the team for the next game and to cheer them on. Perhaps this helped, for the Giants not only beat the Oilers but went on win their next five games, including a close victory over the Eagles and a final-game victory over the Cowboys. The Giants ended up in second place in their division with a 9–7 record but did not make it into the playoffs.

Things went downhill from there for Reeves and the Giants. Neither the offense nor the defense could show improvement and the record over the next two years was a combined 11–21. Dave Brown proved not to be the quarterback they had hoped for, throwing twenty-three touchdowns and thirty interceptions over that course of time. The defense was bolstered by some very promising young players—Michael Strahan at defensive end,

Jessie Armstead at linebacker, and Jason Sehorn at cornerback—but this was not enough to turn the tide. By the end of the '95 season cries of "Dan must go," reminiscent of the cries "Ray must go," were being heard.

Then too, Reeves was having conflicts with the administration. He felt that Young was not getting him the players he needed and there were differences over draft choices. The latter seemed to reach a peak where the Giants, with the seventeenth pick in the draft, selected Tyrone Wheatley out of Michigan. The Giants again were looking for a big back, in this case to replace the aging and periodically injured Hampton, and Wheatley at six feet and 230 pounds seemed to fit the bill. At the time another big back was available, Rashaan Salaam. He was selected four places later by the Bears. There were rumors that Reeves wanted Salaam whereas Young wanted, and selected, Wheatley. Wheatley, though big and fast, never lived up to his promise with the Giants and eventually went to the Raiders. Salaam showed initial promise with the Bears, gaining over a thousand yards in his first season, but lasted only another two years.

With the differences between Reeves and Young becoming problematic and the fans increasingly calling for Reeves to go, it could not be long before he and the Giants parted. In January of 1996 the indoor practice facility of the Giants collapsed due to heavy snow and wind. With the near-collapse of the team during the season, Reeves was gone by the end of the year. He went on to become head coach of the Atlanta Falcons, winning Coach of the Year honors in 1998. That year he took his team to the Super Bowl but once more was not able to taste victory, losing to his old team the Broncos and his old quarterback Elway. Once more early success turned out to be fleeting and he was fired at the end of the 2003 season.

Jim Fassel (1997–2003)

For the third time in six years, the Giants were in search of a head coach. Enter Jim Fassel. To a certain extent Fassel was a known entity to the Giants, having been hired by Parcells in 1991 as quarterbacks coach and then promoted to offensive coordinator by Handley in 1992. Prior to that he had been head coach at Utah State and an assistant at Stanford, where he coached John Elway. After working as an assistant with Handley, whom he knew from his time at Stanford, he worked as quarterbacks coach with the Raiders and offensive coordinator with the Broncos and Cardinals. He had expertise in working with quarterbacks and the hope was that he could develop Dave Brown into the premier quarterback the Giants had in mind when they drafted him. Reflecting on Fassel's earlier work with the Giants as quarterbacks coach, Phil Simms credited him with a lot of his progress, including teaching him the west coast offense, which he loved. He also credited Fassel with teaching him about moving in the pocket and setting his body for a pass after moving.[6]

As it turns out, the selection of Fassel had more than a bit of drama to it. Unbeknownst to others at the time, Parcells was considered for the position of head coach of the Giants. Parcells was about to leave New England and apparently there was the possibility of the Giants signing him. One problem was potential compensation the Giants would have to pay New England but a more important factor was the split within the Giants organization. Young, the general manager, was against hiring Parcells and threatened to quit if the decision was made to hire him. Mara was a strong supporter of Parcells. Tisch, the co-owner, sided with Young, and Mara then agreed to have Young make the offer to Fassel. Just after Young had gone to make the offer to Fassel, Tisch called to say that he had changed his mind and was in favor of the Parcells hiring. Oops! But Young already was off to meet with Fassel at a nearby hotel. By the time they were able to reach Young he already had made the offer to Fassel and the offer had been accepted. Mara and Tisch, being honorable individuals, stood by the offer rather than withdraw it and thereby ended another tenure of Parcells with the Giants before it had even begun.[7]

In many ways Fassel and the Giants might not have had much to look forward to—they were coming off a 6–10 season, coming in last in their division; the offense was last in the NFL, and now would have to do with an unproven quarterback (Brown) and unproven running back (Wheatley). True, the defense had shown some promise in 1996, particularly in the play of some of the younger players, but could they continue to improve under the direction of the new defensive coordinator, John Fox, previously defensive coordinator with the Raiders?

Things did not get off to a promising start in '97. The Giants lost three of their four preseason games and the same in the beginning part of the regular season. Included in those losses were a preseason and regular season loss to the Jacksonville Jaguars, an expansion team led by Tom Coughlin. Neither the offense nor the defense looked particularly impressive. But then things got turned around with the Giants winning nine of their remaining twelve games, with one tie and a loss for a season record of 10–5–1 and first place in their division. During that period Brown was injured and replaced by Danny Kanell, a 1996 fourth-round draft choice with limited prior experience. Also noteworthy was a running game by committee—Charles Way, a 1995 sixth-round draft choice, Wheatley, and Tiki Barber, a rookie second-round draft pick. The defense, under Fox, continued to improve with the play of recent draft choices such as Strahan, Armstead, and Sehorn, and the rookie defensive back Sam Garnes. The defense finished first in the league in takeaways and interceptions, and was third in sacks.

Thus, there was much to cheer about in the '97 season. A strong win against the Redskins in the next-to-last game of the season clinched first place in their division for the Giants. In that game the fans could again roar "Dee-Fense" and cheer for the runs of Rodney Hampton, recovering from arthroscopic knee surgery in what would be his final season with the Giants. And, reminiscent of the Parcells era, the players poured a bucket of Gatorade over Fassel. George Young celebrated Fassel as "The right man at the right time." And Wellington Mara commented, "He knows how to motivate the players."[8] Fassel also was named Coach of the Year—the same honor bestowed upon Reeves after his first year with the team. Young, criticized by Reeves and others for a number of his unsuccessful draft choices, now was praised for using the draft to patiently build the team from within. As a footnote to the regular season, the Giants handily beat the Cowboys, with the players proclaiming that they no longer would be pushed around—they were the new champs in town. In one year the Giants seemingly had gone from rags to riches!

Unfortunately, a post-season loss to the Vikings in the division wild card game ended the year on a more somber note. Although the Giants had a better record, the Vikings were expected to be a strong opponent with a strong running game, terrific receivers, and a rejuvenated quarterback in Randall Cunningham, formerly with the Eagles. Still, the Giants had a strong running game of their own and a strong rushing defense. The thinking was that if the Giants could stop the run, they would win the game.

In the early part of the game the Giants looked as if they would leave with an easy victory, leading by a score of 19–3 at the end of the first half. A second-half Viking score, following a fumble by Barber, brought the Vikings to within six points. However, the Giants followed with a field goal of their own, to again lead by nine: 22–13. With snow again falling in Giants Stadium, and the Giants seeming victors with only a little more than a minute and a half left in the game, the fans were enjoying themselves and yelling derisively at the Vikings players and fans. But the cheers were premature. Cunningham, bearing the brunt of much of the derision from the Giants fans, passed for a touchdown to bring the Vikings to within two points: Giants 22, Vikings 20. Still, with the Giants to receive the ball and limited time left, the Giants appeared to have the game in hand.

As is typical in such situations, the Vikings went for an onside kick. What is not typical in such situations was that they were successful, recovering the ball after it bounced off a Giant receiver playing on the special teams unit: "It came off low, it came to me, I went down, but it took a funny bounce, hit my chest and went away."⁹ Now the Vikings were in position to win the game with a field goal. A successful Cunningham pass, a pass interference call against the Giants, and a Viking run brought the ball to within field goal distance.

As players on both teams knelt in prayer and Giants fans at the stadium and at home crossed their fingers, the Vikings went for the field goal. The ball sailed through the uprights—final score Vikings 23, Giants 22. A nine-point lead had dissolved in the final two minutes of play. It was a late collapse and a crushing loss in a game controlled by the Giants much of the way. Part of the collapse was due to mistakes and part to arguments during the game between Giants players and a resulting loss of focus. The Giants, in many places a young team, were still learning to win. Would the learning process continue and how far would it go? Would Fassel's initial success and selection as Coach of the Year follow Reeves' downward path or were he and the team on a different trajectory?

The following two years, '98 and '99, suggested that Fassel and the Giants might be headed in the direction of Reeves' efforts—downward! In fact, during these years their record was almost identical to that of the Giants during the second and third years of Reeves' tenure: 15–17. Fassel had taken them from last to first in one year. Now they were in the middle of the pack in their division, falling behind the Cowboys, over whom they earlier had proclaimed their superiority. What was the problem? A large part of the problem was the continuing saga of a search for a quarterback to lead the team. By the '98 season Dave Brown had gone to Arizona, playing one game for them that year. He was replaced by Danny Kannell, who had finished out the previous season with a winning record and showed some skill in passing for touchdowns as opposed to interceptions. The Giants lost three of their four preseason games and seven of their first ten regular season games. Kannell was replaced by Kent Graham, who was returning to the Giants after two seasons with the Cardinals, where he had moderate success but also showed a tendency to throw interceptions.

After a mediocre start in '99, where a tendency to throw interceptions was again on display, Graham was replaced by Kerry Collins. This was after the first ten games of the season, the same number of games after which he had replaced Kannell the previous year. Was this to be a game of musical chairs at quarterback for the Giants—Brown, Kannell, Graham, Collins, all in the course of four years?

Kerry Collins was a gamble for the Giants. Coming out of a successful career at Penn State in 1995, he was drafted in the first round (fifth selection) by the expansion team Carolina Panthers. He had much in the way of credentials—big (6'5", 240 pounds), a strong arm, and a successful college career under the legendary Joe Paterno. His college career was capped off with a Nittany Lions victory in the Rose Bowl and All-American honors. He had some success in his early professional years, including leading the Panthers to a berth in the conference championship game in 1996, his second season as a pro. He threw for over two thousand yards in each of his first four years, but also showed a tendency to throw interceptions. The real problems with Collins, however, and what made him a gamble for the Giants, was that he was accused of some racist remarks by teammates and also was reported to have a serious alcohol problem, which perhaps played a role in the reported racist remarks. Could Collins gain the respect of the Giants' players? Could the Giants' brain trust, known for its conservatism and emphasis on personal integrity, take a chance on Collins? Desperate for a front-line quarterback, the Giants decided to take the gamble after consulting with team's psychologist and director of counseling services.

In '99, his first season with the Giants, the gamble did not seem to be paying off. Replacing the injured Graham and starting the last six games, he became the first Giants quarterback since Simms to throw for over three hundred yards in a game and ended up with more than two thousand yards in less than half the season. At the same time, while showing flashes of talent and leadership, Collins could not take the Giants to a winning record in their remaining six games as he threw for more interceptions than touchdowns and also showed a tendency to take sacks. On a more promising note, Collins seemed to click with two young wide receivers, Amani Toomer and Ike Hilliard, as well as with Tiki Barber coming out of the backfield and the tight end Pete Mitchell—each having more than fifty receptions in the course of the '99 season.

On the defensive side of the ball, the Giants certainly would have been expected to build upon their '97 season success. They still had John Fox as their defensive coordinator, and young players such as Michael Strahan and Jesse Armstead were developing into forces on that side of the ball. In fact, both were selected to the Pro Bowl in each of Fox's first three seasons as defensive coordinator. In '97 Armstead set a team record for tackles in a season and Strahan finished the season tied for third in sacks (14) in the NFL. In '98 Armstead again had over one hundred tackles and Strahan had a career-high fifteen sacks. In '99 Armstead again had well over one hundred tackles, including almost one hundred solo tackles, and had nine sacks. Although Strahan's sack total went down, he remained a force on the defensive line. Given the continuing strength of these two players, the decline in defensive performance over these two seasons is hard to understand. Perhaps in '99 it had to do with there being four new additions to the starting defense, including on the line, at linebacker, and at safety.

The 2000 season represented a surprising turnaround, one that hardly could have been anticipated from the four losses in the preseason and eight new starters in the lineup, five on offense and three on defense. Eleven games into the season the Giants had a 7–4 record. They looked improved but at times showed weaknesses, particularly on defense: they gave up a total of sixty-nine points in the tenth and eleventh games, losing both. With many doubting where the Giants were headed, Fasell made a guarantee that the team would make the playoffs. In addition, he told the players and assistants to shut up and follow him or resign. Follow him they did, with five straight wins and the division championship. During that final stretch the offense averaged over twenty points a game and the defense gave up an average of twelve points a game.

For the season, both the offense and the defense showed significant improvement. On offense, Collins enjoyed a terrific season, establishing career highs in passes, completions, passing yards, and touchdown passes. In three games he passed for over three hundred yards. Perhaps he was helped by Sean Payton, who had joined the Giants as quarterbacks coach in 1999 and now was offensive coordinator. The running game also showed improvement, averaging over 125 yards a game, led by the combination of thunder (rookie Ron Dayne, 5'11", 225 pounds, their first-round draft choice, 770 yards) and lightening (Tiki Barber, 5'10", 205 pound, 1006 yards). Toomer and Hilliard again had terrific seasons as receivers, as did Barber as a receiver coming out of the backfield. On defense, the team was second in the NFL against the run and once more was led by Armstead (fifth consecutive season with over 100 tackles), Strahan (9.5 sacks), the veteran Keith Hamilton (strong against the run and team-leading ten sacks), and the newly acquired free agent Michael Barrow. Barrow had been a second-round draft choice by Houston in 1993, picked up by Carolina as a free agent in 1997 and then waived by them after three seasons, and signed by the Giants as a free agent in 2000. Playing middle linebacker he provided tough, smart leadership to the defense.

The Road to Super Bowl XXXV

The Giants again were in the playoffs. They were a considerably different team from the one that lost in the first round of the 1997 playoffs—a new general manager, new uniforms, new offensive coordinator, and only ten remainders from that team. Having won the division championship, the Giants had to play their division opponents, the Philadelphia Eagles, in the conference playoff game. Neither team had great respect at the time and the game was referred to by some as "The Toilet Bowl." The Giants had beaten the Eagles, led by the exciting quarterback Donovan McNabb, twice during the season. However, there was concern about the Giants rushing game since Dayne had been slumping toward the end of the season and Barber was playing with a broken bone in his left arm.

The Giants won the game by a score of 20–10, led at the beginning by a ninety-seven-yard touchdown return of the opening kickoff by Ron Dixon. Dixon was new to the team, a third-round draft choice from a small college, Lambeth University, in Jackson, Tennessee. Dixon had great speed, as shown in the touchdown run. He also had been suspended by Fassel earlier in the season for oversleeping and missing practice. The offense did not put up outstanding numbers and did not score a touchdown but played a controlled game, leaving things up to the defense. The defense was up to the task, sacking the elusive McNabb ("They hit me a lot.") six times, two by Strahan. In addition, cornerback Jason Sehorn intercepted a pass and returned it for a touchdown. Although victorious, the Giants had to be concerned about some aspects of their play—missed scoring opportunities, two fumbles in the first half, one on a botched reverse, and a blocked punt in the final minutes of the game that led to an Eagles touchdown.

On to the conference championship game against the Vikings, victors over the Giants in the 1997 playoff game. This would be a game of strength against strength, the Vikings having a powerful offense and the Giants a strong defense. The Vikings offense was led by another strong, elusive quarterback, Dante Culpepper, two outstanding receivers in Cris Carter and Randy Moss, a strong running back in Robert Smith, and an All-Pro tackle in Korey Stringer. The Strahan-Stringer matchup was described as "614 pounds of fury."[10] The Giants' offense, at times methodical and at other times sloppy, would be playing against a team that had given up an average of over twenty-three points a game.

Atoning for their earlier embarrassing playoff defeat by the Vikings, the Giants demolished their opponents with a 41–0 victory. On offense, Kerry Collins passed for almost 400 yards and threw five touchdown passes. In the biggest rout in NFL championship history, the Giants already led by a score of 34–0 by the end of the half. Not to be outdone, and cheered on by the retired LT and Harry Carson, the defense put on its own remarkable show. The defense more than halved what the Vikings offense averaged in passing yards and receptions, holding the dangerous tandem of Carter and Moss to a combined five receptions for forty-two yards. The defensive coordinator, John Fox, was viewed as a magician with his confusing schemes that made the Vikings offense seemingly disappear. Fassel, whose job at one point seemed to be in question, now was seen as a talented head coach.

5. *The Times They Are A-Changin'* (1991–2003)   131

Turning over his offensive coordinator responsibilities to Payton seemed to enable him to focus on more general aspects of the team. Now he was seen by observers as one of the league's smartest coaches and by his players as a coach who "knows when to push and when to pull" and "a player's coach. He gets behind us and believes in us."[11]

Now the Giants were on to Super Bowl XXXV against the Baltimore Ravens. Whereas the Vikings had presented a challenge in terms of their dangerous offense, the Ravens presented a challenge in terms of their powerful defense. That defense, led by middle linebacker Ray Lewis, was tops in the NFL, allowing an average of ten points a game. In addition, the Ravens, as well as others, viewed Collins as great when he had time to throw but otherwise "skittish" or "fragile." In the words of their defensive tackle, Tony Siragusa, after observing Collins at the line in the opening series: "He was looking at us, the guys who were coming to get him. I thought 'Man, this game is over.'"[12] At the same time, the Ravens' offense seemed at least on a par with that of the Giants. So the question was whether the defense could duplicate its effort against the Vikings offense while the offense hopefully scored some points against the Ravens' vaunted defense.

Unfortunately, neither proved to be the case as the Ravens won by a score of 34–7. The Ravens' defense proved to as dominant as promised, intercepting Collins four times, a Super Bowl record, and holding Tiki Barber to a total of forty-nine yards, only three in the second half. In all the Giants' offense was held to a total of 149 yards. The powerful and fast Lewis not only helped to stop the run but deflected four passes, one of which led to one of the four interceptions. The only points scored by the Giants were on a kickoff return for a touchdown. The Ravens returned a kickoff of their own for a touchdown, matching the Giants' effort, in addition to their being able to score far more than the necessary points to win the game.

The loss, in and of itself as well as in its magnitude, was a disappointing ending for the team, as it is for any team that reaches the Super Bowl and comes up empty-handed. On the other hand, the team and its fans had much to look forward to—an intact coaching staff, an offense with an established quarterback (Collins) and all-purpose running back (Barber), a defense again led by linebacker Armstead and end Strahan, promising rookies from the 2000 draft (Dayne, defensive tackle Cornelius Griffin, wide receiver Ron Dixon), and hopefully some new players from the upcoming draft.

At least initially, the Giants under Fassel did not repeat their record under Reeves—initial success with the head coach acclaimed only to be followed by a downward spiral. Indeed, at the end of the 2000 season the Giants appeared to be on the upswing. However, the promise was not to be fulfilled. Instead, in the words of Yogi Berra, it was déjà vu all over again—success and promise followed by three years of disappointment. The 2001 team was completely intact on offense, yet Collins's rating went down (fewer touchdowns, more interceptions, more sacks), and Dayne and Barber, thunder and lightning, each gained fewer yards than the previous season.[13] The defense had five new starters which, given their quality, should have been an improvement. Kenny Holmes was signed as a defensive end, Cornelius Griffin at defensive tackle and Brandon Short at linebacker were from the 2000 draft, and Will Allen and Will Peterson, cornerbacks, were first- and second-round additions from the most recent draft.

Yet, as the offense scored fewer points, the defense gave up more points, resulting in a 7–9 record and no playoff appearance. Both the offense and defense showed signs of strength at times but at other times were sloppy and made mistakes that resulted in losses. The offense would have an interception or fumble that would stall a drive, and the defense would play well but then give up a long gain. On defense, Armstead and Strahan had Pro Bowl seasons, with Strahan setting an NFL season sack record, but too often the backfield gave up a long gain.[14] And special teams? In one case a fumbled snap on a punt resulted in a winning touchdown for the opposition. A frustrated Fassel commented: "Whatever I focus on, those are the things that blow up on us in the game."[15] In a rare speech to the team, the owner Wellington Mara, in a "fatherly talk," asked the players to examine their commitment and rededicate themselves. Two wins followed, but then two losses in the final games of the season did as well.

Whatever the distress of Giants fans, of course it paled in comparison to that of New Yorkers and Americans generally over the terrorist attacks on the Twin Towers and Pentagon—9/11/2001! And, near the end of the season, after a disappointing loss to Dallas, there was the death of their previous general manager, George Young.

Jesse Armstead

Jesse Armstead grew up in a tough section of Dallas, fighting others to protect his image and playing full-contact football on a field with rocks. In high school as a sophomore he was named by a national recruiting magazine as the best high school player in America. This was repeated the next two years, leading to his recruitment by the University of Miami Hurricanes. He played as a freshman, injured his knee as a sophomore, played well in the following two seasons, but at 6'1" and 225 pounds was thought by pro scouts to be too small to play linebacker in the NFL. In the eighth and last round of the 1993 draft, with the 207th pick, the Giants selected

Armstead. He immediately started to play in all games but, with the arrival of John Fox as defensive coordinator, really came on as an outside linebacker during the 1997 season, when he had a team record tackles, was an All-NFL selection, and was named a starter in the Pro Bowl. Following that, for four straight seasons he was named to the Pro Bowl (1998–2001). A model citizen and gentle, kind family man, Armstead was able to turn the aggression on when it was needed on the football field, breaking the 100-tackle mark in five straight seasons (1996–2000). Strong and fast, he seemed to always be around the ball, whether it was in a sack, stopping the run, or making an interception.

As with virtually all NFL players, age and injury started to take a toll on Armstead, and between 1999 and 2001 his tackle and sack totals started to decline. This, and salary cap problems that forced the Giants to make many cuts, led to his signing a three-year contract with the Washington Redskins. Although he was able to play well for the Redskins, he was released by them after two years. Signed by the Carolina Panthers for the 2004 season, to rejoin John Fox, he did not play for them that season and ended his NFL career there—another Giants star who was a casualty of the salary cap regulation.

Which team would show up for the 2002 season—the thrilling team of 2000 that won its last five regular season games and two playoffs, or the 2001 team that was noted for its inconsistency, mistakes, blunders (a botched reverse here and a collision between backfield defenders there), and lost opportunities? Would the smart head coach of 2000 be on display or the 2001 coach of a team that didn't do much right and did much wrong? How serious would be the loss of their defensive coordinator, John Fox, who had moved on to become head coach of the Carolina Panthers?

The 2002 team had new starters on defense and offense, particularly on the offensive line, which had four new starters and a shift of the right tackle, Luke Petigout, to left tackle. Particularly noteworthy, however, was the addition of their heralded first-round draft choice, tight end Jeremy Shockey. For a decade the Giants had relied on the blocking ability of Howard Cross to fortify that position. Not since the last year of Mark Bavaro's career with the Giants, 1990, had the Giants had a tight end who could enhance the passing game as well as the running game. Shockey already had established himself as a fighter in training camp. When told to sing a song by linebacker Brandon Short, as rookies were required to do, he said he would do it when he was done eating. Short insisted it be done then, leading to a fight between them. Fassel's reaction was: "Wow. I got my guy. This is a real player."[16] Thus, Shockey was to be the new tight end to return that position to its earlier days of glory for the Giants. Along with established wide receivers Amani Toomer and Ike Hilliard, and running back Tiki Barber, Shockey was to be part of a wealth of receivers for Collins to choose among. With Barber and Dayne available to do the running, if the revamped offensive line could hold up the Giants would have a powerful, dynamic offense.

The preseason as well as the first half of the season proved inconclusive as to what kind of team the Giants were to be this year. The promise of a high-powered offense seemed at times to be on hand but at other times proved to be otherwise, as the offense scored a high of twenty-six points and a low of three points in the first eight games. Between them, the offense and defense were averaging about the same number of points obtained and given up, as perhaps befit a 4–4 record. Then, in the second half of the season, the offense, with Fassel taking over play-calling from offensive coordinator Sean Payton, really picked up, increasing its average by almost ten points per game while the defense remained steady, resulting in a 6–2 record and a playoff berth. The offense indeed proved to have great firepower as Collins had a career-high pass completion percentage and threw for over four thousand yards, Toomer set team records for receptions and yards gained, Barber rushed for over a thousand yards and gained almost six hundred more on receptions (fourth in the NFL), and the Pro Bowl–bound rookie tight end Shockey had more than seventy receptions, good for almost nine hundred yards. At the same time, there were sources of concern, particularly in terms of giving up points late in the game and special teams play. Special teams play had been an ongoing problem for Fassel's teams—a botched snap here, a missed field goal there, perhaps due to the limited experience of the coach responsible for them.

The Debacle of the 2002 Season Wild Card Playoff Game

At the beginning of midseason, two wins were followed by two bad losses. The first was a loss to the expansion team Houston Texans, in part due to a bad snap that sailed over the punter's head. Then there was an overtime loss to the Titans. Although the Titans were leaders in their division, the then six-and-six record of the Giants, inconsistent play, and team blunders resulted in Fassel's job being called into question. He received strong support from Collins and Strahan, leaders on offense and defense, both of whom indicated that they wanted him back the next year and that the team would fight for him and give it everything they had in the remaining four games. Nothing was being said by Giants management.

5. The Times They Are A-Changin' (1991–2003)

Victories over the Redskins and Cowboys revived playoff hopes. If they could win the remaining two games, they had a chance. In the next-to-last game they scored a big victory against the Indianapolis Colts, then a team in competition with the Titans for the lead in their division. The offense scored forty-four points, Fassel was credited with a near perfect game plan, and his job seemed to be more secure. The final game of the season was against the division-leading Eagles. A victory did not guarantee a playoff spot but a loss spelled doom in that regard. In an exciting game filled with mishaps, the Giants were able to win in overtime, 10–7, and gain a wild card playoff spot. Of course, the victory and playoff spot were uppermost in the minds of players and fans. On the other hand, the mishaps were cause for concern—four turnovers, two in the red zone, two touchdowns called back because of penalties, seven fumbles, a missed field goal before the winning one in overtime. Inconsistency again was apparent—Collins brilliant at times but fumbling snaps and forcing the ball at other times, Barber running over two hundred yards but also losing three fumbles. Special teams still were an adventure, as when an extra-point kick bounced off the upright but then dropped through. This followed a touchdown play in which Collins was almost intercepted (again) on a pass to Shockey, but Shockey was able to rip the ball from the Eagles' defender. The winning field goal in overtime brought relief to Tiki Barber, who at that point was in tears on the bench, fearing that his fumbles had lost the game and their hopes for the playoffs. In sum, Fassel's team played hard but not necessarily smart. How far could this kind of play take them? How long could it be sufficient for Fassel to keep his job?

Whatever the drama of the misadventures, the Giants were headed into the playoffs with the momentum of four wins, an offense that had come to life, a defense that was strong against the Eagles, and players bonded with one another and their coach through adversity. Their opponent was to be the San Francisco 49ers, leaders in their division, to whom the Giants had lost (16–13) in the season opener. The 49ers were dangerous on offense with the combination of their mobile quarterback, Jeff Garcia, and dangerous wide receiver, Terrell Owens. Owens now was famous, or infamous, for his theatrical stunt earlier in the season—after a touchdown catch he pulled a Sharpie pen out of his sock, autographed the football, and handed it to his financial adviser. The Giants were in decent physical condition although they had to sign a replacement for their long snapper, who tore a ligament in his thumb in the finale against the Eagles.

Well into the third quarter, the Giants appeared to have the game in hand, leading by a score of 38–14 with less than five minutes to go in the quarter. As the score indicates, the Giants were playing both hard and smart. Collins was erasing the memory of his four interceptions in the 2000 Super

Bowl. The defense was holding its own. Then things began to fall apart. The offense stalled, going scoreless over the final nineteen minutes of the game. And the defense collapsed, allowing the 49ers to score twenty-five points in the final seventeen minutes of the game. In this relatively brief period of time, Garcia passed for two touchdowns, ran for one touchdown, completed two two-point conversions, and set up a field goal. The Giants' team seemed to be unraveling, with defensive back Sehorn being beaten by Owens three times in the second half and safety Shaun Williams being ejected with a minute left in the game.

The game was winding down with the Giants behind by a score of 39–38 but with a chance to pull out a victory in the remaining seconds of the game. The field goal kicker, Matt Bryant, was to attempt a field goal from the twenty-three yard line. He had been the hero of the victory over the Eagles in overtime. Could he do it again? A few minutes earlier in the game he had missed a similar field goal attempt due to a low snap that was barely handled by the holder, punter Matt Allen. But the just-hired snapper was a nineteen-year veteran and had practiced well during the week. He was known to Fassel from the coach's days at Arizona and Fassel had faith in him. All that was needed for the Giants to move on, despite their collapse in the second half, was a successful field goal—ball snapped, placed down, kicked, through the uprights, game won.

As typified the Giants' season, it was not to be. Instead, there was what was called "Snapgate." The snap was bad and the placeholder could not set the football for a field goal effort. Instead, he ran toward the sideline, yelled "Fire! Fire!" to signal his teammates that were eligible to go out for an attempted downfield pass. The pass was incomplete but there also was a penalty flag. Perhaps it was against the 49ers—the intended receiver, guard Rich Seubert, had been knocked down while reaching for the ball. But the penalty was called on the Giants for an ineligible receiver, Seubert, whom the referee ruled had not checked in as required as an eligible receiver. The game was over.

As so often during the season, the Giants were undone by a mistake. As it turns out, the Giants were not alone in making a mistake on the last play of the game. The next day the NFL announced that Seubert was eligible and had been interfered with. However, there was another ineligible receiver downfield. The penalties, the interference against the 49ers and the ineligible receiver for the Giants, should have been offsetting and the final down replayed. But it was too late for the mistake to be undone. It was a tough loss, one that Fassel described as hurting as much as any loss he had in his life. As expressed by one of their players, the Giants just weren't good enough.

5. The Times They Are A-Changin' (1991–2003)

Heading into the 2003 season optimists could point to remaining strengths and additions. The key components of the dynamic offense remained—Barber, Shockey, Toomer, and Hilliard. The defense remained completely intact with the young cornerbacks, Allen and Peterson, expected to come up big in their third season with the team. And the Giants had taken steps to improve their special teams, adding a new punter and field goal holder, Jeff Feagles; a new long snapper, Ryan Kuehl; a field goal kicker, Mike Hollis, to compete with the by-now infamous Matt Bryant; and a punt and kick returner with established credentials, Brian Mitchell. Hopes were high among the optimists. Could this be a Super Bowl team? At the same time, pessimists pointed to the record of inconsistency and the need to replace the right side of the offensive line, where last year's starting guard and tackle were lost to free agency. Were the expectations of optimists more wish and fantasy than reality?

The preseason certainly was not encouraging, with the Giants losing three of their four games. Not only that, but special teams appeared to be jinxed—early in the preseason the new long snapper experienced shooting pains in his right arm, diagnosed as elbow tendonitis, and the competitor for place kicking hurt his back while trying to make a tackle. The first regular season game provided evidence for both optimists and pessimists. For the former, there was the victory over the Rams with the defense causing three fumbles and making an interception. For the latter, there were three fumbles on offense, one each by Collins, Barber, and Hilliard. Although some predicted that the debacle of the previous season would make the Giants a stronger, more disciplined team, the jury remained out.

The second game of the season had an aura of excitement to it—it was the homecoming in a sense for the new Cowboys head coach, Bill Parcells. There to welcome and embrace Parcells were many of his former players— LT, Harry Carson, Mark Bavaro, Jim Burt, and others. As a sidelight there was Sean Payton, formerly the offensive coordinator with the Giants but from whom Fassel had taken over play calling, now assistant head coach and passing game coordinator with the Cowboys. The previous season the Cowboys were last in their division. Parcells was expected to make a difference but the Giants clearly seemed to be the stronger team. The game was surprisingly close but with eleven seconds left to play the Giants were ahead, 32–29, about to kick off after a successful field goal by Bryant. How could a game be lost under such circumstances?

Remember Pisarcik? Remember last year's collapses? Bryant's kickoff went to the side, rather than straight, bouncing out of bounds and giving the Cowboys excellent field position. In addition to the snapper who couldn't snap right there now was the kicker who couldn't kick straight. The

Cowboys, amazingly enough, with just seconds remaining in the game, went on to kick a tying field goal, and then a winning one in overtime!

A sidelight to the game was that Bryant's go-ahead field goal was made on second down. Fassel could have run the clock down further before going for the go-ahead field goal, leaving that much less time for the Cowboys to tie the score. However, he was reluctant to run another play, fearing a fumble or other misplay:

> Maybe I'm skittish, maybe I am. But I have a rookie snapper in there and it's a wet field. It's drizzling rain. What's our chances? On the other hand, what's our chances of kicking the ball between the lines, burning about seven seconds, eight seconds off the clock and now they've got six seconds to go in the game, forty yards away from attempting a field goal. It just makes sense to me.[17]

In addition, there was a disagreement between Fassel and Bryant on what the kick was supposed to be, Fassel saying that he told Bryant to squib kick the kickoff up the middle and Bryant saying that he was told to squib kick to the left: "On a squib, you don't really know where the ball is going to go.... There's nothing I can do about it. I shaded it left and it shot straight towards out of bounds."[18]

In addition to the demoralizing loss to Dallas, the Giants had other problems. The offensive line was being reshuffled due to injury and poor play on the part of their rookie tackle. Three of the five positions were now being manned by individuals who were not the original starters at that position. And in the Dallas game, the offense continued to be plagued by fumbles and dropped passes. The Giants were able to pull out an overtime win in the next game but their fundamental problems remained. In the following game, a loss to the Dolphins, there was the all-too-familiar pattern—interceptions, missed opportunities to make interceptions, missed coverages, and overpursuit. On top of everything, Bryant pulled a hamstring on a successful field goal and the punter had to make the field goal attempts until a replacement could be found for the following weeks. The Giants were continually stabbing themselves in the foot. They could make some good plays but just weren't getting the job done.

After the coaches and players emphasized no turnovers and mental toughness, the Giants continued with their mistakes—an interception here, a fumble there, a false start, missed tackles, miscommunications between quarterback and receiver and between defensive backs. Special teams? They were described as a threat—to themselves! Television commentators agreed that the Giants had the talent. How come their play was so sloppy? Fassel was accepting responsibility for setting things right—stopping the turnovers and getting the offense going. He felt that with the players they had the Giants could and should be a winning team. He felt that he could fix things.

But so much for potential. As expressed by Giants defensive tackle Keith Hamilton: "Just because you've got potential, that doesn't mean nothing. Potential will get you out of a job real fast. You don't win games on what you should do."[19] To bring the 2003 season to a close, the Giants continued to make errors, miss opportunities, and lose games, including the last eight games of the season. Fassel was unable to fix things. Against the Eagles, defeat was snatched from the jaws of victory as the Giants gave up an eighty-four-yard punt return for a touchdown with just over a minute left in the game. Midway into the season, in a game against the Falcons, who had a seven-game losing streak and were widely regarded as among the worst teams in the league, the Giants lost by a score of 27–7. By then the chant of "Fire Fassel" had begun. A firing might not be necessary. Fassel said he would resign if the team did not play better. The Giants were reeling while the Cowboys, coached by Parcells, and the Carolina Panthers, coached by John Fox, were having success. In a loss against the Buccaneers, the Giants had four turnovers and nine penalties. Only a few thousand fans stayed to the end of the Giants' 24–7 loss to Buffalo, a game in which Collins was sacked six times and fumbled twice. As in the game against the Falcons, a poor team got better against the Giants. In a loss against the Redskins, there was a penalty for twelve men on the field and two unsportsmanlike conduct penalties that gave the Redskins first downs after they had been stopped. In a blowout loss against the Saints, a field goal attempt was blocked and run back for a touchdown. The television camera showed Fassel in agony as the Giants' offensive line collapsed to allow the block.

With two games left in the season, Fassel announced his resignation. He would coach the last two games but, facing the inevitable, he had decided to resign. How could he go from Coach of the Year and the right man for the job, a coaching genius, to someone who just couldn't get the job done? Was it the loss of Fox, whose team now was bound for the playoffs? Was it the loss of Payton, from whom he took over the play-calling responsibilities and who went on to become a success in Dallas and then as head coach of the Saints, leading them to the playoffs in his first year at the helm? Was it a gamble on the offensive line that didn't pan out? Was it poor selection of free agent players or a series of injuries? Whatever the reason, a man liked and respected by his players was on his way out. As it turned out, things did not get much better for Fassel. After being hired by his friend Brian Billick as offensive coordinator for the Ravens, Fassel was fired during the 2006 season. Billick decided to take over the responsibilities just as Fassel had once decided in relation to Payton. He applied for coaching positions in the NFL and at the college level at Stanford but was unable to obtain one. Despite earlier successes as a quarterbacks coach and then as a head coach in his early tenure with the Giants, the later failures with the Giants and then with the Ravens were too much to overcome.

Changes in the Organization and League

Along with changes in the fortunes of the Giants team, there were significant changes in the organization and league. As noted in the previous chapter, in 1991 Preston Tisch became co-owner of the Giants—the first time the Maras were not the sole owners of the team. Tisch was head of Loews Corporation, a financial company. Now he also would be chairman and chief executive officer. Wellington Mara, now 75, would still be involved in the player-personnel aspects of the Giants. Tisch would be more involved in the business aspects while also trying to have his "ten years of fun." Hopefully this would not take the thirty years his partner jokingly suggested it might, although, as we have seen, the ensuing decade could hardly be described as fun.

Although less involved than he had once been, Wellington Mara continued to attend practices and games. And he continued to have a special status with present and past players. Rarely speaking to the team as a whole, when he did it had an impact upon the players. In 1999, when Mara addressed the team for the first time in thirty years, the players removed their hats out of respect for him. In 2003 he was honored at a surprise party arranged by Frank Gifford. Many distinguished players of the past, including Alex Webster, Sam Huff, LT, and Mark Bavaro joined Gifford in honoring him. Gifford led the toast by thanking Mara for all he had done for the players: "He's done something for almost every Giant I've ever known. And you've never heard him say anything about it. He just doesn't like being in the forefront. But he's touched every one of these guys' lives, including mine, and their families."[20]

Near the end of the 2003 season, Mara recognized the need for changes and promised to improve the product the fans were paying money to see. The players heard this and recognized that the end had come to the patriarch of the organization and, in some ways, the patriarch of the league. Now his eldest son, John, would be getting involved, eventually becoming executive vice-president and chief operating officer. On the Tisch side, in 1991 Preston Tisch's son, Jonathan, also became involved with the team as treasurer. Thus, it was clear that management of the Giants would be passing on to the next generation of the Mara and Tisch families.

Another major change in the organization during this period involved the resignation of George Young after the 1997 season. Partly for health reasons, Young moved on to become the NFL's senior vice president for football operations, a newly created position. During his nineteen seasons with the Giants the team won two Super Bowl championships, reached the playoffs in eight seasons, and won their division title four times. Two of his first-round draft choices became legendary Giants: Simms, drafted in 1979, Young's first draft choice; and LT in 1981. Among the other noteworthy draft choices in the first three rounds were Joe Morris, Carl Banks, Rodney Hampton, Michael Strahan, Amani Toomer, and Tiki Barber. In addition there were noteworthy draft choices in the later rounds, as well as free agent signings. At the same time, there were some noteworthy misses in early round draft choices, particularly at tight end—Dave Young in the second round of 1981, Jamie Williams in the third round of 1983, and Derek Brown in the first round of 1992. His selection of coaches also had somewhat mixed results—Parcells, Handley (described by Young as his worst decision), Reeves, and Fassel. Five times he was chosen NFL Executive of the Year. He died in 2001.

Young's replacement was Ernie Accorsi. Accorsi had joined the Giants in 1994 as assistant to Young. He began his NFL career with the Baltimore Colts, working his way up from public relations director to general manager. In 1983 he selected John Elway with the first pick of the draft, only to have Elway traded by ownership to the Broncos when he indicated that he would play baseball rather than play for the Colts. Accorsi then served as general manager of the Cleveland Browns. During his eight years with the Browns the team made five consecutive playoff appearances.

Clearly Accorsi was experienced and ready to assume responsibilities as general manager and then vice president as well. As we will see, during Accorsi's time with the Giants the job of general manager became much more complicated. Now it included free agency and salary cap issues. In relation to the salary cap, when he became general manager the Giants already were eleven million dollars over the cap with two weeks left within which to get under it. If he left the team over the cap the league could remove players from the roster and make them free agents. Trading players was problematic because there would still be a hit taken against the cap. Thus, Accorsi took over the helm at a time of great difficulty and somewhat limited room to maneuver.

During the 1998–2003 seasons, the period covered in this chapter, Accorsi's record of draft selections showed mixed results. In terms of first-round selections, on the plus side there were the selections of tackle Luke Pettigout and tight end Jeremy Shockey. The selections of defensive backs

Shaun Williams and Will Allen could be described as mixed—both were starters but did not achieve the expected level of play. Disappointing first-round selections were running back Ron Dayne and defensive lineman William Joseph. Dayne's selection, despite its early promise, turned out to be particularly questionable given the availability of Shaun Alexander at the time. The Giants' overall record during this period was 48–48, with the high point being the 2000 season, when the team played in the Super Bowl, and the low point being the collapse of the team in 2003.

During this period there were minor and major changes in the NFL as well. With the retirement of Pete Rozelle, the NFL had to appoint a new commissioner. The nod went to Paul Tagliabue, a lawyer who had represented the league in many cases. Although vastly different in style, and facing new challenges, Tagliabue continued the pattern of success established by Rozelle. During his tenure, the issue of teams moving their franchises and negotiating stadium deals with cities came to the forefront. In 1995 the Raiders moved back to Oakland from Los Angeles, leaving a major city without an NFL team. In 1996 the Cleveland Browns were allowed to move to Baltimore after the league promised the city of Cleveland, which was fighting the move, that it would get an expansion team and league financing of a stadium.

Comparatively minor, although significant, were changes in some game rules—installment of the two-point option after a touchdown, kickoffs starting from the thirty yard line rather than the thirty-five, missed field goals from beyond the twenty yard line leaving the ball where the kick had been missed, and instant replay.

By far of the greatest significance for the league was the movement toward free agency and the initiation of the salary cap. For many years the issue of free agency had been hanging over the league. The 1989 Plan B free agency rules allowed teams to sign players not on another team's protected list of players without compensation—hardly much of a real free agency. The Players Association wanted more, but the owners were resistant to change: "You're not going to get it in ten years, you're not ever going to get it. Don't you see? You're the cattle, we're the ranchers."[21]

In 1992 these rules were declared invalid by the courts, requiring renewed negotiations between the Players Association and league owners. The resulting agreement, worked out in part through the collaborative efforts of Gene Upshaw, executive director of the NFL Players Association and considered one of the great former players, and Paul Tagliabue, who before he became commissioner of the league had represented the NFL in a USFL antitrust suit, was monumental. In allowing free agency after four years in the league, it also provided for a salary cap and player salaries as a percentage of NFL revenues. Instituted in 1993, the salary cap set a limit on what each team could spend on salaries. The limit, the same for every NFL team, was based on a percentage of league revenue. The salary cap, in addition to league rules concerning revenue sharing and order of the draft, created a strong element of parity among league teams. No longer could wealthy teams gain superiority by outspending those with lesser revenue, as was the case in major league baseball. In addition, it meant that some players would greatly increase their bargaining power while others would have to make up the difference with lesser salaries. As with Simms, it also meant that some players would be cut as too expensive whom teams otherwise would have liked to keep. Alone among major professional sports, the NFL player contract was not a binding one on management. Players could not void their contract but could be cut by management without their being paid the remainder of the salary. As protection against this, stars demanded considerable up-front money when they signed. Finally, the cap meant that rookies signed to big contracts had to earn their salaries immediately. Otherwise, they were too expensive to hold in reserve while they learned the game. In particular, quarterbacks just obtained from the draft were pressed into service as quickly as possible rather than their sitting on the sideline for a few years while learning the complexity of reading defenses and calling for play adjustments at the line of scrimmage.

The rules concerning salary cap were complex in terms of what would be counted against the cap, for example, in the case of career-ending injuries to players or up-front money paid to a star whose contract was terminated after one or two years. This increasingly made the general manager's job the most important in professional football. First, the general manager was responsible for hiring the head coach. Always an important matter, it became increasingly important in the time of parity. In cases where team player talent was relatively equal, the difference in success could lie with the coaches. Successful coaches, like star players, now were worth their weight in gold—almost. Parity and free agency made it much more difficult for a team to become a dynasty. When a team did approach such status, as later with the New England Patriots, its success was largely attributed to the coach and general manager. Second, there was continuing responsibility for the draft, increasingly important as new players were forced to play sooner than previously had been the case. Money spent on drafted players had to begin paying dividends virtually immediately. Finally, there was the selection of free agents to fill gaps in team talent. The general manager had to evaluate which of his own potential free agents were worthy of big bucks and which were not, as well as evaluate the talent and monetary value of free agents on the market. Then the general manager had to pray that the free agents obtained played at the anticipated level and remained free of injury. The costs of mistakes were enormous.

Finally, in 2003 another antitrust suit was brought against the league. In this case a suspended Ohio State running back, Maurice Clarett, was prevented by the NFL from entering the draft because of its rule that a player was not eligible for the draft until he had been out of high school for at least three years. Clarett, a sophomore who had led his team to a national championship, sued to overturn the league rule as a violation of federal antitrust laws. The case attracted considerable attention both because of the college star involved and the multiple issues it raised. NFL players themselves held differing views concerning the desirability of the rule, with some feeling that, before the time defined under the rule, players likely were ready neither physically nor psychologically to handle the on-field and off-field pressures of playing in the NFL. In the end, the league rule was sustained and Clarett became just a note in the history of the league's bucking up against antitrust laws.

In sum, the years covered in this chapter involved considerable change in the Giants' team, the Giants' organization, and the NFL. For the Giants, it was a period of mixed success at best. The overall mediocrity of the team was reflected in its 103–104–1 record over the course of the thirteen seasons between 1991 and 2003. There was consistency in team inconsistency and generally a big decline from earlier success. For the NFL there was change but steady progress toward union-management cooperation and overall financial success.

6

The Coughlin-Accorsi-Manning Era and Super Bowl XLII (2004–2008)

The 2003 season started with great hopes for the Giants, perhaps including a Super Bowl. The season ended as a disaster—eight straight losses and near the bottom of the list in The *New York Times* computer ranking. Jimmy Johnson, the onetime head coach and later television commentator, suggested that Fassel had lost the team—"they quit on him."[1] The results had been so bad that there was the feeling that the team needed an overhaul, starting with a new head coach. There were many potential head coaches available, as is typically the case, but there also were seven head coaching vacancies. Thus, the Giants' hunt for a new head coach, now led by Wellington Mara's son, John, and General Manager Ernie Accorsi, potentially involved competition with other teams for the most desirable candidate.

The New Head Coach: Tom Coughlin

Part of the Giants' game plan for a new head coach involved finding a contrast with Fassel. Whereas Fassel was viewed as a "player's coach," the feeling was that what was needed was a head coach who would exercise greater control over the team, if need be a "disciplinarian." Preferably the new head coach would be someone with head coaching experience, or at least considerable experience as an offensive or defensive coordinator, and a proven record as a winner. As soon as Fassel was out, speculation immediately focused on Tom Coughlin. Coughlin was a known entity to the Giants—he had been the wide receivers coach under Parcells during the 1990 Super Bowl season and had been offered the head coaching job after the firing of Ray Handley. In the latter case, Coughlin turned down the offer to remain head coach at Boston College, where he was turning the program around and establishing a winning record. But the Giants were to consider other candidates as well—Charlie Weis and Romeo Crennel, offensive and defensive coordinators respectively of the winning New England Patriots and former coaches with the Giants under Parcells; Lovie Smith, successful defensive coordinator with the St. Louis Rams and former assistant to Tony Dungy with the Tampa Bay Buccaneers; and Nick Saban, formerly defensive coordinator with Bill Belichick in Cleveland and then successful college head coach.[2]

It really did not come as a great surprise when on January 6, 2004, the Giants named Coughlin as their new head coach. In addition to his record with the Giants and success at Boston College, Coughlin had been a successful head coach and personnel manager with the expansion team Jacksonville Jaguars (1994–2002). Under Coughlin, the Jaguars were the most successful expansion team in NFL history. Twice he took them to the AFC championship game and in 1995 was named Coach of the Year. From 1996 to 1999 the Jaguars made the playoffs every year. Coughlin's Jaguars teams were known both for their dynamic offense and few turnovers. During his last year with the Jaguars the team had fewer turnovers than games played, a rarity in NFL history and a far cry from the Giants' 2003 season when they had thirty-five fumbles (18 lost) and twenty interceptions, for an average of more than two a game. As a person, Coughlin fit the Mara ideal—Jesuit-trained, devout, a family man, a person of integrity. In sum, Coughlin had much to recommend him as head coach of the Giants and the team felt confident that he was the right man for the job. With Parcells already with the Cowboys, and Joe Gibbs soon to be signed as coach of the Redskins, and Andy Reid already proving himself a successful head coach with the Eagles, the Giants surely would need a strong, winning hand at the helm. In the words of general manager Accorsi: "If we can't win with this guy, I'm taking up tennis."[3]

At the same time that Coughlin had much to recommend for him, there were other features of his record that raised some questions. Although Coughlin was credited with doing an outstanding job with the Jaguars, the team had losing records in his last three years with them, resulting in his being fired. One explanation was that there were salary cap problems, injuries, and some poor personnel decisions that led to a weakened team. Another explanation was that with his tough disciplinary approach, Coughlin had worn out his welcome with the team.

Which brings us to the second questionable feature in regard to Coughlin's appointment—his approach toward players. On the one hand, there were those who felt that his no-nonsense approach was just what the Giants needed. Thus, a *New York Times* headline read: "A Strict Colonel Tom Is What's Necessary."[4] On the other hand, there were others who questioned whether this was the best approach for today's NFL players. As suggested by Jimmy Johnson: "He wore thin toward the end there at Jacksonville. If you don't communicate and you don't motivate, you are going to wear thin or you're going to have a revolt."[5]

In any case, Coughlin promised Giants fans what they wanted to hear: "It is a tremendous challenge, and I am looking forward to working with these players and reestablishing the New York Giants' tradition of physically controlling the line of scrimmage. We want to win the battle at the line of scrimmage, eliminate the disease of turnovers, and control field position of special teams."[6] This was quite a tall order. In terms of control of the line of scrimmage, on offense the team was to have just one returning lineman at his 2003 position, Luke Petitgout at left tackle; on the defensive line, just Michael Strahan was returning at defensive end with an entire new corps of linebackers. On offense, would there be improvement at quarterback? In 2003 Collins threw more interceptions than touchdowns, was sacked twenty-eight times, and had a noticeable decline in his overall rating. And then there was the problem at running back. Could Tiki Barber cut down on his fumbling while continuing with his outstanding running and receiving? And could the career of Ron Dayne be salvaged? Drafted in the first round in 2000 and, with Barber, the "thunder" part of the "thunder and lightning" tandem in that season, Dayne was left inactive the entire 2003 season. Could he return to form under the tutelage of a new coach and running behind a revamped line?

The Draft of Eli Manning

Whatever the importance and drama of hiring a new head coach, it was at least equaled by that of plans for the draft. The Giants had decided on their new head coach and made some free agent signings to bolster the linebacking corps and defensive and offensive lines. Now it was time to head into the draft with the Giants having the fourth pick in the first round. The pick in the first round always seems critical, particularly when it is as high as the one available to the Giants in the 2004 draft. The selection would be managed by Accorsi and his staff, as well as participation by John Mara and Coughlin as the new head coach. Accorsi's record in first-round picks was somewhat mixed. In 1998 he selected safety Shaun Williams, who showed promise but to date was not contributing as anticipated. In 1999 the pick was Luke Pettigout, again clearly contributing but not reaching the heights of elite offensive tackles. In 2000 there was the selection of Ron Dayne, the Heisman Trophy winner, whose contribution was on the steady decline and who was selected instead of Shaun Alexander who went on to star for the Seattle Seahawks. In 2001 there was the selection of Will Allen, again contributing and showing signs of progress but not one of the elite cornerbacks in the NFL. In 2002 Jeremy Shockey was selected—a winning selection, as Shockey made the Pro Bowl. Finally, in 2003, there was the selection of William Joseph, whose status became that of a reserve defensive lineman. The record was partly complicated by the Giants' often having a low position in the draft. Now, with the fourth pick, the Giants stood in a position to pick an elite player.

There always is a great deal of drama associated with the NFL draft as well as much speculation about which teams will select which players, particularly as regards the first ten slots. For the Giants there was particular drama since this was expected to be one of the last Accorsi drafts and, with three prized quarterbacks available in the draft—Eli Manning, Philip Rivers, and Ben Roethlisberger—there was speculation about the order in which they would be selected. There also was a prized left tackle available, Robert Gallery, always a prime position to be filled in the draft. As the day of the draft approached, the drama heightened with speculation that the Giants wanted Manning but the Chargers, with the first pick, reportedly were going to select him. Rumor had it that the Giants were attempting a trade with the Chargers, with the Chargers getting the Giants' pick, using it to select Rivers, as well as additional draft picks or players from the Giants. Further intensifying the drama were reports that Manning did not want to play for the Chargers, reports that included comments by Manning's father, Archie Manning, himself a former star NFL quarterback. In addition, there were reports that the Chargers really wanted Rivers but were dangling the selection of Manning to up the ante in trade negotiations. Manning, of course, not only had his father's pedigree but also that of his brother, Peyton, already a premier NFL quarterback with the Colts.

On NFL draft day, the excitement of the crowd at Madison Square Garden in New York is incredible. Fans line up hours before doors open to gain access to the event. Some camp out the night before so as to be guaranteed admission. Giants and Jets fans are noticeably present, the draft being held in New York, but fans of a variety of other teams clearly are evident wearing identifying shirts and hats. The fans are there not just to observe, but to express their pleasure or disappointment with their team's selection as well. The television viewing audience is enormous as well. Then, the tension peaks as the Commissioner Tagliabue announces, "With first pick of the draft, the San Diego Chargers select..."—Eli Manning. Giants fans were disheartened, but perhaps not as much as Manning, who grimaced as he went up to the stage and held up a Chargers jersey. With the second pick,

6. The Coughlin-Accorsi-Manning Era (2004–2008)   149

the Raiders selected Gallery, with the third pick the Cardinals selected the wide receiver Larry Fitzgerald, and with the fourth pick the Giants selected Rivers. Roethlisberger was selected by Pittsburgh with the eleventh pick of the draft.

The disappointment of Manning, his family, Accorsi, and Giants fans turned out to be short-lived. The Giants were able to work out a trade with the Chargers, exchanging quarterbacks, and the Giants giving the Chargers their third-round pick in the current draft as well as their first- and fifth-round picks in the 2005 draft.[7] Why this trade was not worked out before the draft never became completely clear. One view was that the Chargers believed that they could keep Manning if they made him their selection and only traded him once it became clear that the Manning family really was unhappy with the selection and a holdout was possible. In a later interview, Accorsi disclosed that the Chargers had wanted defensive end Osi Umenyiora included in the deal, and the trade could only be accomplished when they gave up on this demand.[8] In any case, the Giants' management, Accorsi in particular, as well as the majority of their fans, was delighted with the way things worked out. Manning smiled as he held up a Giants jersey and the fans cheered as Manning arrived at Giants Stadium.

Why were the Giants so keen on obtaining Manning and what were the implications for the current quarterback, Kerry Collins? Manning had a great record at Mississippi (Ole Miss), but so did Rivers and Roethlisberger have great college careers. All were tall and had strong throwing arms. However, Accorsi felt that Manning was special, the quarterback that could lead the Giants to glory in the years ahead: "This is a once-in-a-decade player. This is a quarterback you wait for a long time."[9] Accorsi had gone to see Manning the previous year when it was thought that Manning might be coming out after his junior year. He saw him play against Auburn, a strong defensive team, and he was impressed with what he saw. In later workouts he confirmed much of what Accorsi had seen—great feet, great poise, an excellent arm, great anticipation and touch. Accorsi felt that Manning could be like Brett Favre of the Green Bay Packers, a quarterback who lets his teammates know that they can win and elevates the game of others. In other words, Manning was special: "I have always had this feeling that you have a chance to pick a franchise quarterback maybe once.... To me, when you have a chance to pick somebody like him, you just go pick him. It is that simple.... If he is as good as we think he is, and he stays healthy, he is going to be a standard-bearer for this franchise for a long time."[10]

There was another element to Accorsi's opportunity to pick a franchise quarterback, one that he said comes perhaps only once. In the 1983 draft Accorsi was the general manger of the then Baltimore Colts. With the first pick in that draft, the Colts selected John Elway. Elway did not want to play for the Colts, disliking their coach, and threatened to play baseball for the New York Yankees. Accorsi wanted Elway and felt that an attractive contract could get him to change his mind. However, Robert Irsay, the owner of the Colts, was not prepared to spend that kind of money—five million dollars for five years, a record amount at the time. The Broncos offered draft choices for Elway, as did the Oakland Raiders, and the Patriots offered All-Pro guard John Hannah for him. Accorsi turned the offers down only to learn that the Colts traded the rights to Elway to the Broncos for the Denver first-round choice in the draft, Chris Hinton, a quarterback, and Denver's first-round choice in the following year's draft. Accorsi was not involved in the deal and resigned early in 1984. Elway, of course, went on to become a Hall of Fame player, leading the Broncos to five Super Bowls and two NFL championships. The selection of Manning was a chance to pick the franchise quarterback he missed in Elway. The selection also was expected to be a major part of his legacy with the Giants.

In the meantime, Collins was disappointed to learn of the Manning selection, recognizing that it likely meant the end of his career with the Giants, either that year or the following year when his contract ended. Not only was his passer rating falling but his expensive contract and the likely huge signing bonus due Manning, technically the number one selection in the draft, meant that the Giants would be unable to keep both. Collins had been rejuvenated with the Giants and wanted to finish his career with them. The Giants tried to get Collins to accept a lower salary and viewed him as a potential teacher to the younger Manning. However, Collins didn't want to accept the cut in salary and was released.

Drafting a Quarterback

The success of NFL teams runs from the general manager, through the head coach and assistants, to the players. Part of the success, or failure, of the general manager and head coach involves their ability to evaluate players for the draft and free agency signings. The draft has become a drama unto itself with fans lining up the night before at Madison Square Garden in New York, each fan wanting to applaud or boo as their team's draft selection is announced. For weeks beforehand, the experts come up with mock drafts, and for weeks afterwards there are analyses of which teams did well or screwed up badly. Of course, once more this is part of pro football as entertainment, as the draft is televised with great fanfare and fees to the NFL.

6. The Coughlin-Accorsi-Manning Era (2004–2008)

The first NFL draft was conducted in 1936, the brainchild of the then commissioner Bert Bell. Way back then it followed today's pattern of teams selecting in the reverse order of their finish. Whereas in the early years evaluations were done unsystematically, in the 1960s the Cowboys and 49ers jointly developed a computer model to quantify these evaluations. The Cowboys in particular, under the leadership of Tex Schramm and Gil Brandt, developed systematic evaluations of potential draft selections on critical skills, the weighting of skills varying with the position being considered. Until 1982 college players were evaluated by different scouting groups, a process that was time-consuming and costly. In the early 1980s the process was streamlined, with evaluations done at one site with players on an invitation-only basis. Approximately three hundred players spend the better part of two days taking physicals, being evaluated for strength, speed, agility, and position-specific skills. In addition, players take psychological tests to measure intelligence and various personality traits, some of which are common to all teams and some of which are specific to a particular team.

The issue of the use of psychological tests to evaluate players is an interesting one. A wide variety of tests are used. The one basic test, the Wonderlic Personnel Test, has received the greatest attention. The Wonderlic is a group test of general mental ability and is administered at the combine to all potential draftees. It consists of fifty multiple-choice items administered with a twelve-minute time limit. Illustrative items are:

Soft is the opposite of
1. hard   2. closed   3. secure   4. sad

Two men buy a car which costs $350; X pays $50 more than Y. How much did X pay?

The boy plays baseball. All baseball players wear hats. The boy wears a hat.
1. True   2. False   3. Uncertain

Which number in the following group of numbers represents the smallest amount?
7   .8   31   .33   2

The Wonderlic is considered by professional psychologists as a generally useful and economical method of predicting job performance across a wide domain of jobs and positions. At the same time, questions are raised about its utility for specific jobs for which its utility has not been demonstrated as well as its utility with minority populations. Evidence of its utility in relation to draft selections is a particularly critical point. Critics cite evidence such as the high score of Ryan Leaf and low score of Dan Marino in questioning the utility of the test.

In addition to the Wonderlic, many teams administer one or another of several personality tests. These include the Myers-Briggs Test, based on the thinking of the psychoanalyst Carl Jung; the California Psychological Inventory, a well-researched personality test that measures traits such as dominance, sociability, self-acceptance, and self-control; the Caliper Profile, a personality test that has been administered to almost a million business people and more than four thousand athletes for professional sports franchises; and a Brain Type measure, another test based on Jung's theories that claims to classify each person on one of sixteen brain types that is associated with specific mental proficiencies and deficiencies. These brain types are viewed as inborn traits that greatly determine why people do most of the things they do.

The Giants organization, always concerned with the character of its players, historically has used a version of the California Psychological Inventory and a specially developed sentence completion test to weed out troublemakers. In the sentence completion test the players are asked to complete sentences that begin with stems such as, "The hardest thing about dealing with a coach for me is...," "Referees...," and "The best way to criticize me is...." Approximately ten percent of the potential draftees are given negative reviews or recommendations against being drafted.

The interesting thing about the use of all of these tests is that there is no systematic evidence of their predictive utility in relation to the selection of professional football players. When management is asked about this, the likely answer is, "We know it [the test] works." When asked, "How do you know?" the answer is, "We know from experience." This is true not just for football teams and others sports teams but often for business and industry more generally. But there is obvious room for self-deception here. A critical question in addressing the utility, or validity, of a test is whether accurate predictions are made. In relation to this, there is concern about two types of error—false positives and false negatives. In the case of false positives the prediction is that an athlete will be a successful pro and this turns out to not be the case. In the case of false negatives the prediction is that the athlete will not make it and he turns out to be a success. Both types of error are quite common in the selection process and yet there are not systematic studies of how often they occur, why they occur, and what steps can be taken to reduce their frequency.

When all of the information on the potential draftees is in, generally they are given an overall score and ranked by position. This enables the team to draft by overall talent, often emphasized in the first round in particular—pick the best player available, as well as by position and by need at that position. Often this is not a straightforward process and can involve serious arguments among the participants in the process—general manager, head coach and assistant coaches, director of player personnel, and scouts. Some examples: Parcells thought LT was a great player but he was not a top pick of Bill Belichick, and George Young was high on the running back George Rogers; the scouts loved Dave Meggett but Parcells thought he was too small and questioned, "What am I going to do with the guy?"[11] Also there were power issues. Dan Reeves wanted more input than he had, Jim Fassel had more input than the scouts preferred. When the decisions finally are made it is time for fans to cheer or boo and for the second-guessing to begin.

The fortunes of teams rise and fall on the basis of these decisions. Every team has its record of hits and misses. Here are some illustrative Giants' misses: In 1991 the Giants selected Jarrod Bunch, a running back, in the first round. Brett Favre was available. In 1995 the Giants selected Tyrone Wheatley, a running back, in the second round. Curtis Martin was available. In 2000 Ron Dayne, a running back, was selected when Shaun Alexander, also a running back, was available.

Selection of a quarterback is particularly problematic. As expressed by Brian Billick, one-time head coach of the Ravens and a former offensive coordinator: "Despite all of the one-on-one interviews with quarterbacks, the stacks of game film the psychological profiles, and the physical tests, determining how a college quarterback will fare in the pros is 50–50."[12] The list of quarterbacks recently selected, generally early in the first round, who turned out to be busts is long and painful for those who made the decisions: Tim Couch, Joey Harrington, Ryan Leaf, Rick Mirer, and Akili Smith.

The case of Ryan Leaf is particularly dramatic. Whether he or Peyton Manning would be selected number one in the 1998 draft was considered a toss-up. As it turned out, Manning was selected first by the Colts, and Leaf second by the Chargers. Manning, of course, turned out to be a great quarterback whereas Leaf failed with a number of teams and was out of football while Manning was still throwing touchdowns.

Then there is the case of Joey Harrington, selected third overall in the 2003 draft, who by 2007 was playing with his third team and not starting at that. As one NFL scout reported: "I'm shocked he hasn't done better. Setup quickness, foot mechanics, throwing motion, accuracy. He was an upper-echelon quarterback."[13] One could add here David Carr, originally a first overall draft pick in 2002, who could not make it with either the Houston Texans or Carolina Panthers, and who currently is struggling to make the Giants team as a backup quarterback. Carr may yet rejuvenate his career—he's still only twenty-nine as of this writing and has talent—but he's fallen a long way from what was anticipated for him.

At the other extreme, Johnny Unitas, considered by many to be the all-time great quarterback, was selected by Pittsburgh in the ninth round and then cut by them. He was doing construction work and playing semipro ball until given a chance by the Baltimore Colts. Physically he hardly presented an imposing image. In fact, when the Giants' Charlie Conerly and Frank Gifford observed him during a 1956 preseason game, Conerly said to Gifford: "Look at that goofy sonofabitch."[14] Another noteworthy miss in this regard was in the 1983 draft, when Dan Marino was only selected after three other quarterbacks. Whereas Marino went on to set passing records, none of the others achieved much acclaim in their NFL careers.

In 2004 the Giants in some ways bet the house on Eli Manning as their quarterback for the future. The other two quarterbacks available, Phil Rivers and Ben Roethlisberger, were also considered to be top prospects. After four seasons (2004–2007), Roethlisberger has the best completion percentage, the best total rating, and the best touchdown-to-interception ratio. A few more seasons should tell which of the three deserved to be selected number one.

The 2004 Season: Mediocrity and Inconsistency

The 2004 preseason would revolve around four major issues. First, what could the Giants do to shore up the weak offensive and defensive lines as well as the linebacking corps? There were two free-agent linebacker acquisitions and offensive line draftees, including a guard who was the future son-in-law of Coughlin. Could this be enough to do the job? Second, could Barber continue to gain yards while still holding onto the ball, and could Dayne become the back the Giants thought he was when they drafted him in the first round? Third, there was the question of how quickly Manning could develop and, with the departure of Collins, who would start until he was ready and help to guide him in his development. Fourth, there was the question of how the Giants would respond to Coughlin's tough disciplinary approach, including rules such as hats off and feet on the floor during meetings. In addition, could he cut down on the injuries suffered by the players, something that he referred to as a "cancer" and "a mental thing?"

Coughlin's approach to developing self-esteem and team pride became obvious to the players at their first meeting of the off-season "voluntary" workout program. The workouts lasted twice as long as those under Fassell and this resulted in some players complaining to the Players Association that the new schedule violated the NFL workout guidelines. The Players Association investigated the matter and concluded that the off-season rules had indeed been violated and therefore the Giants were penalized with the loss of two days of organized workouts. In addition, Coughlin was told to stop listing the workouts as mandatory.

The response to Coughlin's approach flared up again when a number of players filed a grievance with the Players Association after being fined for being "late" for a team meeting. According to reports, the players actually were early but not as early as Coughlin demanded: "Players ought to be there on time, period. If they're on time, they're on time. Meetings start five minutes early."[15] Reportedly the star defensive end Michael Strahan also had been fined for arriving "only" two minutes early, finding himself locked out of the meeting. Although no such public grievances were displayed during the season, there were indications that the issue continued to simmer among some players.

After the release of Collins, who went on to sign with the Oakland Raiders, the Giants were in the market for a veteran quarterback. They came up with Kurt Warner. Warner had led the St. Louis Rams to two Super Bowls and had received two NFL Most Valuable Player awards (MVP) and one Super Bowl MVP award while leading the Rams to the Super Bowl XXXIV championship, only to be released for salary cap reasons. Thus, the release of one quarterback, Collins, for salary cap reasons had led to the signing of another quarterback, Warner, who similarly had been released for salary cap reasons. Warner had risen from NFL Europe and the Arena League to NFL stardom, but now seemed to be on the decline due to injuries. Interestingly enough, the Giants had played a role in the Rams' release of Warner. In the first game of the 2003 season, the Giants caused him to lose three fumbles, sacked him six times, and knocked him out of the game with a concussion. He appeared in only one more game, leading to his release prior to the 2004 season. It was not expected that Warner would be what he was, nor that he was to be the Giants' quarterback of the future—Manning clearly held that anointed position. However, it was hoped that he could hold the fort and provide mentoring until Manning was ready. In the early workouts and exhibition games Warner looked good, throwing the ball well and showing good timing and command of the team.

As for the running backs, Coughlin instructed Barber to carry the ball closer to his body and to cradle it with both arms when he was about to be tackled so that it could not be punched out from him by the opponents. In practice defensive players were told to try to slap the ball out of his hands so that he would focus on keeping the ball tight. Over time he became comfortable holding the ball in the prescribed way and his fumble problem largely went away. Dayne was told to lose thirty pounds or not show up. He lost the weight and was given a new opportunity to prove himself. In the preseason opener Dayne ran for over one hundred yards and scored two touchdowns. In another preseason game, however, he fumbled twice at the goal line and missed a block of a blitzing linebacker. Dayne's fumbles and lack of consistency in making first downs on short yardage left him as a question mark for the season.

Finally, the problems on offense and defense appeared to remain unsolved. The offensive line remained a problem. Free agent signings and rookie draft choices suggested the hope of some improvement, but preseason performance left some doubts. Even the play of left tackle Luke Pettigout, the lone returnee at his same position, left something to be desired and drew some criticism from Coughlin. As they headed into the season, there remained questions as to whether the offensive line would be an improvement over last year's, which had allowed forty-four sacks and was described by some as more offensive than effective. The defense similarly remained a question with three new starters at linebacker who, due to injuries, had spent limited time playing together. It is said that football games are won in the trenches—being able to run and being able to stop the run. To many fans it seemed strange that the Giants would allow their offensive and defensive fronts to fall into such a weakened state. Because of these uncertainties and weaknesses, the Giants were predicted to end up last in their division.

As it turns out, the Giants' season can be described in short fashion as one of overall mediocrity and consistent inconsistency! The season began with a bad loss to the Eagles in which the team's weaknesses were evident. However, to the surprise of many, this loss was followed by four straight wins. Warner was throwing accurately and there were hopes that he might be able to return to his earlier form. Barber was running well and holding onto the ball. Included in the string of victories was a game against the Green Bay Packers in which their quarterback, Brett Favre, threw a touchdown after being taken out with a concussion and following which he was taken out of the game. After the game Favre told Warner he didn't remember the touchdown pass and the Packers coach said he never gave Favre permission to return. The doctors had not cleared Favre to go back and he shouldn't have been in the game!

After an open date, a loss and a win, the Giants' record stood at five wins and two losses, better than might otherwise have been expected. However, at this point, midway into the season, there was a disastrous loss to the Chicago Bears, a team with a losing record and a rookie, third-string quarterback. In the game the Giants made only one of fourteen third-down conversions and none of three on fourth down, often needing just a yard for a first down. To give a sense of just how bad things were, consider the following: two interceptions, three lost fumbles, seven sacks, fourteen penalties for over one hundred yards, one of which wiped out a long return. To make things worse, the team, already hit with many injuries, lost their best defensive player, Strahan, for the season with a torn pectoral muscle.

The Chicago loss was followed by another one in which Warner was sacked six times. The offensive line was leaking like a sieve and Warner, never known for his mobility, was the victim of the flood of attackers. Beginning to feel desperate as the season looked to be on the verge of collapse, the Giants turned to Manning, but to no avail—six straight losses before a final game win against the Cowboys in which Barber scored on a three-yard run with eleven seconds left in the game. One of the losses was to the strong Baltimore Ravens, a game in which Manning completed only four of eighteen passes for twenty-seven yards and had two interceptions. There was discussion of whether he was confused, tight, and losing his confidence and that of the players. He improved some after this and ended the season completing more than fifty percent of his passes and throwing for over one thousand yards but with more interceptions than touchdowns.

So how could the 2004 season be summarized? What were the answers to the questions that were there as the season was about to begin? First, the lines were as bad as feared might be the case. On offense, the rushing improved, largely due to the play of Tiki Barber, but there were too many quarterback sacks and too many failures in short yardage situations. On defense, the Giants again were weak against the run, in fact weaker than the previous year. Also noteworthy was their poor defense in the red zone, allowing a touchdown more than seventy percent of the time, a strong contrast with their own lack of success in that area.

Second, there was the question of thunder and lightning. There was a lot of lightning but almost no thunder. Dayne clearly was not the answer to the need for a power runner on short yardage situations. In fact, many suggested it would be better to just leave Barber in the game in such situations. In contrast with Dayne, Barber had an outstanding year—a team record of over fifteen hundred yards rushing, a team record of over two thousand yards gained overall, a team record of nine games in which he gained over one hundred yards, a team record for career receptions with fifty-two in the current season, and a team record of career total yardage, eclipsing that of Frank Gifford by a substantial amount. Barber became the only active player to lead a team in both rushing yards and receptions. One of the two past players to do this was the Hall of Famer Walter Payton.

Third, what about the selection of Manning? Here the jury remained out. There were serious questions raised in his early starts, not unusual for a rookie quarterback, particularly one playing behind a weak offensive line, but signs of progress near the end. Like the team itself, he was inconsistent, at times looking confident and throwing for long gains while at other times looking confused by the speed of the game. Asked about Manning's performance, the Giants' GM, Ernie Accorsi, said that he remained confident in the wisdom of his selection and expected Manning to show big gains in the coming year. At the same time, others could hardly avoid noticing the contrast with the record of Roethlisberger — 13–0 regular season record and voted NFL Offensive Rookie of the Year. The third quarterback in the drama of the '04 draft, Phil Rivers, hardly played as backup to the Chargers' Pro Bowl quarterback Drew Brees.

Fourth, what about Coughlin and his relationship with the players? Again, the jury remained out. Reviewing the team's record for the year, Coughlin himself gave it a mixed evaluation — improved turnover ratio and special teams performance, but little or no improvement in reducing penalties and performance in short yardage and red-zone situations. Particularly troublesome was the continued problem of injuries, with twelve players finishing the season on injured reserve. Coughlin was puzzled by the situation while acknowledging that it was a problem throughout the league, one that was particularly problematic given the salary cap that prevented a team from paying for high-priced reserves. There were no big flare-ups with the players, as had occurred earlier in the season, but questions remained about just how committed the players were to Coughlin and how eager free agents would be to come on board and play for him. Accorsi said he was not worried about either. According to him the players played hard and to win ("When you compare this season to last year it is night and day"[16]), and that players recognized the Giants as a great organization to play for. Accorsi also remained optimistic about the future of the team with the expected improvement of Manning, the recovery of key players from injury, and expected free agent signings.

The 2005 Season: More Inconsistency

With his work cut out for him but cap money to spend, Accorsi set out to use the free agency market to improve the team's defense and offense. Noteworthy among the signings were Antonio Pierce to play middle linebacker, Kareem McKenzie to play right tackle, Plaxico Burress to play wide receiver, and Jay Feeley to be place kicker. Pierce had not been drafted out of college but developed into an outstanding linebacker with the Redskins. Along with adding strength to the team, his signing weakened a division rival. Negotiations with Burress had been an on-again and off-again proposition, with the Giants at one point calling off all negotiations, but his addition brought big play possibilities to the offense. In all, the addition of four starters through free agency appeared to greatly strengthen the team.

In the draft, the Giants were without a first-round pick due to the previous year's trade with the Chargers to get Manning. In the second round they selected a cornerback, Corey Webster, to strengthen that weak area. In later rounds they selected two defensive ends to strengthen the defensive line and a big back, Brandon Jacobs (6'4", 267 pounds), to provide some thunder in case Dayne continued to falter. Here too the Giants felt that they had added strength to the team.

The Giants looked good in their opening victory over the Arizona Cardinals. Although rusty from missing three preseason weeks with an elbow injury, Manning played well and seemed to be able to establish a connection with Burress. In addition, Jacobs was able to make a third-and-one first down, looking like the short yardage back that Dayne wasn't.

By midseason the Giants looked like a vastly improved team with a 6–2 record. In the second game of the season, against the Saints, Manning moved well in the pocket and made good decisions. Shockey, who once again seemed to be a target for passes after a season spent largely blocking, declared Manning to be ready for a breakout game. This appeared to be the case in the fourth game of the season, a victory over the Rams in which Manning threw four touchdown passes and the Giants became the highest-scoring team in the NFL. This was being declared the "dawn of the Manning era" and the Giants were described as an offensive powerhouse. In addition, at this point the team was plus ten in takeaways.

After further victories, Manning was praised for his poise, and headlines read "Eli's Arrived" and "Manning Gives Giants Something To Believe In."[17] Big receptions were being made by Burress, Barber was running well, including running for over two hundred yards in one game, the best of his career, and Jacobs continued to make short yardage gains, including one game in which he had two touchdown runs of one yard each. On defense, end Osi Umenyiora was coming on strong to complement Strahan, the two becoming one of the top sack tandems in the league.

However, the midseason record and signs of progress did not mean that all was well with the Giants, as was clearly demonstrated in their two losses. In the first, a 45–23 loss to the Chargers, the team rejected by Manning, the defense gave up touchdowns on the first three drives of the game. In the second, a loss in overtime to the Cowboys, the Giants were badly outplayed despite the closeness of the score. Once more the Giants' defense proved vulnerable, in particular to the pass. At that point the Giants were next to last in the NFL in pass defense. And despite other signs of being an offensive powerhouse, the Giants' offense proved to be feeble, failing on their first nine third-down attempts and converting three Cowboys turnovers into only six points. In addition, they were suffering from penalties, many at critical times, something that would drive the disciplinarian Coughlin crazy. In sum, there continued to be evidence of inconsistency on both offense and defense, both within games and between games.

The Giants faced a tougher schedule in the second half of the season and it began with a loss to the Vikings in which the inconsistency of earlier games appeared full blown—special teams gave up touchdowns on punt and kickoff returns, Manning made bad throws and bad decisions, the offense scored one touchdown in five red zone (green zone, according to Coughlin) appearances, and Coughlin was left seething over the poor performance. The Giants recovered to defeat the Eagles, who were playing without their quarterback Donovan McNabb, but this was followed by an ugly loss to the Seahawks in which the Giants had sixteen penalties, including eleven false starts and five penalties on the left tackle Pettigout, and missed on three field goal attempts, one of which would have won the game had it been made. Although they were able to beat the Cowboys the following week, and the defense appeared to be coming on, Manning had his worst game of the season—only twelve completions in thirty-one attempts, two interceptions, and a rating of 27.9!

The Giants won three of their remaining four games, ending the season with an 11–5 record, but inconsistency clearly was a problem and injuries, both on offense and defense, had piled up. On the plus side, Tiki Barber continued to prove himself to be a fantastic running back, breaking his and the Giants' single season rushing record and ending up a close second to Alexander for the league rushing leadership. Barber led the league in total yards from scrimmage, proving himself to be an adept receiver coming out of the backfield. Fans constantly chanted "Tiki, Tiki" and many considered him a strong candidate for Most Valuable Player. Plaxico Burress proved himself to be a dangerous and exciting receiver and Shockey returned to form, again being selected to the Pro Bowl. The defense showed signs of improving, particularly with the play of Strahan and Umenyiora, and that of Pierce until he was injured near the end of the season.

On the negative side, the pass defense was weak, with the cornerbacks often being burned by the opponents' speedy receivers. The linebacking corps showed weaknesses during the season and was completely depleted by injuries by the end of the season. Perhaps most significant of all, however, was the inconsistency of Manning. There remained questions about his decisions and accuracy as he threw seventeen interceptions, tied for second in the league. Once more there was a striking contrast with the performance of Roethlisberger, who went on to become the youngest starting quarterback in the NFL to lead his team to a Super Bowl victory and ended with seventeen touchdowns and only nine interceptions.[18]

With their 11–5 record, the Giants made the playoffs, with their opponents being the Carolina Panthers, led by their former defensive coordinator John Fox. The game proved to be a disaster for the Giants, the final score being 23–0, an unfortunate end to the season that at times showed so much promise. In the game Manning was intercepted three times and Barber was held to just forty-one yards. The Giants had just thirty-five offensive plays, with nine first downs, and were never inside the thirty-nine yard line of the Panthers. On the other side of the ball, the Panthers' star receiver, Steve Smith, alone had as many receptions as Manning had completions and their running back gained over one hundred and fifty yards. Linebacker Pierce watched from the sideline on crutches, one of four Giants linebackers missing the game due to injury. After the game a disheartened Barber suggested, "In some ways we were outcoached."

The 2006 Season: More Disappointments

Two years into the Coughlin regime, and one year from the end of the Accorsi period,[19] the Giants were showing signs of improvement but problems remained. First, the offensive line showed signs of improvement but were still plagued by penalties. Second, the defensive line was showing improvement until injuries hit them. Clearly there was a need to upgrade at linebacker, with the exception of middle linebacker Pierce. Third, perhaps of greatest need was improvement at cornerback, particularly the need for a cornerback who could provide man-to-man coverage of the opponent's leading receiver. Fourth, whether Manning was the franchise quarterback Accorsi expected him to be remained an open question. At times Manning looked outstanding, poised and in command of the offense. At other times he was inaccurate, had poor pocket presence, and seemed incapable of consistently bringing his game to a higher level. Finally, Coughlin appeared to have an improved relationship with the team, but how much the players were behind him, as illustrated in Barber's comment after the playoff loss, was another open question.

Accorsi has said that the foundation of a football team is made up of the quarterback, a pass rusher, the left tackle, and cornerbacks. The Giants had what they still hoped was their franchise quarterback. They also had two superior pass rushers in Strahan and Umenyiora. Pettigout was adequate at left tackle but not outstanding, and aging besides. An upgrade here seemed desirable. Cornerback clearly was a problem, with disappointing performances by first- and third-round 2001 draft choices Will Allen and Will Peterson. In addition there was the need for improvement at linebacker, historically a strong suit of Giants teams.

Turning to the free agent market, Accorsi signed LaVar Arrington, a three-time Pro Bowl linebacker whose play during the 2005 season had declined due to injury and friction with the coaching staff. When first drafted, Arrington was being compared to Lawrence Taylor. The Giants hoped he had something of LT left in him. In addition Accorsi replaced much of the defensive backfield, signing two free agent cornerbacks and a safety while releasing the two disappointing cornerbacks they had drafted five years before.[20]

With the approach of the draft, the last for which Accorsi would be responsible, expectation was that the Giants might draft their left tackle of the future, a promising linebacker, or a cover corner. When time came for their first-round selection, to the surprise of many the Giants traded down and then selected Mathias Kiwanuka, a defensive end. Wisdom has it that you draft in terms of talent rather than need, particularly in the early rounds. However, Kiwanuka was not among those most highly rated by the experts at the time the Giants were making their selection and clearly he did not fit the need category. In the second round they selected the receiver Sinorice Moss and in the third the linebacker Gerris Wilkinson.

While the jury concerning Accorsi's record of draft selections would remain out for a while, particularly until the Manning selection had played out, the picture at the time of his retirement was at best mixed. During his nine-year tenure as general manager, Accorsi had eight first-round selections, one year's selection having been given up in the Manning trade. By the beginning of the 2007 season, four of these eight selections were still with the team—Shockey, Joseph, Manning, and Kiwanuka. These were his last four first-round selections, none of the first four (Shaun Williams, Luke Pettigout, Ron Dayne, and Will Allen) still being with the team. Of the twenty-five selections made in the first three rounds, at that time fourteen no longer were on the roster. Although some of these players were lost to free agency, as is true for any team, many just did not achieve the status expected when they were drafted. Particularly disappointing in this regard were the first-round selections of Ron Dayne in the 2000 draft, Will Allen in the 2001 draft, and William Joseph in the 2003 draft.

Despite what appeared to be some clear upgrades, the Giants appeared to still have some weaknesses as the 2006 season approached. Certainly there remained uncertainties on both offense and defense. Yet many felt that the team was ready for Super Bowl competition. The first game of the season, against the strong Indianapolis Colts, would perhaps indicate just how competitive the Giants were. In addition, there was great interest in the competition between the brother quarterbacks, Eli and Peyton Manning, in what some referred to as "The Brother Bowl"—the first time in the history of the NFL that brothers faced one another as starting quarterbacks. Peyton had by now established himself as a premier quarterback and as a future Hall of Famer. On the other hand, Eli still was trying to turn his potential into performance. In the game the Giants showed what they were capable of—for good and for bad. On the positive side, they out rushed and out gained the Colts. On the negative side, they had more turnovers and penalties and missed two interception opportunities. In the battle of quarterbacks, Eli acquitted himself well while completing almost two-thirds of his passes, two for touchdowns, and a total of 247 yards. His passer rating was better than that of his brother. In the end, the Giants lost by a score of 26–21 because of their errors and inability to capitalize on opportunities.

The following week's game against the Eagles again illustrated the mixed bag that seemed to constitute the 2006 Giants. The Giants started slowly and by the fourth quarter were behind by seventeen points. Lo and behold, they scored seventeen unanswered points in the quarter, tying the score, and then added six more in overtime on a touchdown pass from Manning to Plaxico Burress. Manning was sacked six times by the blitzing Eagles but he completed two-thirds of his passes, including all of his overtime passes, three for touchdowns, for a total over three hundred yards—career highs for completions and yardage. With his rating over one hundred, Giants fans were becoming believers in Manning!

The following week, in a game against the Seahawks, Manning again threw three touchdown passes but the team played poorly in the loss. At one point they were behind by thirty-nine points as the offense committed four turnovers and the defense gave up five touchdown passes! Despite free agent signings and the draft, the defense was giving up thirty points a game and its pass defense was ranked near last in the league. In a comment reminiscent of that of Tiki Barber after the playoff lost to Carolina, Shockey said: "We got outplayed and outcoached. Write that down." The defensive leader Antonio Pierce added: "Right now we're a horrible team."[21]

So which team were the Giants—the one that could look so dominant or the one that could look so feeble? The Giants went on to win their next five games, arriving at midseason with a 6–2 record, suggesting that the former might be the case. The defense was showing signs of improvement and the offense was performing well with Manning passing to Burress and Shockey, and Barber consistently gaining over one hundred yards a game. Despite his outstanding performances, during this period Barber announced that this would be his last season. Although the leading rusher in the NFL at the time, at the age of thirty-one Barber felt that his body increasingly needed time to recover from games and that it was time to turn to another job, television, that was less punishing in that regard.

The first game of the second half of the season brought the Giants back to reality as they lost to the Bears, with the defense reverting to its earlier level and Manning playing poorly against the strong Bear defense. Two plays in particular sealed the fate of the Giants. In one, a short field goal attempt was returned over one hundred yards for a touchdown as some Giants players walked toward the sideline, unaware of the return. In the other, the Giants allowed a first down on a third-down play in which the Bears needed over twenty yards for a first down.

By now injuries were beginning to mount and the Giants followed the loss to the Bears with three more losses, bringing their record to an even 6–6. In a disastrous loss to the Titans, the Giants were leading by twenty-one points going into the fourth quarter and yet ended up losing the game. In one critical play the rookie defensive end Kiwanuka, playing well while pressed into service with an injury to Strahan, had the Titans quarterback in his grasp for a sure sack. Afraid of being called for a penalty, he released him too soon, thus freeing him to complete a long pass. Asked whether he had previously been in a game like this, one Giants player commented: "Have I been in a game like this? Only in a nightmare, maybe."[22]

Three-quarters of the way through the season, the Giants seemed to be reeling. After a game against the Jaguars in which he gained just twenty-seven yards, Barber blasted the coaching staff. Coughlin, disturbed by Barber's comment, noted that Barber's performance had increased tremendously under Coughlin's stewardship. Manning, who seemed to have arrived, was having his troubles. "Where did he go?" was a question being asked by many as his completion percentages and passer ratings headed downward. What was particularly troubling in this regard was that at the same time that Manning was having his troubles, Phil Rivers, originally picked by the Giants and then traded at a high cost for Manning, was performing well, showing poise and demonstrating leadership as he led the Chargers to a winning record.

The Giants split their remaining two games, ending the season with an 8–8 record. In the next-to-last game of the season, the final home game for Barber, an angry crowd walked out early as the Giants were humbled by the Saints. The Saints were led by their new head coach, Sean Payton, like John Fox of the Panthers a former assistant coach on the staff of the Giants. The Giants now had lost seven of eight games and fans were calling for Coughlin to be fired. With a win in their final game of the season, the Giants earned a playoff berth against the Eagles. In this, his last regular season game as a

Giant, Barber rushed for a franchise record 234 yards and scored three touchdowns.

Despite the playoff achievement, the players were confused by their losses, given what they felt was a team loaded with talent. While continuing to play hard, they were not playing smart and appeared to be tiring of Coughlin's tough disciplinary approach. On the one hand, there was the view of Tiki Barber. Although publicly Barber emphasized the physical toll taken on his body as the cause of his retirement, in his book he said that "if Tom Coughlin had not remained as head coach of the Giants, I might still be in a Giants uniform.... He [Coughlin] robbed me of what had been one of the most important things I had in my life, which was the joy I felt playing football. I had lost that. He had taken it away.... Under his coaching I lost my passion for the game."[23] On the other hand, Michael Strahan's view of Coughlin underwent a change. Whereas at the beginning his view was negative—"I began to question whether I could play even one year under this man.... I didn't want to play for him. I wanted nothing to do with the man"—it later changed toward the positive. He continued to feel that Coughlin missed a human element but "liked Tom enough that I truly did not want him fired at the end of '06."[24] Others, within and outside the organization, continued to have their reservations.[25] In the meantime, during the 2006 season penalties were up and injuries weren't down. Either the Giants were underachievers or they were just mediocre. A playoff game loss to the Eagles proved inconclusive in this regard.

Tiki Barber

A children's story book, *The Little Engine That Could*, tells the story of a little engine that pulls enormous loads because it thinks it can. For the Giants, Tiki Barber was the little engine that could, and did!

Barber was drafted out of the University of Virginia in the second round (thirty-sixth pick overall) of the 1997 draft. The same year his twin, Ronde, was drafted as a defensive back by the Tampa Bay Buccaneers. At 5'10" and two hundred pounds, Barber was considered small for a full-time running back and was projected as a third-down back and kick or punt returner. In his rookie season he earned the starting running back position in preseason and performed well in his first five games until he was sidelined by a posterior cruciate ligament tear of his right knee. The following two years, 1998 and 1999, he was primarily used as a third-down back. The following year, 2000, he started in most of the games and had more than two thousand all-purpose yards, breaking the team record held by Dave Meggett. He was active in rushing, punt returns, and receptions, scoring a team-high nine touchdowns.

The following three years, under head coach Jim Fassel, Barber continued as the starting running back and led the team in rushing, gaining over a thousand yards in 2002 and 2003. During these three years he averaged seventy receptions and over five hundred receiving yards. He credited then offensive coordinator Sean Payton with much of his development: "Sean was a great influence on my career. He finds ways to utilize his guys' strengths. He did that with me and revolutionized my existence as a football player and turned me into who I am now, or at least started me down the path into who I am now."[26] Barber was the workhorse of the offense, but he had one problem—fumbles! Not known during college or early in his NFL career as a fumbler, Barber had developed a tendency toward fumbling. Fassel had no choice but to continue playing Barber, who by 2003 had become the Giants' career leader in all-purpose yards and receptions, but clearly the fumbles were hindering the ability of the offense to score points.

When Coughlin took over as head coach in 2004, he paid particular attention to the way Barber was carrying the ball and noticed that he often held it too far from his body. Barber would walk and run holding the football tight to his body. This adjustment worked and his fumbling difficulties no longer were the problem they had been. With the addition of a young quarterback, Eli Manning, his role as the workhorse and backbone of the offense became even greater.

It is not easy to describe Barber's greatness as a runner. He was not a power runner, nor one with blazing speed. He did not dance around or fake out defenders. Rather, he had the ability to find the opening, follow blockers, and head upfield. This, together with his ability to come out of the backfield to make key receptions, made him a darling of the fans. "Go Tiki, Go Tiki" was a familiar chant. What was characteristic of him, beyond his talent for running, was his cheerfulness. After almost every tackle he would get up smiling, frequently pat the opposing player on the back, occasionally help the opposing player get up. He never hot-dogged it, showboated, or trash-talked an opposing player. It was hard not to like him, impossible not to respect him as a runner and a person.

Many, perhaps most, consider Tiki Barber to have been the best running back in Giants history. Let the records speak for him:

1. Giants record for career rushing yards, over three thousand yards more than his runner-up, Rodney Hampton.
2. Giants record for single-game rushing yards—234 against Washington in his last regular season game as a Giant.

3. Giants records for career and single-season rushing attempts.
4. Giants record for average per carry (4.7). Only two Hall of Famers, Jim Brown and Barry Sanders, had a higher average per carry.
5. Giants record for the longest run—a ninety-five yard touchdown run.
6. Giants record for number one-hundred yard rushing games (38).
7. Giants record for rushing touchdowns (55), despite often being replaced on short-yardage situations near the goal line.
8. Giants record for career total yards (rushing, receiving, returns), over seven thousand yards ahead of Frank Gifford, second among Giants.
9. Giants single-season record total yardage record, set in 2005, the second-highest total in NFL history.
10. Giants all-time leading receiver with 586 receptions.
11. Giants record for receptions in a game—thirteen.
12. Over ten thousand rushing yards and over five thousand receiving yards, only the third player in NFL history to mark this achievement, the other two being Marcus Allen and Marshall Falk.

The 2007 Season: It All Comes Together

With the disappointing performance over the last half of the 2006 season, changes definitely were in order. Now there was speculation about whether Coughlin, approaching the last season of his contract, would be fired. With the retirement of Accorsi, a new general manager would be hired. Would that person make the decision in regard to Coughlin or would the decision be made independent of that appointment? The latter seemed unlikely since ordinarily part of a GM's responsibility is the selection of the head coach. Yet, shortly after the playoff loss to the Eagles, and prior to the selection of a GM, co-owners John Mara and Jonathan Tisch announced that Coughlin would be given a one-year extension on his contract and remain as head coach of the Giants. Evidently part of the decision was an agreement between Coughlin and the owners that changes in the coaching staff were necessary. The offensive coordinator, John Hufnagel, had already been demoted near the end of the season. Now he was formally replaced by the team's quarterbacks coach, Kevin Gilbride. Gilbride had called plays during the last game of the season and the playoff game against the Eagles, games in which the team scored a total of fifty-seven points. The new quarterbacks coach was Chris Palmer, who previously had worked with Coughlin on the Jaguars staff and had a record of tutoring successful NFL quarterbacks. Also gone was the defensive coordinator, Tim Lewis, replaced by Steve Spagnuolo, previously the linebackers coach of the rival Eagles. Spagnuolo had spent eight years under the tutelage of the esteemed Eagles defensive coordinator Jim Johnson. The Eagles defense was known for attacking and blitzing. Finally, with the retirement of the special teams coordinator, replaced by his assistant Tom Quinn, there was a complete change in the major coordinator coaching positions. Strangely enough, Coughlin remained while the offensive and defensive coordinators he selected were gone.

Within a week of the announcement that Coughlin would be retained, the Giants announced the appointment of Jerry Reese as senior vice president and general manager. Reese had been with the Giants since 1994, serving most recently as director of player personnel. The third African-American in NFL history to be appointed general manager, Reese originally was appointed by George Young and later worked closely with Accorsi. In appointing Reese, the Giants in this case chose continuity over change. Reese and Coughlin already had a working relationship and were said to be of one mind concerning directions needed to be taken to improve the team. Central in this regard was improvement in the play of Manning: "Eli's progress right now is not where we want him to be. Obviously, it's not where we want it to be. We want him to be a Pro Bowl guy that can lead us into the Super Bowl. That's our goal and that's what we're going to do with Eli."[27]

Given the many weaknesses demonstrated during the late-season collapse of the Giants, Reese got off to what seemed to be a slow start in the free agency market, the only signing of some import being that of a linebacker. The problem at left tackle, in some ways heightened by the release of Pettigout, apparently was to be solved by David Diehl, who had moved over to tackle from guard when Pettigout was injured. The need at linebacker, in addition to the free agent signing, was to be filled by the move of Kiwanuka from defensive end to linebacker. In the draft, the first for which Reese was fully responsible, the Giants were looking to fill needs at left tackle, linebacker, and cornerback. In the first round, highly rated players were available at all three positions. The Giants chose to go with Aaron Ross, a cornerback from Texas. The Giants reportedly had tried to trade up to get one of two cornerbacks rated higher than Ross but, feeling the price to be too high, in the end settled for the one they'd ranked third. Highly rated linebackers and a highly rated left tackle were available at the time they made the cornerback selection.

In the next two rounds they selected a wide receiver and defensive tackle, leaving the positions of offensive tackle and linebacker to be covered in later rounds or by members of the current roster. In all, the free agent signings and draft selections left many fans and experts wondering. One expert ranked the Giants near last in quality of upgrading as a result of the free agency and draft, in particular noting that they had failed to address "glaring needs" on the offensive line.[28] With cap room to spare, perhaps the Giants had in mind signing players to be released by other teams during the preseason. If not, they were taking a big gamble on the coaching staff and players already on the roster.

Some Big Questions

As the Giants entered the 2007 season, a number of questions were prominent, some old and some new. First, once more there was the question of Coughlin's relationship with the players. Aside from changes he made in coordinators for offense and defense, there was the question of changes he might make in how he related to players. As noted, in his 2007 book, Tiki Barber made it clear that much of his retirement had to do with Coughlin, that Coughlin had taken away his passion for the game.[29] But as also noted, Strahan, in his book, indicated that although he initially wanted nothing to do with Coughlin, at the end he liked Coughlin enough that he wanted to end his career playing for him.[30] From the fans' standpoint, many were tired of seeing his tirades on the sidelines, seeming to always criticize and never encourage. For his part, Coughlin seemed to recognize that he needed to be less of a rule-governed tyrant and more of a motivator. So the question was whether Coughlin could identify the necessary changes and make them in a way that would make sense to the players.

Another old question, the big one, was whether Manning could become the franchise quarterback he was expected to be. Comparisons with Rivers and Roethlisberger remained, with Manning typically faring poorly in relation to them. With three years under his belt, and with flashes of excellence, it was time for Manning to show whether he was worth what the Giants had given to get him.

The first new question involved the defense. First, how would the Giants fare under their new defensive coordinator, Steve Spagnuolo? Could Spagnuolo bring to the Giants the same strong, aggressive defense characteristic of the Eagles? To complicate his situation, Strahan held out during preseason and indicated that he was considering retirement. Finally deciding to return for the season, having missed preseason, would Strahan be in condition to play? About to turn thirty-six and having suffered injuries the past two seasons, was he well past his prime and no longer able to contribute as he had in the past? And then there was the question of whether Kiwanuka could make the transition to linebacker after showing so much promise as a defensive end. Questions also remained about the defensive backfield. Could the rookie Aaron Ross, their first-round pick in the draft, make an immediate contribution at cornerback?

The second new question, or set of questions, involved the offense. How would the Giants make up for the loss of Barber? Brandon Jacobs showed signs of being a capable runner, but not one capable of making the diverse contributions for which Barber was known. And, having lost Pettigout to free agency, would David Diehl be able to make the transition from guard to the key position of left tackle? If not, Manning was in for a long season regardless of how much progress he had made.

Finally, the Giants kept all eight players taken in the draft, half on offense and half on defense. Since rookies typically play an important role in terms of depth and special teams, would the new general manager's picks be strong enough to carry their weight in these critical areas? The Giants were not given high marks by outside observers for their free agent and draft additions. If these additions did not strengthen the team, and answers to the other questions were less than spectacular, the Giants and their fans were in for a long 2007 season. Indeed, on the Fox Sports show prior to the opening game against the Cowboys, commentators Terry Bradshaw, Howie Long, and Jimmy Johnson all predicted that the Giants would be worse than the previous year, that Manning would be mediocre, and that Coughlin would be gone by the end of the year.

The Season Unfolds

The first two games of the season seemed to confirm what had been predicted, at least as far as the team was concerned. In the first game, the defense was a sieve, giving up forty-five points. Particularly troublesome were the struggles of Kiwanuka, in his new job as linebacker, in pass coverage. Manning played a good game, throwing four touchdown passes, three to Plaxico Burress. In all, the offense scored thirty-five points against a strong Cowboys defense. However, Manning was hurt on a two-point conversion attempt necessitated by an earlier botched point-after-touchdown try.

In the second game, a 35–13 loss to Green Bay, the defense again was porous. By the end of the first two games it had given up eighty points, allowed seven touchdowns, and allowed a completion percentage closing in on seventy percent. No surprise, it was ranked near the bottom of the league. Although Manning played reasonably well, the team made the kinds of errors that Coughlin was so desperate to correct—a penalty against Shockey for spiking the ball after a touchdown, a penalty against Toomer for taunting, and a fumble by the rookie Ahmad Bradshaw on a kickoff return.

To the surprise of most, and the relief and delight of Giants fans, the team went on to win its next six games. Although four of these victories were against weak teams (Jets, Falcons, 49ers, Dolphins), two were against division rivals (Redskins, Eagles). A critical point seemed to occur in a come-from-behind victory in the third game, against the Redskins, in which the defense made a successful goal-line stand with less than a minute left in the game and the Redskins needing a touchdown and point-after-touchdown to tie the score. During this stretch Manning showed signs of progress but also continued inconsistency. At times he showed greater command of the game and authority at the line of scrimmage, as well as a particular connection with Burress. However, at other times he would be off-target and give up the ball on an interception or a fumble. The defense seemed to be coming on, particularly in terms of blitzes and quarterback sacks, as it became more comfortable with Spagnuolo's system. The field-goal kicking of Tynes continued to be a problem, as were errors such as personal fouls and too many men in the huddle.

The Giants ended the first half of the season with a 6–2 record, better than might have been expected, particularly given their play during the first two games. The question was whether they would continue on an upswing in the second half or fade as had been the case in prior years. A bye week presumably would allow them to heal some injuries and focus on what needed to be corrected to produce greater consistency. Also worthy of note in the first half was the first regular season game in a foreign country, the Giants-Dolphins game at Wembley Stadium in England, and Amani Toomer's breaking of previous Giants records for receptions and touchdown receptions.

Unfortunately, the bye week did not seem to accomplish what had been hoped for, and the Giants had a 4–4 record for the second half. In the first game of the second half the Giants again faced the Cowboys. The result was not much different: Cowboys 31, Giants 20. Both the offense and defense were inconsistent and there seemed little doubt that the Cowboys were the better team. Long gains by Giants players were wiped out by penalties, seven in the second half alone, and Manning was sacked five times. In contrast, Romo, the Cowboys' quarterback, again threw four touchdown passes and never was sacked.

In the next game, the Giants eked out a nail-biter victory against the Lions. However, there was a cost to the game—a broken fibula on Kiwanuka, putting him out for the season, and a hamstring injury to Jacobs. Although the Giants split their next two games, they did not look good. In fact, in the first game, against Minnesota, they looked ugly, ugly, ugly! The offense was described by the announcers as "inept" as Manning was intercepted four times by a poor pass defense, there was poor communication between him and the receivers, and there were penalties such as illegal formation and false start. Altogether, the offense gave up more points than it scored: 21 versus 17! In the other game, a victory against the Bears, Manning was intercepted twice, once in the end zone, and fumbled the ball deep in Bears territory. As Yogi Berra would say, it was once more beginning to look like déjà vu all over again.

In the remaining four games there was much of the same but perhaps near the end a sign of difference. In an ugly victory against the Eagles, in which an Eagles try for a field goal to tie the score hit the upright, Manning played well but Jacobs fumbled twice deep in Eagles territory and the Giants failed to score a touchdown when they had the ball first and goal at the two. In contrast, in a later win Manning played poorly, throwing two interceptions and losing two fumbles, one at the opposition's eleven, while Jacobs and Bradshaw each gained over a hundred yards rushing. Was it possible for the passing game and running game to get it together at the same time? Was it possible for both offense and defense to play well in the same game? With a 9–4 record, and a chance to secure a wild-card berth, against a Redskins team that had lost most of its recent games and was using a quarterback who had not started in ten years, the Giants went down to defeat. Not only did they lose the game, but they lost the services of Shockey for the rest of the season due to a broken fibula. As John Madden commented: "They might make it into the playoffs but they are not a playoff team."[31]

As the Giants entered the final game of the season against the undefeated Patriots, they had a difficult decision to make—should they play their regulars? The Patriots could be expected to play hard with an undefeated season at stake. The Giants already were in the playoffs, in that sense they had little to gain with a victory and a lot to lose with a bad loss or injuries. Many felt it made sense to rest the regulars but Coughlin decided to play them and go for a win. In a valiant effort, the Giants lost by a score of 38–35, after at one point leading by more than a touchdown. Manning had perhaps the best game of his career—22 of 32 for 251 yards and four touchdowns, and a passer rating of 118.6! Coughlin appeared to have made the correct decision as, despite Madden's comment, the Giants indeed looked like a playoff team. The good news was that the game might give the Giants momentum entering the playoffs. The bad news was that three valuable players—center O'Hara, cornerback Madison, and linebacker Mitchell—suffered injuries that probably would keep them out of the coming playoff game against the Buccaneers.

The March to Super Bowl XLII

The Giants made it to the playoffs but they hardly were favorites to progress very far. Their won-loss record in their last six games was three and three, and most observers would agree with Madden's saying that they were "not a playoff team." Their last game against the Patriots was a valiant effort but it still was a loss, and three starters had to leave the game. Manning had a good game but he had been inconsistent all season, as also was true for the Giants team as a whole. In the meantime, their first playoff game was to be against the Tampa Bay Buccaneers, ranked second in the NFL in overall defense and first in pass defense. Although not a powerhouse offense, the Bucs were led by the mobile Jeff Garcia, who had given the Giants fits in his previous employment with the 49ers and Eagles.

NFC Wildcard Game, Giants vs. Buccaneers, January 6, 2008, at Tampa Bay: The game against the Bucs started poorly for the Giants, with the offense totaling a minus three yards in the first quarter while the Bucs scored on their opening drive. The game looked like it could be an ugly one for the Giants. Now that they were playing without the three starters who were hurt in the Patriots game, the decision to play that game with the regulars began to look questionable. However, the Giants gained the momentum after the first quarter and went on to win by a score of 24–14. After the opening drive for a touchdown the defense held the Bucs scoreless until near the end of the game. The substitutes played well, in particular Corey Webster in place of Sam Madison. A second-round draft choice in 2005, until then Webster had been a disappointment and benched during the 2007 season. On offense, Manning had his second excellent game. Was this a sign for the future or the laying of the groundwork for another disappointment? In any case, it was on to Dallas to meet the conference champions, a team who already had beaten them twice this season.

NFC Divisional Playoff Game, Giants vs. Cowboys, January 13, 2008, at Dallas. In many ways the Giants and the Cowboys were contrasting teams. The Cowboys were led by Tony Romo, an undrafted player who had made All-Pro while the Giants were led by Manning, the first player selected in the draft who had yet to prove himself to be among the elite quarterbacks in the league. Romo was a fun-loving guy who dated stars and had just spent part of his time off with one of these stars in the Cabo San Lucas area of Mexico. In contrast, Manning seemed to always have the same facial expression and had just become engaged to, of course, a non-celebrity. Having won their division and a place in the playoffs before the last game of the season, the Cowboys had chosen to rest their starters during the final game and to give the players time off during the bye week they had while the

Giants were playing the Bucs. The Cowboys were rested; would they be sharp? The Giants had gained some momentum from their play in the last two games; would they be able to continue it against the strong Cowboys? The Cowboys had twelve All-Pros, the Giants one (Osie Umenyiora). In the words of Giants defensive leader Antonio Pierce, it was the "All-Pros" against the "All-Joes." Many did not give the Giants a chance. Terry Bradshaw, Howie Long, and Jimmy Johnson on the Fox Sports pre-game show all predicted a win for the Cowboys.

Near the end of the first half the Cowboys led the Giants by a score of 14–7, with their big offensive line able to hold the Giants' pass rush in check and their defense playing strong against the Giants' offense. Then, with little time left in the half, Manning led the Giants on a seven-play, seventy-one-yard touchdown drive in less than a minute. Giants fans could feel good about a tied score at the end of the half and could look forward with hope to the second half.

The hope of the fans immediately was dashed at the start of the second half—the Giants went three-and-out on their possession, and then the Cowboys scored on their first possession. It looked like the Cowboys had regained their momentum. But the Giants' defense stiffened, holding the Cowboys to three points in the second half, while the Giants' offense was able to score on Manning's second touchdown pass to Toomer: final score, Giants 21, Cowboys 17.

The Giants' defense had found its mojo as it harassed Romo. The Cowboys' line coach and assistant head coach could be seen screaming at his line to knock the Giants back from the line of scrimmage. Particularly noteworthy on the defense was the play of the defensive backfield. With one starting cornerback, Madison, out for the game, and the other starting cornerback, Ross, hurt during the game, the Giants had to play the reserve cornerback Webster and an unknown player just signed off the practice squad! On offense, Manning had another good game, throwing for two touchdowns, showing good command of the game, and having neither an interception nor a fumble. With three good games in a row, Giants fans were beginning to believe that Accorsi might have made the correct decision.[32] Accorsi remained confident in Manning, believing it was not a question of whether but only a question of when. With the win it was on to Green Bay for the conference championship and the right to play in the Super Bowl.

NFC Championship Game, Giants vs. Packers, January 20, 2008, at Green Bay. Once more the Giants were coming in as underdogs, in this case to the Green Bay Packers. Picking the Packers to win, Jimmy Johnson described them as strong on offense, strong on defense, and strong on special teams. Both the Giants and the Packers were among the youngest teams in the

NFL, except that the Packers were led by the thirty-eight-year-old Brett Favre while the Giants were led by the relative novice Manning. During the year Favre had broken the career touchdown record set by Dan Marino and the career victory record for quarterbacks set by John Elway. Many considered him among the greatest quarterbacks of all time, perhaps the greatest. Along with Elway, he was known for his ability to lead teams to come-from-behind victories. In fact, in defeating the Seahawks the previous week, he had given his team the confidence to win after being down by two touchdowns. In contrast, Manning was just beginning to establish himself as a quality quarterback after his third straight excellent game. Another sidelight to the game was the fact that both starting running backs had been overshadowed by other running backs while in college and virtually overlooked in the draft.[33]

Along with the drama of a championship game with the winner to play the Patriots in the Super Bowl, there was the drama of the weather. With temperatures below zero, in the negative twenties when the wind-chill factor was considered, this was Ice Bowl II, following Ice Bowl I, a 1967 game played in even colder weather at Lambeau Field. Favre chose to play without gloves, Manning to play with a glove on his left hand. During the week of preparation, note had been made that Manning played better in warm weather. This idea would certainly be tested in this game. Amazingly enough, many players chose to play without long sleeves. The football was described as hard and slick, perhaps difficult to throw, perhaps difficult to catch, certainly difficult to kick. In a pre-game demonstration of just how cold it was, Jimmy Johnson poured water into a glass and it was frozen within minutes. It was cold!

On their initial possession of the first quarter, Manning led the Giants on a fourteen-play, seventy-one-yard drive that ended with a Tynes twenty-nine yard field goal: Giants 3, Packers 0. Early in the second quarter Manning led the Giants to another score, a thirty-seven-yard field goal by Tynes: Giants 6, Packers 0. Both drives involved completed passes to Burress, who seemed to be having his way with the Packers' cornerback. Shortly after the second Giants field goal, the Packers came back with a dramatic touchdown. The Packers' kickoff receiver had fumbled the Giants' kickoff, recovering the ball on the Packers' ten-yard line. Then, on first and ten with his feet almost in his own end zone, Favre found his receiver, Donald Driver, wide open at the thirty. He ran untouched for the remaining seventy yards for a ninety-yard Packers touchdown and the lead: Packers 7, Giants 6. What had happened on the play was that Webster, who had played so well the previous week, tried to jam the Packers' receiver at the line. Instead, Driver tossed Webster aside. By the time Webster had recovered, Driver was open and free to run the rest of the way. Suddenly the lead had changed for the first time in the game.

Near the end of the second quarter the Packers scored on a field goal: Packers 10, Giants 6. That drive was aided by an illegal interference call against the Giants when the Packers seemingly had been stopped with a third and ten. Taking the kickoff with limited time left in the half, the Giants were driving and seemed to be about to score a touchdown when Burress, while falling to the ground, dropped a Manning pass within five yards of the goal line. Giants fans were hoping for a call of a completed pass with the ground causing the fumble, but this was not to be. At the end of the half the score remained Packers 10 and the Giants 6.

The Giants opened the third-quarter scoring with a one-yard touchdown run by Jacobs: Giants 13, Packers 10. The lead had changed for the second time. Actually, the touchdown came after two almost heartbreaking plays by the Giants. In the first, Manning almost was intercepted. In the second, on the play just before his touchdown run, Jacobs fumbled the ball near the goal line but fortunately it was recovered by the Giants. On the other hand, the Giants' drive was aided by a Packers illegal contact penalty and a roughing the passer penalty. A tense, hard-fought game was beginning to be demoralizing for fans of both teams as solid play was occasionally brought down by penalties or missed catches.

Now it was the Packers' turn. Still in the third quarter, the Giants' kickoff was returned to their own thirty-nine yard line, putting the Packers in excellent field position. After a few plays, the Giants seemingly were going to be able to prevent a touchdown score when Madison, the old pro cornerback returning to play after being kept out of two games with an abdominal strain, was called for an unnecessary roughness penalty. The ball now was on the Giants' twelve-yard line, following which Favre threw to this tight end for a touchdown: Packers 17, Giants 13. The lead had changed for a third time.

The Giants' came right back. Following a good kickoff return by Hixon, the Giants drove for fifty-seven yards in seven plays, capped off by a four-yard run by Bradshaw: Giants 20, Packers 17. The lead had changed for the fourth time. Each of the Giants' running backs, Jacobs and Bradshaw, the new thunder and lightning, had scored a touchdown. With this touchdown the Giants ended the third quarter with the lead. The Giants might yet make it to the Super Bowl, something that had seemed inconceivable after their loss to the Packers in the second game of the season.

But early in the fourth quarter the Packers scored a field goal to tie the score: Giants 20, Packers 20. Here too there was a heartbreaking play for Giants fans. With the Packers driving toward the end zone, the Giants' cornerback R.W. McQuarters intercepted a Favre pass. But then McQuarters fumbled the ball into the hands of a Packers lineman at the Giants' nineteen. With limited time left, the interception at first looked like it had brought the Giants to victory. Instead, the fumble had allowed the Packers to come back to tie the game.

With the score tied and limited time left, the game now was about to come down to a field goal try by Tynes. Actually, the Giants previously had two opportunities to "ice" the game. In the first, Bradshaw had a nifty fifty-two-yard touchdown run, only to have it called back on a holding penalty on Snee, Coughlin's son-in-law, no less. In the second, Tynes missed a forty-three-yard field goal with under seven minutes to play. Returning to the sideline, Tynes received the scorn of Coughlin for all watching the game on television to see. Now, with four seconds left, Tynes had the opportunity to redeem himself with what would be a game-winning thirty-six yard field goal. It was not to be. The snap was high, Feagles did a good job in bringing it down and placing it down, but the timing was slightly off and Tynes kicked it far to the left. Overtime!

The captains went out for the coin toss for overtime. The Giants called tails, it was heads. The Packers chose to receive, the Giants to have the wind at their backs. Giants fans could see it coming—Favre pulling out another one of his game-ending scores. But the heartbreak now was for the Packers players and fans. On the second play of overtime, Favre was intercepted by Webster, who brought the ball back to the Packers' thirty-four. Webster had redeemed himself for the earlier blown coverage that had led to a Packers touchdown. A frustrated and dejected Favre left the field knowing that he might have just lost the game for the Packers. What he did not know at the time was that the interception would be the last pass as a Packer.

With the interception, the Giants had the ball but their drive stalled on the twenty-nine yard line of the Packers. With third and five, what were the Giants to do—go for the first down or go for the field goal with a kicker who already had missed two from less than the distance required? Before Coughlin had a chance, Tynes raced out onto the field, eager to redeem himself. Seeing the confidence and intent in the kicker's eyes, Coughlin sent Feagles, the holder, out there. The snap was good, the hold was good, the kick was good: Giants 23, Packers 20, in overtime!

The previous week, Favre had left the Lambeau playing field joyful, having a snowball fight with his teammates. This week he left dispirited, not only unable to once more bring his team to victory but in this case playing a role in its defeat. On the other side of the ball, in what always is a dramatic contrast, the Giants' players were joyful. Webster and Tynes had redeemed themselves. Burress, playing injured for much of the season, had eleven catches for 154 yards. Manning ended the game throwing for 254 yards on twenty-one completions of forty attempts. He had played his fourth excellent game in a row, passing well, holding onto the ball, and generally taking command of the offense. The defense, a sieve during the first two games, once more had played strong, holding the Packers to a field goal in the final quarter and then reeling in the interception that led to the winning field goal. Coughlin, whose job had been in question at the end of the last season and at times during the current season, hugged his players and was hugged by them. At least for the time being, his job was secure. And Strahan, the old warrior who had debated whether to return for the season, was joyful as he hung around on the field to shake hands with joyful Giants fans. Later he was to remind his teammates that what they had achieved was special but that they had to focus on the game ahead. The Giants were going to the Super Bowl!

Super Bowl XLII, Giants vs. Patriots, February 3, 2008, at Glendale, Arizona: In Arizona, the climate was vastly different from that in Green Bay. With the roof of the stadium closed, weather would not be a factor in any case. The Patriots had many All-Pros, including three on their offensive line, the Giants one. The high-powered Patriots offense was led by the quarterback Brady and receiver Moss, the combination having set records for touchdown passes and receptions. The Patriots, having beaten the Giants at the end of the regular season, were going for a perfect nineteen-game season. The Giants, who at mid-season hardly seemed like Super Bowl contenders, were there to prove that their playoff victories were not flukes and to capture the gold. The Giants came in as two-touchdown underdogs. On the pre-game Fox Sports show, all three analysts picked the Patriots to win. Only the comedian picked the Giants. Even many Giants fans were placing bets on the Patriots, despite the heresy involved.

The opening drive was a promising one for the Giants as they held onto the ball for nearly ten minutes. Manning completed a number of third-down passes and Tynes made a field goal: Giants 3, Patriots 0. Although disappointed that they could not get a touchdown in the red zone, or what Coughlin called the green zone, the Giants still could feel good about the way their offense had functioned. However, the good feeling did not last for long as the Patriots took the kickoff, returned it to their own forty-three, and then marched down the field for a touchdown: Patriots 7, Giants 3.

The Giants again were driving deep into Packers territory when a Manning pass to the rookie receiver Smith was bobbled and intercepted by the Patriots. What had happened too often early in the season seemed about to bite the Giants again here in the Super Bowl. Later in the half the Giants had another scare as Bradshaw fumbled a handoff, but fortunately they recovered. Then, later in the half, the ball was knocked from the hands of Manning. The Giants' Smith recovered the ball after Bradshaw had illegally batted the ball for a penalty. The Giants were unable to move further but were lucky not to have lost the ball on each occasion. In the meantime, the Giants defense was strong against the vaunted Patriots offense. With less than two minutes left in the first half, at a time when the Patriots typically mounted a strong drive and it was critical for the Giants defense to hold, the Giants' Tuck knocked the ball from the hands of Brady. The Giants recovered the ball. The defense had held. The score at the half: Patriots 7, Giants 3. Although the Giants had missed opportunities in the red zone, the defense had played well. The Giants were in contention; they had not been blown out as some had anticipated.

In the third quarter the Giants made another error, twelve men on the field, leading to a Patriots first down. Fortunately the defense, like Giants defenses of old, held. Neither team scored as the score at the end of the quarter remained Patriots 7, Giants 3.

Early in the fourth quarter the Giants mounted a touchdown drive led first by a forty-five-yard completion from Manning to the rookie tight end Kevin Boss, playing in place of the injured Shockey, and later a five-yard touchdown pass to David Tyree, the reserve wide receiver and special teams specialist. Tyree had caught only four passes for thirty-five yards during the regular season. Clearly this was something unanticipated by the Patriots: Giants 10, Patriots 7.

About midway through the final quarter Manning almost was sacked but managed a pass to Burress. Burress, playing on a bad ankle and a bad knee, was unable to make the catch and the Giants had to punt. Later, with under three minutes left in the game, the Patriots marched down the field, finishing off their drive with a third-and-goal touchdown pass from Brady to Moss. Strangely, on the play Webster had been left alone to cover Moss in single coverage. Clearly Webster was no match for him. Patriots 14, Giants 10.

Were the Patriots about to pull off a late-game win as they had so often in the past? Certainly Moss thought so as he celebrated his touchdown reception. With less than three minutes in the game, the Giants took the kickoff but were only able to return it to their seventeen—a long way to go but time enough to do it. The Giants moved to their own forty-three yard line when they were faced with a third and seven. Manning looked to pass, had difficulty finding a receiver, and then lofted a pass in the direction of Toomer. The ball seemed to hang in the air as Toomer neared the sideline with a defender near him. Somehow Toomer was able to catch the ball while keeping his feet in bounds. But he was short of a first down by a yard! A field goal was unlikely to do the Giants any good—they needed a touchdown. But first they needed a first down, which Jacobs was able to obtain on a short gain into the Patriots' line.

Could Manning now come through with a final winning drive? Accorsi, the now retired general manager who selected Manning and continued to believe in him, sat nervously at the game: "If he's going to be what we thought he was going to be, he does it now."[34] Could the Giants achieve the unimaginable? Could Manning validate the faith in him shown by Accorsi and others?

On two plays it seemed as if this was not to be. On one, Manning almost lost a fumble and on another he was almost intercepted. Then, with just over a minute left to play, Manning seemingly was about to be sacked but miraculously was able to escape and loft a pass in the direction of Tyree. Tyree leaped for the ball with the Patriots' defender on him. Somehow Tyree was able to catch the ball, holding it against his helmet while falling to the ground. It was amazing that Manning was able to make the throw, and now it was amazing that Tyree was able to make the catch, described as one of the greatest catches in Super Bowl history. The Giants now were on the Patriots' twenty-four yard line, with just under a minute left to play, still needing a touchdown. After two more plays the Giants approached the line with a third and eleven and forty-five seconds left to play. Manning completed a pass to the rookie Smith, who fell out of bounds just past the first-down marker. Perhaps Smith had redeemed himself for the earlier bobbled pass that led to the interception. With thirty-nine seconds left, the ball on the New England thirteen, Manning lofted a pass to Burress in the end zone. Burress faked a turn toward the center of the end zone and then cut to the corner, eluding the Patriots' defender, the same defender who previously had made the interception. Now wide open, Burress made the easy catch: Giants 17, Patriots 14!

The Giants kicked off to the Patriots, who had thirty-five seconds and three time outs left to get to approximately the Giants' thirty-two yard line and attempt a game-tying field goal. Although the Giants and their fans were ecstatic, the game was not yet over. An incomplete pass from Brady was followed by a sack of Brady, the fifth of the game for the Giants. The Patriots called a time out with nineteen seconds left. Approaching the ball with a third and twenty from their own sixteen yard line, Brady lofted a long pass downfield to Moss—incomplete. With one chance left, Brady again lofted a long pass that fell incomplete. The Giants had done it—they had pulled off what was described as one of the biggest upsets in Super Bowl history: Giants 17, Patriots 14!

To cap it all off, Manning was named the MVP of the game. In all, he had completed nineteen of thirty-four attempts for 255 yards and two touchdowns, both in the fourth quarter. Accorsi's pick looked to be a good one. The faith he, the players, the coaches, and the management had in Manning appeared to be well served. For two successive years a Manning was the MVP of the Super Bowl, Peyton the previous year and Eli this year.

The Questions Answered

The questions raised at the beginning of the year could now be answered. In terms of Coughlin's relationship with the players, clearly there was a difference. Coughlin made an effort to be more relaxed with the players while still emphasizing the discipline and commitment that were basic to him. He relied more on the input of players than had been true in the past and retained the support of the veteran Strahan. In all, he had led the team to victory after season-beginning losses that appeared to doom the team. His job was secure.

In terms of defense, the new defensive coordinator Spagnuolo had done an incredible job. After the first two games in which the defense looked horrible, the defense came on to be one of the strong points of the Giants team. To cap it all off they held the Patriots to two touchdowns, but forty-five net yards rushing, and sacked Brady five times for a total loss of thirty-seven yards. A vital part of that defense was Strahan, who had indeed returned for the season and was able to perform at a high level.

In terms of offense, Diehl was able to make the transaction to left tackle, as the offensive line generally did an excellent job on the run and in pass protection. None of them made All-Pro but as a group they proved themselves to be a cohesive, effective unit. There was no single back to achieve what Barber had done, but Jacobs played well and the rookie Bradshaw came on as the season progressed, making many important gains as he provided a speedy change of pace from the power-running Jacobs. Finally, there was the big enchilada—Manning. After some ups and downs, Manning looked as if he was the quarterback the Giants projected him to be when they drafted him. In the course of the final game of the season, three playoff games and the Super Bowl, Manning demonstrated an ability to take control of the offense, to be the leader who could lead the team to victory.

Finally, the new general manager, Reese, had a Super Bowl victory in his first year. He had handled relations with the coaches and veterans well and the players selected in the draft played an important role in the success of the team. With a relatively young team, with established leadership and a crop of rookies who were already making contributions, the Giants could look forward to the future. At the same time, in a few months they would a huge loss with the announced retirement of Michael Strahan.

Michael Strahan

Giants fans hold many images of Michael Strahan. First, there is the image of Strahan in a crouch, showing his bulging bicep muscles after making a sack. Often double-teamed, typically he was able to put pressure on the quarterback even when unable to make a sack. Second, there is the image of Strahan sliding along the line from his position at right defensive end, stopping the opposition's running back for a loss or small gain. Since he is primarily known as a stellar sacker of opposing quarterbacks, his prowess as a run stopper often was overlooked. According to former general manager Ernie Accorsi, Strahan played the run better than any great pass rusher he had seen. Third, there is the image of Strahan stepping back in pass coverage as one of the other defensive players blitzes. At 6'5" and 275 pounds, Strahan still was agile and athletic enough to step back on pass defense. In fact, he had two touchdown interceptions, one for forty-four yards and another for twenty-four yards. Finally, there is the gap-toothed smile present while doing one of his many interviews or commercials, making him a natural on television sports shows. His book *Under the Helmet* is a down-to-earth account of what it is like to play in the NFL.

Strahan was selected out of Texas Southern in the second round of the 1993 draft. Strahan's career with the Giants started slowly as he experienced a foot injury in 1993 and a knee injury in 1994. Over the first four years he averaged but 4.5 sacks a year. However, in 1997 he had a breakout year with fourteen sacks and fifty solo tackles. This was the beginning of a stretch during which he would be named to the NFC Pro Bowl squad in six of seven years (1997–2003). During that stretch his play climaxed in 2001 when he set an NFL single-season record with 22.5 sacks, in the process eclipsing Lawrence Taylor's Giants sack record of 20.5 established in 1986. During that season he also had sixty-two solo tackles, seven forced fumbles, and a touchdown on a fumble recovery. At the end of that year he was named the Associated Press Defensive Player of the Year, the *Sports Illustrated* Player of the Year, and Associated Press and *Sports Illustrated* first-team All-Pro, along with many other honors. Another banner year was in 2003 when he had 18.5 sacks, sixty-four solo tackles, and again was named to the first-team All-Pro squad by the Associated Press and *Sports Illustrated*. A Pro Bowl year in 2005 was sandwiched between two years in which he was slowed by injury. After considering retirement before the 2007 season and missing the preseason, he returned to play a valuable role in the Giants' march to victory in the Super Bowl. In that game, which turned out to be the final game of his career, Strahan had one sack, three tackles, two quarterback hurries, four hits, and a knocked-down pass.

In June 2008 Strahan announced that he was retiring. Along with tutoring younger defensive line players and being the inspirational leader of the defense, Strahan set the following Giants records: most career sacks; most sacks in a single season; most NFL Pro Bowl selections by a Giants defensive lineman (7); and most games played. Considered to be one of the best defensive ends in NFL history and a future Hall of Famer, in the course of his career Strahan had over 140 sacks, almost 800 tackles, and over twenty forced fumbles.

In announcing his retirement, Strahan said: "I think after fifteen years, the man upstairs said: 'Michael, I let you stick around for fifteen years. I gave you a ring. Now don't be stupid.' So I'm trying not to be stupid."[35]

The Giants and the NFL: The Present and the Future

The lives of the Giants and the NFL are intertwined. Notably, when the NFL was having a problem selecting a commissioner, Wellington Mara played an important role in the process. And when the Giants were having a problem selecting a general manager, Pete Rozelle stepped in and helped them hire George Young. In this final section, three issues are considered that are relevant to the futures of both organizations: changes in management, NFL football as an entertainment business, and the problem of injuries to players and proper medical care for them.

Management Changes in the Giants and the NFL

In October of 2005 Wellington Mara died at the age of eighty-nine. Three things were central to Mara's life: family, religion, and the Giants. As a family man, he was the devoted father of eleven children and grandfather of forty grandchildren. As a religious man, he was a devout Catholic who attended Mass daily. As a team man, he was a central part of the Giants for almost his entire life.

Starting with his participation as a ballboy when his father bought the team in 1925, he became co-owner with his brother Jack in 1930 and remained actively involved with the team virtually until the end of his life. Beyond involvement as president for many of these years, he was known for his presence at virtually all games and practices, as well as for his helpful involvement in the personal lives of many players. Those former players who were devoted to him ranged from the more conventional, such as Gifford and Barber, to the more unconventional, such as LT and Shockey. At the surprise party he organized to honor Mara in 2003, Gifford talked of how he had touched the lives of so many players. Upon his death, Gifford said: "He was my boss, my father figure, and my dearest friend."[36] Shockey, one of the few players invited to see Mara when he was dying, had the following to say upon Mara's death: "We're two different people, two different backgrounds, and raised in two different areas. It was very special to me to get to know him and to see that he took time out of his day to get to know me and to try to mold me into a better person.... He wasn't worried about me as a football player. He was worried about me as a person."[37] Seven busloads of players, past and present, came to his funeral, an expression of how beloved he was by them.

Beyond his involvement with the Giants, Mara played a key role in the development of the NFL. He always was a voice of reason and integrity in the complex and often stormy dealings of the league's owners. Of particular note here was his role in the development of the policy of sharing television revenue on a league-wide basis rather than on an individual team basis. As co-owner, with his brother Jack, of one of the larger television markets, the latter would have been advantageous to the Giants. But the two Maras saw the advantages of the former for the league as a whole. He also played a key role in many of the contracts negotiated between the owners and players as well as in the selections of league commissioners. Upon his death, Commissioner Tagliabue said: "Wellington Mara represented the heart and soul of the NFL. He was a man of deep conviction who stood as a beacon of integrity."[38] For all of these contributions he was elected to the Pro Football Hall of Fame in 1997.

Shortly after Mara's death there was the death of his partner Preston Robert Tisch. Tisch became half-owner of the team in 1991, purchasing the half owned by Wellington's nephew Tim. Tisch was a successful businessman who also had served in the federal government as postmaster general. As chairman and co-chief executive officer, Tisch handled many of the business aspects of the Giants as well as playing an active role in the NFL organization. A long-time football and Giants fan, Tisch previously had tried to buy the Jets and also had considered buying the Dallas Cowboys as well as other teams in the NFL and in other sports. When the opportunity came up to purchase half ownership of the Giants, he jumped at it and successfully completed the purchase a few months after the Giants won Super Bowl XXV. When he purchased the Giants he told his partner

Wellington Mara that he just wanted ten years of fun. Mara told him that "to have ten years of fun in pro football you'll need to be in it for thirty years."[39] With three playoff years and a Super Bowl trip in his almost fifteen seasons with the Giants, Tisch would appear to have had many years of fun. Upon his death, Coach Coughlin said: "It's just incredible that we've lost two pillars, two great men, two pillars of the community in a span of twenty-one days."[40]

With the passing of Mara and Tisch, the future of the Giants clearly was in the hands of their sons, John Mara as president and chief executive officer, Chris Mara as vice president of player evaluation, Steve Tisch as chairman and executive vice president, and Jonathan Tisch as treasurer. With the arrival of Reese as the senior vice president and general manager, the changing of the guard in the organization was complete.

As the Giants were settling into their administrative transition, the NFL had to deal with its own administrative issues, in particular a new contract with the players' union and a new commissioner. Talks between the NFL and the players' union initially did not go well. Although the current contract ran through the 2007 season, a failure to reach agreement on a new contract would limit the salary cap, restricting teams from going after free agents and leading some teams to cutting players to get under the cap then in force. Of particular contention was the percentage of revenue to be available to pay players within a salary cap, an issue further complicated by disagreement among owners whose teams generated greater revenue and those whose teams generated less revenue. Many feared that an agreement would not be reached and prayed for someone such as Wellington Mara to enter: "We need the ghost of St. Wellington to appear with some of the forefathers."[41]

In the end, after many days of tense negotiations and fears of an impasse, a deal was reached. The deal, covering six years and thereby ensuring labor-management peace through the 2011 season, raised the salary cap. This provided room for teams to keep high-priced players and go after expensive free agents, something that played to the advantage of the players. In addition, provision was made for higher-revenue teams to contribute more to the salary fund than lower-revenue teams. Peace again would reign within the NFL, leaving the fighting for the playing field.

With the contract between players and management settled, Commissioner Tagliabue indicated that he would retire prior to the beginning of the 2006 season. Tagliabue, with his own style, built upon the foundation established by Pete Rozelle. During the period of his tenure as commissioner (1989–2006), Tagliabue oversaw the expansion of the league from twenty-eight teams to thirty-two teams, the signing of lucrative television contracts, the building of many new stadiums, and the establishment of agreements with the players, union that included free agency and salary caps.

After considering a number of candidates, the league settled on Roger Goodell, until then the league's executive vice president and chief operating officer, as the new commissioner. Although Goodell was fortunate to enter the commissioner's office with the player contract issue settled through 2011, he quickly found that he had to deal with issues of player involvement in off-field questionable or illegal activity, issues surrounding the treatment of player concussions, and, into the season, the illegal taping of the Jets' defense signals on the part of Bill Belichick and the New England Patriots. The latter threatened to become a major issue as a member of congress, Senator Arlen Specter, was prepared to investigate the entire issue of taping and was upset that Goodell had destroyed the relevant tapes.

In his desire to preserve the image of the league, in April 2007 Goodell led the league to formulate a new Personal Conduct Policy that involved the possible suspension of players for off-field activities that violated the PCP. By late August of 2007 four players had been suspended for off-field conduct. Goodell set up a committee to review and make recommendations concerning the handling of concussions. This led to policy guidelines that were stricter than previously had been the case. In the Belichick case, Goodell took away one of the Patriots' first-round draft choices and fined both Belichick and the Patriots. Life already was not easy in the commissioner's office, but the image of the league appeared undiminished. In the meantime, the season had ended on a high note with a record-setting television audience, almost one hundred million viewers, watching an exciting Super Bowl.

Football as an Entertainment Business

What we're in business to do is entertain and please and involve the fans—that's what we do for a living.[42]
—Bill Polian, Bills GM

This isn't a game—this is business.
—*Forbes*, 9/20/04, p.140

We're football players. We get paid to provide entertainment.[43]
—Giants running back Derrick Ward

For fans, NFL football is sport, an opportunity to kick back and relax, to let the competitive juices flow, to vicariously be a star athlete, to bond with family and friends. For owners and players it may have some of the aspects of sport but most of all it is business, the entertainment business, and big business at that. Who would have guessed in 1925 when Tim Mara bought the Giants that by 2007 the team would be worth a billion dollars and partnering with another team, the Jets, in building a privately financed stadium for well over a billion dollars? With an estimated $250 million in annual revenue, the Giants could afford to privately finance their half of the cost of the stadium. Could Preston Robert Tisch, a smart businessman and at the time chairman of one of the country's most successful financial companies, have known in 1991 that his seventy-five-million-dollar investment for half ownership of the Giants would by 2007 be worth five hundred million?

In its early days the teams were struggling financially. Today each of the thirty-two teams is estimated to be worth at least half a billion dollars and probably half of them worth close to a billion dollars. In 1950 the Cowboys franchise was bought for fifty thousand dollars plus five hundred and fifty thousand dollars for players, six hundred thousand dollars in all. In 1989, Jerry Jones bought what many consider to be America's team for $140 million. Not quite twenty years later Jones's investment was estimated to be worth close to $1.5 billion! A once-struggling NFL is now estimated to bring in seven billion dollars in annual revenues. NFL football is big business.

Professional football has become a part of American life. Season tickets are passed on from generation to generation and are a source of battle in divorce settlements. Special family events are scheduled around football Sundays, playoff games, and, of course, Super Bowl Sunday. Governments can put pressure on the NFL to grant them a local franchise and the NFL can put pressure on Congress to grant it special exempt status from antitrust laws. How has professional football been able to gain such status?

Part of its success undoubtedly had to do with the skill of Pete Rozelle, a former public relations person and commissioner from 1960 to 1989. Rozelle not only was skillful at handling disputes among owners and between owners and players, he was enormously successful at managing the promotion of football as entertainment. During his tenure as commissioner, professional football became one of the most watched programs on television, both regular channel and cable.

As the popularity of television viewing and football viewing increased in tandem, television stations competed for the rights to broadcast games and television revenues became the mainstay of team revenues: "Television is the engine that drives the train."[44] From a time in the sixties when CBS paid $4.65 million a year to televise NFL games and each team made well under a million dollars a season in television revenues, to the present when the total television package is well over three billion dollars a year and each team makes approximately $100 million a year, television has been a financial boon to the NFL. The Super Bowl is the most-watched television program, with the size of international viewing audiences increasing each year. Advertising rates for a thirty-second Super Bowl commercial have gone from $1.6 million in 1999 to $2.4 million in 2004, a fifty percent increase in just five years. At $2.4 million for a thirty-second commercial, it's eighty thousand dollars a second!

Although television revenues form the major portion of team revenues and have fostered economic parity, they are not the only form of revenue. These other forms have fostered team inequality rather than equality. There are beginning to be haves and have-nots from a financial standpoint. Whereas some teams derive the vast majority of their income from shared revenue, other teams derive the majority of their income from non-shared revenue. Foremost among these non-shared forms of revenue are those associated with stadiums, particularly newly built stadiums with many luxury boxes. The NFL has embarked upon a huge program of supporting the privately financed construction of new stadiums, contributing up to $150 million toward the construction of each such stadium. Included here is the new Giants-Jets stadium. In order to pay off the more than one-billion-dollar cost of the stadium, both teams are moving toward higher-priced tickets and the selling of personal seat licenses. The seat licenses are like a stock that can be sold, at a profit or at a loss. Most experts predict an increase in value of such licenses but, of course, stocks can go down as well as up. The problem for the fan holding a season ticket is not just the financial risk involved with the personal seat license but the initial investment of purchasing the license. Seat licenses range from $1,000 to $20,000, beyond what many fans who have choice seats say they can afford. This is all aside from the sale of luxury boxes and naming rights, as well as the increase in season ticket prices. The Giants team expects to bring in perhaps $400 million from the licenses, but the organization claims that it did not have as a goal the maximization of profits. For the Giants and the league, the questions will be whether the time comes where they price themselves out of the reach of most fans and whether parity ultimately will be replaced by haves and have-nots.

Violence, Injury, and Medical Treatment

Football is a violent game. For some players and fans the violence is a sidebar to other aspects of the game; for others it is part of the game's drama and excitement. For many players football is like war:

Johnny Unitas: "It's the closest thing there is to all-out war."[45]

Michael Strahan: "Everything in our professional lives is predicated on violence and aggression.... Our lives have all these military connotations and war terms like blitz, bomb, firing bullets, and in the trenches."[46]

Tiki Barber, quoting General U.S. Grant before a game: "The art of war is simple enough. Find out where the enemy is. Get to him as soon as you can. Strike at him as hard as you can and keep moving on."[47]

Harry Carson: "A football season is the closest thing to war I can imagine.... Each season is a war. You got the soldiers. Some guys are asked to carry the machine guns and some are asked to carry the ammunition."[48]

Not only do football players draw the analogy to war, but it works the other way around as well. Those on the battlefield draw the analogy to football:

R. Jadick, author of *On Call in Hell*: *A Doctor's Iraq War Story:* "Marines think of combat the way football players think of the Super Bowl. Combat is what we train for. We learn how to engage the enemy. You can't put your heart and soul into that kind of training for years just to be left at home when the big game comes."[49]

G.C. Schroen, in an account of the CIA in Afghanistan: "Gary thought of his football team just before the start of the second half in a game they were winning handily. Happy, cocky, confident, totally enjoying themselves."[50]

General David Petraeus, expressing battlefield sentiments similar to those of of Bill Parcells and other head coaches: "I've always maintained that a commander has the highest of highs and the lowest of lows, and that probably gets more intense the closer you get to the front."[51]

As Michael Strahan indicates, many football terms are taken from the battlefield: helmet, blitz, bomb, shotgun, ground attack, firing bullets, in the trenches, flak jackets, hurt by friendly fire, a play resulting in collateral damage, the "war room" on draft day, etc. Analogies are drawn between successful generals and successful head coaches, General Patton and Vince Lombardi providing one such illustration. The camaradery of a football team during a game is likened to that of a platoon on the battlefield. Pride is taken in the team as a combat unit. Not only that, but football players are fond of calling themselves gladiators, which also is true of special forces troops in the military: "Nowadays professional football players are the Roman gladiators."[52] And, for both there is the sense of invincibility, partly based on training and partly on the basis of equipment. They are, they believe, despite what they see around them, indestructible: "Bring on Caesar's gladiators! Bring on the lions, the swords, the spears and anything else because, for now, I am invincible."[53]

All of this is part of the violence that is part of the game. The approach of the players ranges from an attempt to make a good play, to an attempt to intimidate, occasionally to an attempt to cause pain or an attempt to cause injury. Often the line between one and the other becomes a blur. Strahan indicates that "our careers and job are based upon inflicting pain, not injury."[54] The great Ravens linebacker Ray Lewis states: "I don't hit people to hurt them physically. I hit people to take their souls."[55] Lawrence Taylor, who loved to hit, was in extreme distress when he hit Joe Theisman and heard the sound of the bone breaking in Theisman's his leg. For Harry Carson a great hit could provide so much pleasure that it was "like an orgasm."[56]

Has violence increased in the NFL? That is hard to say, although it would not be surprising given the stakes for players, coaches, and management. According to Bill Parcells, "violence, and doing things to trigger violence, is getting out of control in this league and making me concerned."[57] In any case, there is some evidence that injuries are up. A 2004 *Sports Illustrated* article suggested that "the NFL's casualty list doesn't seem longer this year. It is longer."[58] According to the article, the number of players on injured reserve (IR) was up thirty-nine percent over the comparable '98-'03 period.

Despite league efforts, the problem of injuries remains a serious one for players and teams. During 2007 particular attention was paid to the problem of concussions. This followed evidence suggesting that players were playing despite multiple concussions and that past players with such concussions sometimes later suffered from deficits in brain functioning and depression. Players described multiple concussions during a season that went unreported, some involving brief periods of loss of consciousness. After a period of study and notoriety, the NFL announced new safety procedures involving the handling of concussions. Beyond injuries such as concussions, attention began to be drawn to the problem of obesity with its implications for the development of cardiovascular disorders and diabetes. By some estimates more than fifty percent of the NFL players are obese by medical standards with the problem being particularly acute among offensive and defensive linemen.[59]

Why so many injuries and, if there is an increase in their frequency, why? One part of the problem would appear to be the increase in size and weight of the players. In the words of John Fox, head coach of the Carolina Panthers: "We've got a violent game and these guys are human projectiles."[60] These projectiles have become larger and faster, with greater consequent damage when they meet their target. Consider a comparison of linemen for the Giants from the years 1933, 1962, and 2007. Relative to the linemen from the 1933 team, the members of the 2007 offensive line averaged four inches taller and ninety-seven pounds heavier! For the 1933 team, the great center Mel Hein was considered large at 6'2" and 225 pounds. Sean O'Hara, the center on the 2007 Giants, stands at 6'3" and weighs in at 303 pounds.

Comparing the members of the offensive line for the 1962 and 2007 seasons, the linemen for the 2007 season averaged 2.4 inches taller and 73 pounds heavier. The largest offensive lineman on the 1962 team was the left tackle, Roosevelt Brown, standing at 6'3" and weighing 255 pounds. For the 2007 Giants, not one starting lineman on offense weighed less than 300 pounds. The 2007 starting left tackle, David Diehl, stands at 6'5" and weighs in at 319 pounds.

Another part of the injury problem may be that some players continue to play, either because of being coerced by the coaches or because of the culture of toughness, before they are physically ready to continue playing. Most players express the view that you do whatever it takes and gut it out as a badge of honor. Aside from competitive spirit, coaches have a lot on the line (i.e., their jobs) in terms of their best athletes continuing to play. Bandages, tape, shots, almost whatever it takes will be used to keep an essential player in the game. But playing in pain also is part of the macho culture of football. According to Phil Simms: "It's about your manhood.... It's the ultimate macho thing for men. It's testing your manhood, what you're made of."[61] In addition to the fear of being cut, players fear being viewed as soft, part of the gladiator mentality. Players respect their teammate who plays while in pain and toughens it out. As described by Harry Carson: "Players deny that they are hurt even when they're limping or their arm is dangling. They seem convinced the risk of being hurt worse is a better gamble than loss of esteem in the eyes of their opponent, teammates, and coach."[62]

As long as violence sells, as long as there is a culture of toughness, as long as jobs are on the line, there will be injuries in football, probably including some that would not occur were things otherwise. The NFL has taken the problem seriously but at times has not been as forthright in coming to grips with the problem as it might have been. When artificial turf was first introduced, players complained of injuries due to their cleats being caught in the turf, the ground being too hard, and the turf causing skin burns. Only after a while did the league come to grips with the problem. For a period of time there were suggestions of a problem with concussions and the way they were being handled, but it was only in 2007 that the league came to grips with the problem. Already there are signs that concussions are being handled differently, but the problem of players not recognizing or reporting concussions probably remains. It remains not unusual to see a player slowly get off the ground, shaking his head ("Clearing the cobwebs"), and walking back to the huddle while seeming dazed, but continuing to play. There remains the struggle between keeping professional football the exciting game it is while keeping injuries down, of continuing to have football players be the gladiators fans love while doing away with the excesses that ultimately are costly to both player and management alike.

To 2008 and Beyond

Entering the 2008 season, both the Giants and the league generally appear to be in good shape. Administratively, the Giants have an organization set in place that appears to be cohesive. At the league level, Goodell appears to have weathered the storm of the Belichick-Patriots case and appears to be dealing effectively with upholding the image of the league.

As the Giants enter the 2008 season, there is the motivation to repeat what was accomplished in the 2007 season and recognition that opposing teams will be targeting them more than in the past. Player-wise, the Giants are without three leaders, both Barber and Strahan having retired and Shockey traded to New Orleans in July for two 2009 draft choices. Will the Giants need a leader and, if so, who will emerge? Is Manning ready, by tenure and temperament, or will someone else become the team leader? Fans will be watching to see whether Manning builds upon his playoff successes, whether Coughlin continues to maintain his relative composure, whether the Giants can have a high-powered offense without Shockey, and whether the defense can continue to improve without Strahan. As things stand now, things look bright for the future of the Giants and the NFL.

Chapter Notes

Chapter 1

1. Two chapters in *Total Football II*, 1999, give the history of football before the NFL as well as that of the NFL.
2. Mara, Introduction to *What Giants They Were*, by R. Whittingham, 2000, p. viii.
3. Mara, Foreword, *The Giants*, by R. Whittingham, 1987, p. ix.
4. Eskenazi, 1976, p. 26.
5. Hein, in Whittingham, 2000, p. 37.
6. The sneaker story as told by Wellington Mara and the whiskey story appear in Whittingham, 1937, pp. 43, 44.
7. Badgro, in Whittingham, 2000, p. 49.
8. Hein, in Whittingham, 2000, p. 182.
9. In 1937 Steve Owen utilized a platoon system in which two teams of relatively equal ability would play both offense and defense in alternating quarters.
10. Mara, in Whittingham, 1987, p. ix.
11. Anderson, 1985, p. 43.
12. Of course, this was prior to the time when plays could be sent in from the sideline to a receiver in the helmet of the quarterback.

Chapter 2

1. Gifford, 1993.
2. Gifford, in Whittingham, 2000, p. 5.
3. Gifford, 1993, p. 97.
4. Kyle Rote describes the time when Doc Sweeney had to sew up Gifford's split lip: "Doc Sweeney, who was not averse to having a nip or two in cold weather, was mucking around getting ready to stitch up Frank's lip. Finally he got to it and started to stitch the lip, but the problem was he hadn't gotten around to threading the needle. When he realized that, he went off to get some thread and Frank was sitting there with the needle stuck through his lip. Finally the doc got some thread and sewed it up, but I recall Frank wasn't all that happy about the situation" (in Whittingham, 2000, p. 67).
5. Gifford, 1993, p. 133.
6. Katcavage, in Whittingham, 2000, p. 71.
7. Gifford, 1993, p. 185.
8. Gifford, 1993, p. 80.
9. Maraniss, 1999, p. 167.
10. MacCambridge, 2004, p. 108.
11. *Total Football*, 1999, p. 318.
12. Whittingham, 2000, p. 117.
13. *Total Football*, 1997, p. 290.
14. Whittingham, 2000, p. 84.
15. Litsky, obituary in the *New York Times*, 6/11/2004, p. B10.
16. Gifford, 1993, p. 108.
17. Whittingham, 2000, p. 73.
18. *New York Times*, September 21, 1964, p. 38.
19. Whittingham, 2000, p. 186.
20. Gifford felt disliked by Howell, who is described as asking Gifford whether he wanted to be a football player or a movie actor, reflecting some of the sentiment of the players (Gifford, 1993, p. 97).
21. Summerall, in Whittingham, 2000, p. 123.
22. Landry, in Whittingham, 2000, p. 62.
23. Whittingham, 1987, p. 96.
24. Summerall, in Whittingham, 2000, p. 59.
25. Gifford, 1993, p. 174.
26. Anderson, 1985, p. 59.
27. *New York Times*, December 29, 1958.
28. Gifford, in Whittingham, 1987, p. 144.
29. Tittle, in Whittingham, 2000, p. 123.
30. *New York Times*, October 30, 1962, p. 58.
31. Huff, in Whittingham, 2000, p. 117.

32. Gifford, 1993, p. 188.
33. Eisen, Giants' home page, 9/7/03.
34. Gifford, 1993.
35. MacCambridge, 2004, p. 169.
36. Eskenazi, 1976, p. 57.
37. MacCambridge, 2004, p. 164.
38. Gifford, 1993, p. 105.
39. Gifford, 1993, p. 80.
40. MacCambridge, 2004, p. 172.
41. *Total Football*, 1999, p. 512.
42. Whittingham, 2000, p. 68.
43. MacCambridge, 2004, p. xiv.

Chapter 3

1. Steinbreder, 1994, p. 115.
2. Whittingham, 1987, p. 143, p. 171.
3. The New York Titans drafted for two years, 1962 and 1963, before they became the Jets.
4. As quoted in Eskenazi, 1976, p. 213.
5. Huff, in Whittingham, 2004, p. 135.
6. Modzelewski, in Whittingham, 2004, p. 110.
7. Gifford, 1993.
8. Eskenazi, 1976, p. 146.
9. Eskenazi, 1976, p. 151.
10. Lest one be too critical of the Giants' draft choice in this case, note should be made that the Green Bay Packers used their first-round number-one pick to select another of the quarterbacks on Mara's list, Randy Duncan, who never played for them or any other NFL team.
11. *New York Times*, September 21, 1964, p. 38.
12. Tittle, in Whittingham, 2000, p. 186.
13. Wood then played one season for New Orleans before returning to the Giants to see limited duty during the 1968 and 1969 seasons.
14. MacCambridge, 2004, p. 206.
15. MacCambridge, 2004, p. 207.
16. *New York Times*, March 8, 1967, p. 58.
17. Asinof, 1968, p. 102.
18. Webster, in Whittingham, 2000, p. 132.
19. *New York Times*, November 27, 1967, p. 80.
20. *New York Times*, November 12, 1968, p. 58.
21. *New York Times*, November 20, 1978, p. C1.
22. Gifford, 1993, p. 188.
23. Whittingham, 2000, p. 132.
24. Gifford, 1993, p. 279.
25. Gifford, 1993, p. 279.
26. Whittingham, 1987, p. 168.
27. Whittingham, 1987, p. 171.
28. An earlier television contract had been signed in 1960 for $8.5 million over five years. The change in value illustrates the increased popularity of professional football among the viewing public.
29. MacCambridge, 2004, p. 221.
30. MacCambridge, 2004, p. 224.
31. In 1973 another rival league, the World Football League, started. Without TV revenue, the teams were in red ink and the league folded by the end of 1974.
32. Frank Gifford replaced Keith Jackson in the second year of *Monday Night Football*.
33. MacCambridge, 2004, p. 312.
34. Asinof, 1968, p. 228.
35. Asinof, 1968, p. 203.
36. Harry Carson became the Giants' starting middle linebacker in 1976.
37. MacCambridge, 2004, p. 320.

Chapter 4

1. Steinbreder, 1994, p. 135.
2. *New York Times*, December 9, 2001, p. A55.
3. At the time there was only one player in the division weighing over 300 pounds. The heaviest player on The Hogs, tackle Joe Jacoby, weighed in at 295.
4. At the time, "Charlie the Tuna" was a comical character in a tuna fish commercial.
5. Parcells, 1987, p. 113.
6. The game was against the Cincinnati Bengals. In the same game, Bavaro set a Giants record with twelve receptions in one game.
7. Hasselbeck is the father of two later NFL quarterbacks, including one who was a reserve quarterback with the 2005 Giants.
8. Whittingham, 2000, p. 240.
9. *New York Times*, January 5, 1987, p. C1.
10. *New York Times*, January 5, 1987, p. C1.
11. *New York Times*, January 11, 1987, p. C1.

12. *New York Times*, January 26, 1987, p. A1.
13. *New York Times*, January 26, 1987, p. C10.
14. Parcells, 2000, p. 4.
15. *New York Times*, September 13, 1989, p. D23.
16. *New York Times*, September 13, 1989, p. D23.
17. *New York Times*, January 11, 1991, p. A23.
18. *New York Times*, January 21, 1991, p. C1.
19. *New York Times*, January 21, 1991, p. C5.
20. *New York Times*, January 24, 1991, p. B11.
21. *New York Times*, January 27, 1991, p. 13.
22. *New York Times*, January 28, 1991, p. C8.
23. Taylor, 2003, p. 101.
24. Carson, 1987, p. 76.
25. Parcells, 1987, pp. 91–92.
26. Parcells, 2000, p. 101.
27. Madden, quoted in Taylor, 2003, p. 47.
28. *Total Football II*, 1999, p. 355.
29. Taylor, 1987; Taylor, 2003.
30. Taylor, 1987, pp. 76, 80.
31. Mara, in Whittingham, 2000, p. 97.
32. Taylor, 2003, p. 34.
33. Parcells, 2000, p. 52; Taylor, 2003, p. 41.
34. Taylor, 2003, p. 57.
35. Taylor, 1987, p. 57.
36. *New York Times*, December 20, 1981, p. S1.
37. Taylor, 2003, p. 89.
38. *New York Times*, November 26, 1982, p. D7.
39. *New York Times*, November 26, 1982, p. D8.
40. Taylor, 1987, p. 189.
41. *New York Times*, December 26, 2005, p. D2.
42. Taylor, 2003, p. 105.
43. Taylor, 2003, p. 114.
44. Anderson, *New York Times*, November 29, 1988, p. B15.
45. Taylor, 2003, p. 156.
46. *New York Times*, November 28, 2003, p. D1.
47. *New York Times*, November 28, 2003, p. D1.
48. Whittingham, 2004, p. 41.
49. Whittingham, 2004, p. 147.
50. *New York Times*, January 6, 1990, p. B7.
51. Steinbreder, 1994, p. 214.
52. *New York Times*, June 16, 1994, p. B18.
53. Simms, 2004, pp. 20–21, 157.
54. Simms, 2004, p. 135.
55. Parcells, 1987, p. 92.
56. Steinbreder, 1994, p. 184.
57. In his 1987 book, Parcells did not explain why he was so sure that Young had tried to replace him. In his 2000 book he explained that he and Schnellenberger shared the same agent.
58. Parcells, 1987, p. 243.
59. Parcells, 1987, p. 235.
60. Parcells, 2000, pp. ix-xii.
61. Parcells, 2000, p. 121.
62. Burt, 1987, pp. 71, 7.
63. Hostetler, 1991.
64. Halberstam, 2005.
65. *New York Times*, December 21, 1997, p. D1.
66. Parcells, 1987, p. 150.
67. Parcells, 1987, p. 162.
68. Although most would agree that Parcells rates as one of the great football coaches of all time, a *New York Times* article in 2005 suggested that without Bill Belichick as his defense coordinator he was somewhat ordinary. With Belichick he had a 117–73–1 regular season record, an 11–5 record in playoffs, and 2 Super Bowl titles. In contrast, without Belichick his record was 44–47–0 during the regular season, 0–2 during the playoffs, and no Super Bowl titles (December 4, 2005, p. 8.11).
69. Carson, 1987, pp. 102–3.
70. Parcells, 1987, p. 220.
71. *New York Times*, November 28, 2003, p. D9.
72. Tisch was chairman of the Loews Corporation, a large conglomerate, and had served as postmaster general in the Reagan administration.
73. Steinbreder, 1994, pp. 201, 208.
74. Parcells, 1987, p. 161.

Chapter 5

1. Bob Dylan, "The Times They Are A-Changin'," copyright 1963.

2. Asked whether he would have hired Belichick as head coach had he known that Parcells would resign, General Manager George Young commented: "There are rotisserie baseball leagues and fantasy football leagues. That question fits into that game" (*New York Times*, May 19, 1961, p. B14).

3. *New York Times*, May 17, 1991, p. B9.

4. Wannstedt became head coach of the Chicago Bears, then of the Miami Dolphins, and currently is head coach at the University of Pittsburgh.

5. *New York Times*, January 16, 1994, p. S1.

6. Simms, 2004, p. 53.

7. The story is told by Accorsi in Callahan, 2007.

8. *New York Times*, December 14, 1997.

9. Chris Calloway, quoted in the *New York Times*, December 28, 1997.

10. *New York Times*, January 10, 2001, p. D3.

11. Dusty Zeigler and Joe Jurevicious, as quoted in the *New York Times*, January 15, 2001, p. D1.

12. Callahan, 2007, p. 87.

13. Interestingly, in the 2000 draft the Giants had their choice between Dayne and Shaun Alexander. The Giants selected Dayne, the Seahawks Alexander. Results in the first season seemed to justify the selection of the Giants. On the other hand, by the end of the 2001 season Dayne was on the bench while Alexander was gaining over one thousand yards. Alexander went on to gain over a thousand yards in each of the next four seasons, leading the Seahawks to the Super Bowl at the end of the 2005 season. On the other hand, Dayne's gains and playing time declined until he was gone from the Giants and playing for the Broncos in 2005. Released by the Broncos, he joined the Houston Texans in 2006. At the same time, it is worth noting that Tiki Barber might not have emerged as the running back he became had Alexander joined the Giants and starred for them as he did for the Seahawks.

14. Concerning Strahan's final sack of Bart Starr in the season-ending game against Green Bay, some suggested that Starr had allowed himself to be sacked by his friend Strahan. Whatever the merits of this claim, it was clear that Strahan had had a great season and had become a stellar defensive end.

15. *New York Times*, December 11, 2001, p. S1.

16. Feinstein, 2005, p. 180.

17. *New York Times*, September 17, 2003, p. D5.

18. Matt Bryant, quoted in the *New York Times*, September 17, 2003, p. D5.

19. *New York Times*, October 21, 2003, p. D3.

20. Giants.com, September 8, 2003.

21. Schramm of the Cowboys, quoted in MacCambridge, 2004, p. 384.

Chapter 6

1. Fox TV, November 10, 2004.

2. All of these candidates eventually went on to become head coaches—Weis at Notre Dame, Crennel with the Cleveland Browns, Smith with the Chicago Bears, and Saban with the Miami Dolphins. Weis and Smith were clear early successes, while Saban had mixed results with the Dolphins and returned to college coaching. Crennel, after some difficult seasons, in 2007 brought the Browns to a near playoff spot.

3. Callahan, 2007, p. 91.

4. *New York Times*, January 7, 2004, p. D3.

5. *New York Times*, January 1, 2004, p. D6.

6. *New York Times*, January 7, 2004, p. D1.

7. The Giants' first-round pick of the 2005 draft turned out to be significant. The Chargers used it to select Shawn Merriman, who became an outstanding linebacker.

8. Interview with Michael Eisen, June 1, 2004, Giants.com.

9. *New York Times*, April 25, 2004, p. D9.

10. Interview with Michael Eisen, June 1, 2004, Giants.com.

11. Boisture interview, September 23, 2003.

12. *New York Times*, February 23, 2003.

13. *New York Times*, November 14, 2007, p. 9.

14. MacCambridge, 2004, p. 93.

15. *New York Times*, September 14, 2004.

16. 2004 Postseason Guide, *Touchdown: The Official Newsletter of the New York Giants*, p. 21.
17. *New York Times*, October 28, 2005, p. D6; November 7, 2005, p. D3.
18. Rivers again played little behind Brees on the Chargers.
19. During the season Accorsi was given a one-year extension as he agreed to remain as general manager for one year before retiring.
20. One of the cornerbacks, Peterson, had been injured during the previous season. After being released by the Giants he joined the Eagles and changed his name to Will Peterson.
21. *New York Times*, September 24, 2006, pp. D1, D7.
22. *New York Times*, November 27, 2006, p. D1.
23. Barber, 2007, pp. 14, 196, 202. Barber also was critical of GM Accorsi: "Ernie Accorsi never demonstrated any special belief in me or felt that I could grow into an elite player" (p. 91).
24. Strahan, 2007, pp. 54, 58, 69.
25. Shannon Sharpe, former NFL star and then commentator on *The NFL Today* television show, said about playing for Coughlin: "I would rather die in an abandoned building alone, and my family not know what happened, than play for Coughlin" (*New York Times*, January 23, 2007, p. D2).
26. *New York Times*, December 21, 2006, p. D3.
27. Jerry Reese, *Touchdown: The Official Newsletter of the New York Giants*, 2006 Postseason Issue, p. 6.
28. Peter Schrager, Fox Sports.com, May 18, 2007.
29. Barber, 2007.
30. Strahan, 2007.
31. *Monday Night Football*, December 16, 2007.
32. In fairness to the quarterback the Giants traded for Manning, Phil Rivers, it should be pointed out that Rivers led his team to a tough win against the Indianapolis Colts and then, despite a knee injury in that game, played valiantly in a loss to the Patriots.

33. Ryan Grant, the starting running back for the Packers, played behind two future NFL running backs and was not drafted. After a year on the practice squad of the Giants and then a year on injured reserve, during which he almost lost the use of his left arm in an accident, he was traded by the Giants to the Packers. The week before, he had run for over two hundred yards against the Seahawks.
34. *New York Times*, February 10, 2008, Sports Sunday, p. 5.
35. *New York Times*, June 11, 2008, p. D2.
36. *New York Times*, October 29, 2005, p. D3.
37. *New York Times*, October 27, 2005, p. D3.
38. FoxSports.com, October 25, 2005.
39. *New York Times*, November 16, 2005, p. D1.
40. *Touchdown*, 2005 season issue, New York Giants.
41. *New York Times*, March 9, 2006, p. D6.
42. MacCambridge, 2004, p. 368.
43. *New York Times*, December 1, 2007, p. D2.
44. *Total Football*, 1999, p. 513.
45. Quoted in MacCambridge, 2004, p. 262.
46. Strahan, 2007, pp. 31, 216.
47. Barber, 2007, p. 100.
48. Carson, 1987, p. 28. p. 145.
49. Jadick, 2007, p. 65.
50. Schroen, 2005, p. 348.
51. Quoted in Atkinson, 2004, p. 254.
52. Barber, 2007, p. 120.
53. Strahan, 2007, p. 8.
54. Strahan, 2007, p. 147.
55. Quoted in Freeman, 2003, p. xxxi.
56. Carson, 1987, p. 18.
57. Parcells, 2000, p. 161.
58. *Sports Illustrated*, November 11, 2004, p. 61.
59. *Fox Sports News*, March 3, 2005.
60. *Sports Illustrated*, October 11, 2004, p. 61.
61. Simms, 2004, p. 20, p. 157.
62. Carson, 1987, p. 133.

Bibliography

Anderson, D. (1985). *The Story of Football*. New York: Wm. Morrow & Co.
Asinof, E. (1968). *Seven Days to Sunday*. New York: Simon & Schuster.
Atkinson, R. (2004). *In the Company of Soldiers*. New York: Holt.
Barber, T. (2007). *Tiki*. New York: SSE.
Burt, J. (1987). *Hard Nose*. Harcourt Brace Jovanovich.
Callahan, T. (2007). *The GM: The Inside Story of a Dream Job and the Nightmares that Go With It*. New York: Crown.
Carroll, B., M. Gershman, D. Neft, & J. Thorn. (1999). *Total Football II*. New York: Harper Collins.
Carson, H. (1987). *Point of Attack*. New York: McGraw-Hill.
Chandler, B. (1984). *Violent Sundays*. New York: Simon & Schuster.
Eskenazi, G. (1976). *There Were Giants in Those Days*. New York: Grosset & Dunlap.
Feinstein, J. (2005). *Next Man Up*. New York: Little, Brown & Co.
Freeman, M. (2003). *Bloody Sundays*. New York: Wm. Morrow.
Gifford, F. (1993). *The Whole Ten Yards*. New York: Random House.
Halberstam, D. (2005). *The Education of a Coach*. New York: Hyperion.
Hostetler, J. (1991). *One Giant Leap*. New York: Putnam.
Izenberg, J. (1990). *No Medals for Trying*. New York: Macmillan.
Jadick, R. (2007). *On Call in Hell*. New York: New American Library.
Lewis, M. (2006). *The Blind Side*. New York: Norton.
MacCambridge, M. (2004). *America's Game: The Epic Story of How Pro Football Captured a Nation*. New York: Random House.
Maraniss, D. (1999). *When Pride Still Mattered: A Life of Vince Lombardi*. New York: Simon & Schuster.
Neft, D.S., & R.M. Cohen. (1991). *The Football Encyclopedia*. New York: St. Martin's Press.
Parcells, B. (2000). *The Final Season: My Last Year as a Head Coach in the NFL*. New York: Wm. Morrow.
Parcells, B. (1987). *Parcells: Autobiography of the Biggest Giant of them All*. Chicago: Bonus Books.
Schroen, G.C. (2005). *First In: An Insider's Account of How the CIA Spearheaded the War on Terrorism in Afghanistan*. New York: Ballantine.
Simms, P. (2004). *Sunday Morning Quarterback*. New York: Harper Collins.
Steinbreder, J. (1994). *70 Years of Championship Football*. Dallas, TX: Taylor Publishing Co.
Strahan, M. (2007). *Inside the Helmet*. New York: Gotham.
Taylor, L. (1987). *LT: Living on the Edge*. New York: Times Books.
Taylor, L. (2003). *LT: Over the Edge*. New York: Harper Collins.
Whittingham, R. (1987). *The Giants: An Illustrated History*. New York: Harper & Row.
Whittingham, R. (2000). *What Giants They Were*. Chicago: Triumph Books.
Williams, D. (1990). *Quarterback: Shattering the NFL Myth*. Chicago: Bonus Books.

Index

AAFC (All-American Football Conference) 16
ABC 45
Accorsi, E. 26, 41, 145, 149, 158, 161, 162, 167, 168, 174, 180, 181, 182
Adams, G. 87
AFL (American Football League) 5, 6, 11, 42, 46, 52, 53, 67, 68
Agajanian, B. 33
Aikman, T. 123
All-American Football Conference see AAFC
Allegre, R. 80, 81, 89, 90, 96
Allen, M. 136, 137
Allen, W. 132, 142, 148, 162
Ameche, A. 37, 38, 39
American Football League see AFL
Anderson, N. 91
Anderson, O. 75, 88, 93, 95, 96, 104
Archer, T. 75, 99
Armstead, J. 124, 125, 128, 131, 132–133
Armstrong, T. 91
Arnsbarger, B. 60, 64
Arrington, L. 162
Atkins, D. 33
Austin, B. 20, 28

Badgro, R. 8, 9, 11, 12
Bahr, M. 90, 92, 93, 94, 96, 96
Baker, S. 92, 94, 95
Banks, C. 80, 81, 86, 88, 96, 121, 141
Barber, T. 122, 125, 126, 128, 129, 130, 131, 132, 134, 135, 137, 141, 147, 154, 155, 156, 157, 159, 160, 161, 163, 164, 165–167, 169, 170, 181, 184, 192
Barnes, E. 20, 49
Barrow, M. 129
Baugh, S. 11, 15, 24
Bavaro, M. 79, 81, 85, 94, 96, 105, 133, 137, 140
Bednarik, C. 23
Belichick, B. 77, 92, 96, 118, 119, 121, 153, 186
Bell, B. 16, 43, 151
Benson, B. 101

Berry, R. 37, 38, 39
Billick, B. 139, 153
Blaik, E. 28
Blount, M. 104
Boss, K. 179
Bradshaw, A. 171, 172, 176, 178, 179, 181
Bradshaw, T. 104, 174
Brady, T. 128, 179, 180, 181
Brain Type 152
Brandt, G. 151
Brees, D. 158
Briscoe, M. 71
Brooklyn Dodgers 8
Brooks, M. 121
Brothers Bowl 163
Brown, D. 107, 123, 124, 125, 127, 141
Brown, E. 33
Brown, J. 25, 34, 35, 36, 44
Brown, P. 16, 18, 30, 32, 36, 44, 45
Brown, R. 18, 20, 26, 28, 30, 35, 44, 45, 191
Brunner, S. 75, 77, 105
Bryant, M. 136, 137, 138
Bryant, P. 76
Bunch, J. 153
Burress, P. 159, 160, 163, 170, 171, 175, 176, 177, 179, 180
Burt, J. 78, 83, 84, 93, 111, 137
Butkus, D. 50

California Psychological Inventory 152
Caliper Profile 152
Canadian Football League 19, 21, 42, 46
Cannon, B. 67
Carpenter, R. 77
Carr, D. 153
Carr, J. 5
Carson, H. 76, 79, 84, 86, 97, 98, 110, 111, 113, 116, 130, 137, 190, 191
Carter, C. 122, 130
Carthon, M. 80
Casares, R. 33
CBS 45, 67, 69, 187
Chandler, D. 20, 38
Clarett, M. 144

Clements, V. 55, 57
Cohen, A. 10
College All-Star Game 12, 13
Collins, K. 127, 129, 130, 131, 132, 134, 135, 137, 139, 147, 149, 150, 154
Collins, M. 80, 90, 96
Conerly, C. 15, 17, 20, 22, 24, 28, 29, 33, 34, 35, 36, 38, 39, 40, 42, 45, 50, 107, 154
Cordileone, L. 27
Cosell, H. 69
Couch, T. 153
Coughlin, T. 118, 120, 125, 147, 158, 164, 169, 172, 178, 185, 192
Covert, J. 92
Craig, R. 82, 93
Crennel, R. 146
Cross, H. 92, 122
Csonka, L. 61, 64
Cuff, W. 11, 12
Culpepper, D. 130
Cunningham, R. 102, 126
Cuozzo, G. 53

Danelo, J. 100
Danowski, E. 9, 11, 12, 15
Davis, A. 68, 115
Dayne, R. 129, 130, 131, 132, 142, 147, 153, 154, 155, 157, 162
Defense 20, 35
DeOssie, S. 121
Dess, D. 49
Diehl, K. 171, 181, 191
Ditka, M. 92
Dixon, R. 130, 131
Dorsett, T. 100
Dorsey, E. 90
Driver, D. 175
Dungy, T. 116, 146

Edwards, H. 61
Ehrhardt, R. 105
Elliot, J. 88
Elway, J. 85, 86, 120, 124, 141, 149, 150, 175
Everett, J. 89
Ewbank, W. 52

Fassel, J. 118, 124, 126, 130, 131, 138, 139, 141, 145, 153
Favre, B. 149, 153, 156, 175, 177
Feagles, J. 137, 177
Filchock, F. 15
Filipski, G. 33
Fitzgerald, L. 149

Flaherty, R. 7, 8, 10, 11
Fortunato, J. 33
Fouts, D. 60
Fox, J. 125, 128, 130, 133, 139, 161, 154, 190
Frederickson, T. 50, 52, 55, 121
Friedman, B. 7, 8, 19

Garcia, J. 135, 136, 173
Garnes, S. 126
Gatorade 78, 83, 84, 110, 126
Gibbs, J. 76, 83, 146
Gibson, B. 5, 61
Gifford, F. 18, 20–24, 27, 29, 35, 36, 37, 38, 39, 40, 44, 45, 49, 62, 65, 69, 140, 154, 157, 184
Gilbride, K. 167
Gipp, G. 4
Gogolak, P. 68, 70, 95
Goldberg, J. 103
Goldsteyn, J. 61
Goodell, R. 186
Graham, K. 123, 127, 128
Graham, O. 17, 18, 32
Grange, R. 5, 6, 9
Gray, E. 75
Green, D. 83, 89, 116
Greene, J. 104
Grier, R. 20, 34, 42, 44, 45, 49, 62
Griese, B. 53, 56
Griffin, C. 131, 132
Griffing, G. 51
Grim, B. 55, 56
Grimm, R. 83
Groh, A. 118
Grosscup, L. 50, 53
Groza, L. 18
Guglielmi, R. 51

Haji-Sheikh, A. 77, 78
Halas, G. 5, 10, 110
Haley, C. 93
Ham, J. 98, 104
Hamilton, K. 129, 132, 139
Hampton, D. 91
Hampton, R. 90, 92, 118, 121, 122, 124, 126, 141
Handley, R. 107, 109, 118–120, 141, 145
Hapes, M. 15
Harrington, J 153
Hasselbeck, D. 80
Haynes, M. 76, 77
Hein, M. 8, 9, 12, 13, 14, 15, 21, 190
Heinrich, D. 34
Heisman, J. 4
Hickerson, G. 35

Hill, H. 33
Hilliard, I. 128, 134, 137
Hixon, D. 176
Hollis, M. 137
Holmes, K. 132
Horn, D. 53, 56
Hornung, P. 44
Hostetler, J. 91, 92, 94, 95, 106, 107, 111, 118, 119, 120
Howard, E. 90, 93
Howell, J.L. 22, 24, 30, 35, 41, 43, 49, 62, 98, 140
Huff, S. 20, 24, 30, 35, 41, 43, 49, 62, 98, 140
Hufnagell, J. 167

Jacobs, B. 159, 170, 171, 172, 176, 181
Jacobson, L. 57
Jacoby, J. 83
Jennings, D. 75, 77, 78
Johnson, J. 145, 147, 174, 175
Johnson, P. 87, 90, 121
Johnson, Randy 57, 59, 60
Johnson, Ron 55, 57, 60, 79, 83
Jones, C. 56
Jones, H. 52, 55, 58
Jordan, H. 35
Joseph, W. 142, 148, 162
Jurgensen, S. 59

Kanell, D. 125, 127
Karras, A. 44
Katcavage, J. 20
Kelley, B. 98
Kelly, J. 91, 94
Kilmer, B. 59
Kinard, T. 77
King, P. 35
Kiwanuka, M. 162, 164, 168, 169, 170, 171
Knight, B. 109
Kotar, D. 78
Kratch, B. 111
Kuehl, R. 137

Lambert, J. 104
Landeta, S. 82, 83, 91, 118
Landry, G. 53, 56
Landry, T. 16, 18, 20, 20, 25 , 29–30, 32, 33, 41, 42, 76, 110, 120
Lane, B. 24
Lanier, W. 71
Lavelli, D. 18
Leaf, R. 151, 153
Leemans, A. 11, 12, 13, 15
Lewis, R. 131, 190

Lewis, T. 168
Lipscomb, B.D. 37, 38
Lofton, J. 94
Lombardi, V. 21, 22, 24, 28, 36, 42, 68, 110, 189
Long, H. 174
Looney, J.D. 49, 121
Lott, R. 93
Luckman, S. 15, 40

Mackovic, J. 109
Madden, J. 97, 172
Madison, S. 172, 173, 174, 176
Manley, D. 89
Manning, A. 148
Manning, E. 85, 147, 154, 157, 160, 161, 162, 163, 168, 169, 171, 172, 173, 175, 178, 179, 180, 181, 192
Manning, P. 148, 153, 163, 181
Manuel, L. 84
Mara, C. 185
Mara, Jack 6, 11, 13, 14, 64, 183, 186; death 64; Hein contract 14; ownership 43
Mara, John (son of W) 140, 145, 147, 167, 185
Mara, T. (father) 5, 9, 14, 16, 43, 46, 64, 187
Mara, T. (son of Jack) 65, 73, 113, 184
Mara, W. 6, 8, 13, 14, 21, 26, 31, 33, 36, 45, 49, 50, 58, 63, 64, 68, 73, 98, 103, 125, 126, 140, 183; AFL merger 53, 68; death 183; family feud 53; and Fran Tarkenton 54, 55; Hall of Fame 184; and NFL 116, 183, 185; ownership 43; relationship with players 113, 132, 140; sneakers game 10; USFL 85, 116
Marchetti, G. 37, 38, 39
Marino, D. 151, 154, 175
Marshall, L. 78, 81, 88, 93
Martin, G. 79, 81, 82, 85, 86
Mauch, G. 10
May, M. 83
McConkey, P. 78, 88
McMahon, J. 122
McMichael, S. 91
McNabb, D. 130, 160
McQuarters, R.W. 177
McVay, J. 61, 64
Meggett, D. 88, 89, 90, 96, 118, 121, 122, 153, 165
Meredith, D. 67, 69
Mirer, R. 153
Mitchell, B. 137, 172
Mitchell, P. 128
Modell, A. 114

Modzelewski, D. 20, 32, 35, 41, 49, 62
Monday Night Football 20, 23, 69, 71, 89
Monk, A. 89
Montana, J. 74, 79, 82, 83, 92, 104
Moore, E. 88, 121
Moore, L. 37, 38
Morrall, E. 52
Morris, J. 78, 79, 81, 82, 87, 89, 90, 96, 110, 122, 141
Morton, C. 60, 61, 64
Moss, R. 130, 178, 179
Motley, M. 17, 18, 44
Mowatt, Z. 85
Murchison, C. 30
Muster, B. 92
Myers-Briggs Test 152
Myrha, S. 39

Nagurski, B. 10
Namath, J. 52, 53, 54, 67
National Football League (NFL): All-NFL, All-Pro 12, 13, 22, 26, 40, 76; antitrust suit 114, 115, 144; championship games 9, 11, 12, 15, 16, 32, 36, 37, 39, 46, 83, 92, 130; draft 13, 53, 71, 74, 147, 150, 151, 159; drugs, substance abuse 78, 116; free agency 69, 114, 141, 142, 147, 180; Hall of Fame 12, 13, 14, 23, 25, 26, 51, 56, 60; injury 188–191; MVP award 24, 42, 180; name 5; parity 143; Personal Conduct Policy (PCP) 186; Plan B 114, 142; Players Association 46, 69, 70, 142, 154, 185; playoff games 79, 82, 91, 122, 134; Pro Bowl 14, 24, 25, 26, 57, 160, 182; race 16, 17, 44–45, 70, 116; salary cap 107, 133, 141, 142, 143, 146, 155, 158, 185, 186; strikes (players) 69, 75, 87, 100, 102, 114; sudden death 39, 71; Super Bowl 30, 82, 84, 91, 188; television 45, 65, 67, 68, 114, 187–188; violence 188–191; wildcard playoff 79, 173
NBC 45, 67, 69
Neale, G. 41
Nelson, K. 87
New York Giants: drafts 162, 170; drug problems 106, 112; free agents 170; name 6; personal seat licenses 188; playoff games 106, 126, 129, 130, 134, 173; purchase 5; stadium (Giants-Jets) 188; Super Bowls 82, 84, 91, 94, 106, 129, 131, 173
Newman, H. 8, 9, 10, 11
Nitschke, R. 35, 42, 98
Nolan, D. 20
Norwood, S. 96

Oates, B. 88, 95
O'Hara, S. 172, 190
Owen, S. 7, 10, 18, 19, 22, 26, 29
Owens, T. 135

Page, A. 56
Palmer, C. 167
Parcells, B. 76, 77, 80, 90, 94, 97, 105, 108, 109–113, 118, 119, 120, 125, 141, 145, 189; and Bill Belichick 77; coach of the year 82; and Dallas Cowboys 101, 107, 112, 137, 146; favorite game 89; Gatorade 78, 83, 84, 110; retirement 86–87; superstitions 111; team drugs problem 77, 101, 112, 116; Tuna name 76
Parker, J. 105, 140
Paterno, J. 73, 128
Patterson, E. 80
Patton, J. 20
Payton, S. 129, 131, 134, 137, 139, 164
Payton, W. 60, 115, 157
Perkins, R. 74, 76, 101, 104, 109
Perry, W. 91
Peterson, W. 132, 137, 162
Pettigout, L. 141, 147, 156, 160, 162, 168, 170
Pierce, A. 160, 161, 163, 174
Pisarcik, J. 61, 75, 137
Price, E. 18

Quinn, T. 168

Ramsey, S. 61
Reagan, R. 4
Reasons, G. 93
Reed, A. 94
Reese, J. 168, 181, 185
Reeves, D. 74, 85, 86, 107, 120–121, 123, 141, 153
Reid, A. 146
Rhodes, R. 116
Rice, J. 79, 82, 93, 122
Rivers, P. 148, 149, 154, 158, 164, 169
Roberts, W. 82
Robinson, Jackie 16, 45
Robinson, John 73
Robinson, S. 80
Robustelli, A. 20, 30, 32, 33, 35, 41, 46, 49, 63, 73
Rockne, K. 4
Roethlisberger, B. 148, 149, 154, 158, 160, 169
Rogers, G. 98, 153
Romo, T. 171, 173, 174
Rosenbloom, C. 68

Ross, A. 168, 170, 174
Rote, K. 18, 20, 22, 38, 41, 46
Rowe, H. 16, 18
Rozelle, P. 43, 45, 47, 68, 71, 73, 142, 183, 185, 187
Rozelle Rule 69
Rutledge, J. 77, 85, 105
Rypien, M. 89, 90

Saban, N. 146
Salaam, R. 124
Sayers, G. 50
Schnelker, B. 38
Schnellbacher, O. 16, 18
Schnellenberger, H. 109
Schramm, T. 30, 151
Schroeder, J. 84
Sehorn, J. 124, 125, 130, 136
Seubert, R. 136
Shell, A. 116
Sherman, A. 17, 23, 24, 27, 42, 49, 50, 53, 54, 58, 62, 119
Shockey, J. 133, 135, 137, 141, 148, 159, 162, 163, 170, 172, 184, 192
Shofner, D. 27, 34, 35, 40, 51, 62
Short, B. 132, 133
Shula, D. 64, 74
Simms, P. 74, 75, 81, 83, 85, 86, 87, 90, 91, 95, 104–108, 110, 118, 119, 120, 123, 124, 128, 141, 143, 191
Sims, B. 177
Singletary, M. 91
Siragusa, T. 131
Smith, A. 152
Smith, B. 95, 96
Smith, L. 146
Smith, R. 130
Smith, S. 178, 179, 180
Snead, N. 40, 55, 57, 59, 60, 61, 64
Sneakers, Game 1 9, 19
Sneakers, Game 2 32
Snee, C. 177
Soar, H. 11, 12
Spagnuolo, S. 168, 169, 171, 181
Speedie, M. 18
Spurrier, S. 53, 56
Stabler, K. 53, 56
Stagg, A. 3
Strahan, M 123, 125, 128, 129, 131, 132, 134, 141, 147, 155, 159, 160, 161, 165, 169, 178, 181, 182–183, 190, 192
Streater, S. 99
Stringer, K. 130
Strong, K. 8, 10, 11, 12, 13, 15
Stroud, J. 18, 20, 28, 35, 49

Summerall, P. 20, 29, 35, 36, 37
Svare, H. 20, 41
Svoboda, B. 20, 41
Sweeny, D. 51

T-formation 14, 15, 17, 24
Tagliabue, P. 142, 184, 185
Taliaferro, G. 17, 44, 51
Tarkenton, F. 40, 53, 54, 55, 61
Taylor, L. (LT) 75, 76, 80, 81, 82, 83, 84, 88, 90, 93, 95, 96–104, 110, 113, 120, 121, 123, 130, 137, 141, 153, 162, 182, 184, 190
Theisman, J. 102, 190
Thomas, A. 23
Thomas, T. 94, 95
Thompson, R. 49, 74, 104
Thorpe, J. 4
Timberlake, B. 52
Tisch, J. 140, 167, 185
Tisch, P.R. 113, 125, 140, 184, 187
Tittle, Y.A. 27–28, 40, 42, 49, 50, 61, 62
Toomer, A. 128, 134, 137, 141, 170, 174, 179
Topping, D. 16
Triplett, M. 20, 33, 38
Trump, D. 101
Tuck, J. 179
Tunnell, E. 17, 18, 20, 25–26, 35, 41, 45
Tynes, L. 171, 175, 177, 178
Tyree, D. 180

Umbrella defense 18
Umenyiora, O. 149, 159, 160, 161, 174
Unitas, J. 37, 38, 39, 153
United States Football League see USFL
Upshaw, G. 142
USFL (United States Football League) 81, 101, 115

Van Brocklin, N. 24, 54
Van Duser, J. 73
Van Pelt, B. 57, 75, 76

Walker, H. 81, 101, 115
Walsh, B. 73, 82, 104
Walton, J. 40
Wannstedt, D. 120
Ward, D. 186
Warner, G. 4
Warner, K. 155, 156, 157
Washbington, J. 92
Washington, K. 16, 44
Watters, R. 122
Way, C. 125

Webster, A. 20, 34, 36, 38, 39, 41, 49, 55, 58, 60, 62, 63, 88, 121, 140
Webster, C. 159, 173, 174, 176, 177, 178
Weinmeister, A. 16
Weis, C. 146
WFL *see* World Football League
Wheatley, T. 124, 125, 153
White, R. 60
Wietecha, R. 18, 20, 28, 35
Wilkinson, B. 49
Wilkinson, G. 162
Williams, D. 71, 89, 116
Williams, J. 141
Williams, S. 136, 142, 147, 162
Winslow, K. 104
Wonderlic Personnel Test 151
Wood, G. 28, 51, 53
Woolfolk, B. 75, 77
World Football League (WFL) 64

Yary, R. 57
Yelvington, D. 28
Young, B. 17
Young, D. 141
Young, G. 73, 74, 86, 99, 107, 109, 112, 119, 120, 121, 124, 125, 126, 132, 141, 153, 168, 183
Young, S. 115, 122
Youso, F. 35